My Co
BURG

Montréal

Epoisses

Paris

AREA OF DETAIL

MORVAN

DIJON

Saulieu

ANNE WILLAN

A KITCHEN IN BURGUNDY

PHOTOGRAPHS BY
LANGDON CLAY

CASSELL & CO.
LONDON

First published in the United States in 2000 by Clarkson N. Potter/Publishers
Member of the Crown Publishing Group

First published in the United Kingdom in 2000 by Cassell & Co.

Text copyright © Anne Willan, Inc., 2000

Photographs on pages 211, 214 (top), 227, 282, 287, 288, 291, 292, 295 © Anne Willan, Inc., 2000
Other photographs © Langdon Clay, 2000

A CIP catalogue record for this book is available from the British Library

ISBN 0 304 35438 4

Printed and bound in China

Cassell & Co.
Wellington House
125 Strand
London
WC2R 0BB

Recipe Editor: Molly Stevens
Kitchen Director: Randall Price
Recipe Testing and Development: Stephanie Cockey, Amy Miller, Alex Sanger, and Justine Wyld
Consultants: Jane Suthering (food styling) and Wist Thorpe (wedding photography)

PAGE 1: *A view through an arched door of the old stables at Château du Feÿ.*
PAGES 2–3: *The rolling hills stretch to infinity from the terrace at the château.*
PAGES 4–5: *Charolais cattle in a Burgundian meadow.* PAGES 6–7:
The ancient vineyard of La Chainette in the center of the city of Auxerre.

PAGES 8–9: *Just five miles from us, the sturdy gatehouse of Villeneuve-sur-Yonne.* PAGE 10: *My château kitchen.* PAGE 11: *This small farm supplies vegetables to one of our nearby three-star restaurants.*

This book is dedicated to the memory of my parents,
whose love of the land taught me so much.

CONTENTS

This is a personal story, an adventure that begins on a cold March day in 1982 and ends, for the moment, with a wedding and a glass of Champagne. We bought Château du Feÿ as a weekend retreat, but it has become so much more: a home for the family, the source of much good eating, and a passport to life in the French countryside—past and present. Through Château du Feÿ we have made many friends, from cheesemakers to chefs to owners of grand châteaux. All have that commitment to region and lifestyle that makes time stand still. Two hundred years ago, the young Napoleon Bonaparte sensed the same appeal. "Search out a small piece of land in your beautiful valley of the Yonne," he wrote to a friend in 1796. "I will purchase it as soon as I can scrape together the money. I wish to retire there."

It is this magic I have tried to evoke in *From My Château Kitchen.* In doing so, working with Roy Finamore has been a pleasure: I owe him double thanks for selecting Langdon Clay, the perfect professional, as photographer. My associates Randall Price and Molly Stevens have applied their outstanding testing and editing talents to the recipes. Many Burgundian friends and neighbors have dealt patiently with my questions, and the Maringe family kindly opened their historic home to our photo team.

There are others without whom this book would never have been possible. Chef Fernand Chambrette, now retired, was a comrade in arms almost from the foundation of La Varenne Cooking School in 1975. He brought his former sous-chef, Claude Vauguet, and together they gave me a privileged view of French cooking from the inside. Later it was a talented chef of a younger generation, Jean-Michel Bouvier, who became a pillar of La Varenne. But closer to the heart of this book is the château caretaker, Roger Milbert, whose instinctive appreciation of the fruits of the earth has done so much to educate me, and our many visitors here, in the traditions of rural France.

As a writer, I depend greatly on my London agent, Andrew Nurnberg, assisted by his New York associate, Robin Straus. For working wonders with my draft manuscript, I am indebted to my old friend Margo Miller, the quintessential Bostonian. I also thank our children, Simon and Emma, for their tolerance of that tedious refrain, "Mum's busy." Lastly, there is my husband, Mark Cherniavsky, whose contribution to this book is beyond measure.

Anne Willan
Château du Feÿ
89300 Villecien

Rolling hills near the château.

CHAPTER I

The Adventure Begins

We first saw Château du Feÿ through the chill, sheeting rain of a March afternoon. The shutters were barred and the wrought-iron gates tightly shut. The only sign of life was a thin thread of smoke sliding down a lean-to roof against what appeared to be a sizable pigeon house. The main house had an abandoned look and Mark and I retreated, baffled. And discouraged. Why was it taking so long to find our future home?

Mark and I were born in England but have come to think of ourselves as European. We met in Paris. We have lived and worked all over, Mark as an economist for the World Bank, and I, after a spell of cooking in France, as a food writer in New York City. Washington, D.C., was home in the early days of our marriage. Even our surname of Cherniavsky (Mark's father was Russian) adds another dimension. Now it was time to settle ourselves and, as the French say, to declare a passion. There were cookbooks I wanted to write, and I dreamed of teaching cooking. So, for more reasons than we could articulate, we were gravitating toward France with its historic past, where so much of life centered on the table. Mark got himself transferred to Paris and the adventure could begin. At first we were content with an apartment with a view of the Eiffel Tower, making only visits to the countryside, but after a year or two we became restless. As every Parisien and Parisienne will tell you, they really come from *la France profonde,* France itself, the real France. Our little corner of all that had still to be found.

When we returned a week later to Château du Feÿ, the sun was out and a familiar, cheerful figure stood on the steps. It was Philip Hawkes. A Briton based in Paris, Philip has dealt in French real estate for more than two decades. He led us into the main hall and with the theater that makes him so good at his job, he flung back the tall window shutters in each room. Light streamed in.

Now there are châteaux and châteaux. Some are massive, boxy and grand, so you feel like a goggle-eyed tourist; if you tried to live in them you'd be a perpetual visitor. But the appeal of Le Feÿ was immediate: it did not dazzle or confront but it embraced us. We had seen it in sun and in gloom and we know now that it looks well in any weather, faced as it is in rosy brick and the buff Burgundian stone. The house is long, only a room deep in the central part that runs between two wings. It was built about 1640, a time when the staircases were placed in each wing rather than the center of house to allow a clear vista, or enfilade, through the main rooms. At each end mirrors would be placed to reflect and enlarge the perspective, and so it is at Le Feÿ. To the right of the central hall is the *grand salon,* to the left, the *salle à manger.* Philip snapped on the lights and the mirrors worked their magic, doubling and redoubling the twinkling chandeliers to infinity. Mark and I exchanged glances. After the dozen pathetic wrecks we had inspected so far, stripped of paneling, fireplaces, doors, anything worth cash, this looked promising. In one splendid eighteenth-century mansion, complete with chapel and dairy, we lost count of the rooms after fifty-seven. We could not understand why a charming Directoire pavilion only 25 miles from Paris remained unsold after two years—until we stood still and listened. The trickle of running water was still audible, and no wonder: the place was built on a marsh.

High on its wooded hill, Château du Feÿ seemed to have none of these defects. The roof was sound, having been recently repaired; electricity and water were in working order and there was even central heating. As we toured the rooms—there did seem to be rather a lot of them—I tried to control a rising excitement. We stood on the terrace and admired the panoramic view, rare for local châteaux, we learned later. Châteaux the size of Le Feÿ were really working farms and most sheltered in a valley, near an attendant village that could supply the needed labor. From Le Feÿ nine different villages can be seen, two of them on what used to be château land and all of them witness to the age-old fertility of Burgundian soil.

Our tour of the extensive outbuildings passed by in a blur of stables, barns, and a dairy. A battery of rabbit hutches lined one wall. I scarcely registered the swimming pool and tennis court, both on the wish list of our two almost-teenage children, Simon and Emma. Somewhere was an oak wine-press, somewhere else a massive stone wheel, possibly for crushing walnuts. The well was not only huge but

PREVIOUS PAGES: *Seasonal melancholy adds its own charms to the buildings at Château du Feÿ. Birds once sheltered in the impressive array of pigeon holes (center).* OPPOSITE: *Marie Antoinette presides in the* grand salon.

20

medieval. And, yes, we were right, there was a vast pigeon house. The sheer size of it told us something about the former importance of Le Feÿ. Estates can be measured in acres or hectares, but also in pigeons. Our first, and perhaps still favorite, Le Feÿ statistic concerns the ten thousand birds this *pigeonnier* could have housed. An eighteenth-century landowner had the right to a pair of pigeons per *arpent*— about an acre—of land. Pigeons are succulent birds, good eating, and they supply valuable guano for fertilizer, but they are greedy and no respecters of property. In the fields they gobbled up loose corn and wheat at the expense of poor folk who hoped to glean grain for themselves. So hated were pigeons that a château's *droit de seigneur* (right of ownership) was suppressed at the Revolution in 1789 and many pigeon houses were demolished. Now they are once more a prized possession and admired as architectural curiosities, sometimes small masterpieces of technical and artistic invention.

As it happens, the rooms under the pigeon house were also home to two people without whom our life at Le Feÿ would be less richly rooted in Burgundy. We had crossed the gravel courtyard and were making for the vegetable garden, where I could see a sprightly figure in blue overalls. We'd been told the property came with a caretaker and his wife, a Monsieur and Madame Milbert. Philip Hawkes now made the introduction. Handshakes and civilities were exchanged. Monsieur Milbert's upper lip sported a dead cigarette, a permanent feature, we would later learn. The area of the garden was astonishing, a great square of precisely a hectare (2.2 acres). I was impressed that it was in immaculate order despite the seasonal lull—something to tell my mother, who judged people by their gardens. Monsieur Milbert was setting seed potatoes, working from neat piles at the end of each well-tilled trench. Some friendships are made over wine; ours began with the potato.

ABOVE: *Rich pastures and fields of grain, dotted with centuries-old farms, sum up the traditional wealth of Burgundy.* OPPOSITE: *A warming gratin (left) is made with potatoes supplied by Monsieur Milbert, autocrat of the garden.*

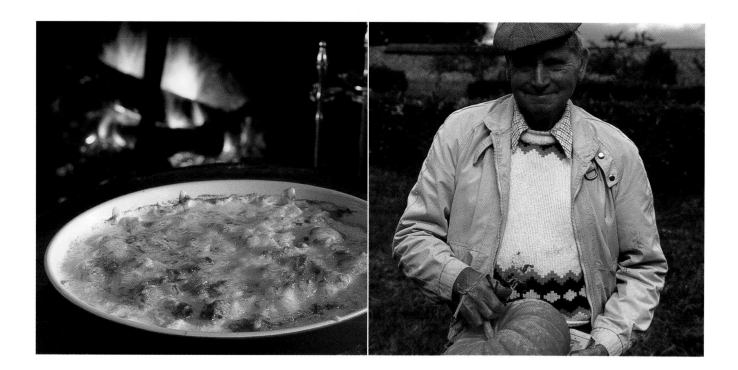

Gratin of Potatoes with Bacon and Cream
Gratin Dauphinois au Lard

Monsieur Milbert's potatoes are a cook's delight—he grows Belle de Fontenay, which soften to floury lightness for *frites,* purées, and gratins like this wonderfully rich Burgundian variant of my favorite *gratin dauphinois.* The potatoes are first simmered in milk (this extracts the tannin they contain, which is likely to curdle the gratin) and then in cream with diced bacon and a topping of Gruyère cheese. (Don't be put off by the word *lard* in the French title; it simply means bacon.) This recipe makes enough for six to eight hearty side portions. I always make large quantities as potato gratin reheats well.

1½ lb/750 g potatoes
2½ cups/600 ml milk, more if needed
pinch of grated nutmeg
salt and pepper
1 tablespoon vegetable oil
a 4-oz/125-g piece of lean smoked bacon, diced
1¼ cups/300 ml heavy cream, more if needed
1 garlic clove, finely chopped
½ cup/50 g grated Gruyère cheese

a 9 x 13-inch/23 x 33-cm gratin or shallow baking dish

Peel the potatoes and cut them into ⅛-inch/3-mm slices, preferably using a mandoline. Put them in a saucepan with the milk, nutmeg, pepper, and a little salt. Stir to mix and bring them to a boil. If necessary, add more milk so the potatoes are covered. Simmer, stirring occasionally, until the potatoes are just tender, 10 to 15 minutes.

Meanwhile, heat the oil in a frying pan, add the bacon, and fry, stirring, until browned. Lift it out and drain it on paper towels. Use the bacon fat to grease the baking dish. Heat the oven to 375°F/190°C.

Drain the potatoes, reserving the milk for another use such as soup. Wipe out the saucepan and put back the potatoes with the bacon, cream, and garlic. Heat gently and simmer, stirring occasionally, until the potatoes are very tender, 5 to 10 minutes. They break up easily, so stir carefully. The mixture should be quite creamy and liquid, not stiff. If necessary, stir in more cream. Taste and adjust the seasoning. Pour the potatoes with the cream into the baking dish, spreading them evenly. Sprinkle the top with the grated cheese.

Bake the gratin until golden brown and the edges are bubbling, 15 to 20 minutes. Test the center with a small knife—the blade should feel hot when withdrawn.

Burgundian Leek Quiche

Leeks are the only vegetable to last through the winter at Le Feÿ, and their soldierly ranks provide the Milbert table with a touch of green until the first baby peas arrive in June. I first came across this way of cooking leeks with tomato and white wine in an old Burgundian cookbook and find it makes a tasty quiche. Add a simple green salad and you have lunch or supper for six to eight people.

FOR THE PÂTE BRISÉE

1 ½ cups/175 g flour
1 egg yolk
½ teaspoon salt
3 tablespoons cold water, more if needed
6 tablespoons/90 g butter

FOR THE LEEK FILLING

¾ lb/375 g leeks
2 tablespoons vegetable oil
1 onion, thinly sliced
½ cup/125 ml white wine
6 oz/175 g tomatoes, peeled, seeded, and chopped
2 garlic cloves, crushed
salt and pepper
1 tablespoon chopped parsley

FOR THE CUSTARD

1 egg
2 egg yolks
½ cup/125 ml milk
½ cup/125 ml heavy cream
large pinch of grated nutmeg

a 10-inch/25-cm pie pan with removable base

Heat the oven to 375°F/190°C, and put a baking sheet to heat on a shelf low down in the oven. Prepare and blind-bake a 10-inch/25-cm pâte brisée pie shell using the ingredients listed above and the technique described in the glossary (page 298).

For the leek filling, trim the roots and tough green tops from the leeks—the tops can be saved for the stockpot. Cut all the leeks in half lengthwise. Set them cut-side down, and chop them into ½-inch/1.25-cm pieces. Rinse the pieces very thoroughly in cold water to remove any grit trapped between the leaves, and drain them in a colander.

Heat the oil in a saucepan, add the onion, and sauté until lightly browned, 5 to 7 minutes. Add the wine and boil until it is reduced by half. Stir in the leeks, tomatoes, garlic, salt, and pepper. Cover the pan and turn down the heat. Cook gently, stirring often, until the leeks are almost tender, 12 to 15 minutes. Take off the lid and cook over high heat until the liquid has evaporated and the leeks are meltingly tender, 5 to 7 minutes longer. Stir in the parsley, taste, and adjust the seasoning.

For the custard, whisk the egg and egg yolks with the milk, cream, nutmeg, salt, and pepper until mixed. Spread the leeks in the pie shell and pour over the custard. Bake the quiche on the hot baking sheet in the oven until the custard is set and browned, 35 to 40 minutes. Serve the quiche warm.

ABOVE: *Hearty leeks are a mainstay of markets throughout the winter.*
OPPOSITE: *A few winter greens survive in our garden—even through the severest Burgundian frosts.*

As we drove back to Paris, less than two hours away on the autoroute, we mulled over what we had seen. Mark had long ago defined our requirements for a country house: an attractive building in good repair, a caretaker on the property or nearby, a location south of Paris for more sun, easy access to a highway, and express trains to the capital. And, of course, the price had to be right. Château du Feÿ had all these attributes and more, much more. The property included no fewer than three other houses vacant for rental—the former farmhouse, and the gardener's and gamekeeper's cottages. The main building was classified as a *monument historique* in recognition of its architectural merit. It was far, far grander than anything we had envisaged. Yet it cost the same as a three-bedroom family apartment in central Paris.

A week later we returned to find other potential buyers taking a tour with us, sharp thinking on the part of Philip Hawkes. With rivals on our heels, the property was even more attractive than we had remembered. This time on the way home we were silent. What do you say when you've fallen in love? Just like marriage, buying property remains a gamble however carefully you calculate the odds. (Mark and I were married in Central America at the registry office in San Jose, Costa Rica, after the formality of a week's engagement, but that's a story for another time.) So we took the gamble, offered the asking price, and were accepted. A week later we departed on business to the United States, which has long been our second home, and many times in the following months I wondered what we had undertaken.

I soon found out. At 7:30 A.M. on July 20, 1982, the first moving truck edged its way under the wisteria into the château courtyard. The children and I had started the day with café crème (plus brioche on the house) at the local truckstop, the only place open at that hour. I stood on the château steps directing traffic while Simon and Emma, twelve and ten and full of purpose, galloped up and down the twisting staircases to the Oak, the Green, the Dutch, and half a dozen other bedrooms. We had already given them names, conferring immediate possession. Our motley collection of English, French, and American furniture, reflecting our peripatetic lifestyle, seemed to fit just fine.

By noon we urgently needed refreshment and so, it seemed, did the movers. Their return from lunch was punctuated by an ominous crash, marking the demise of a pretty blue and white planter. By night all of us were at the end of our tether. When the men balked at unpacking the last few cartons, Mark simply upended the contents onto the salon floor while I watched in trepidation. It was with relief and a sense of finding home at last that we retired to the nearest bistro. It was our first meal out and we were rewarded with a genuine, wine-dark boeuf bourguignon.

Traditional Beef Bourguignon

Few dishes are better known, yet more often maltreated, than boeuf bourguignon. It requires well-aged beef, marbled with fat (Burgundians would specify the local Charolais breed), and with plenty of connective tissue to dissolve during cooking to enrich the sauce. Suggested cuts are blade or chuck, nearest to the French cut of *paleron*, and the four pounds called for in this recipe will make enough to serve at least six hungry people (leftovers are always appreciated). A full-bodied wine is essential and lots of it—we use a fruity pinot noir from the nearby Auxerrois area. Above all, boeuf bourguignon must be cooked slowly, never at more than a simmer, for up to three or even four hours if need be, until the generous chunks of meat are tender but not falling apart. This recipe may seem complicated as it calls for vegetables to be strained out of the sauce before adding the cooked garnish of bacon, onion, and mushroom, but this is the secret to its rich, mellow flavor.

4 lb/1.8 kg stew beef

FOR THE MARINADE

2 bottles (750 ml each) red wine
2 onions, sliced
2 carrots, sliced
a large bouquet garni
4 garlic cloves, crushed
2 teaspoons black peppercorns
3 whole cloves
2 tablespoons vegetable oil

FOR COOKING THE BEEF

2 tablespoons vegetable oil
¼ cup/30 g flour
1 quart/1 liter veal or beef stock, more if needed
salt and pepper

FOR THE GARNISH

1 tablespoon vegetable oil
a 1-lb/500-g piece of lean bacon, diced
30 to 40 baby onions, peeled
1 lb/500 g mushrooms, quartered
½ cup/125 ml veal or beef stock

FOR THE CROÛTES

8 slices of white bread, ¼ in/6 mm thick
oil for frying
2 tablespoons chopped parsley

For the marinade, combine all the marinade ingredients (except the oil) in a saucepan and bring them slowly to a boil. Lower the heat and simmer the marinade for 5 minutes, then let it cool. Meanwhile, trim any sinew and most of the fat from the beef, cut it into 2-inch/5-cm chunks, and put it in a deep, nonmetallic bowl. When the marinade is completely cooled, pour it over the beef. Spoon the oil over the meat to keep it moist, cover the bowl, and refrigerate for 1 to 2 days, depending on the intensity of flavor you want. The longer it sits, the deeper the marinade penetrates.

When you are ready to cook the beef, heat the oven to 300°F/150°C. Lift the beef from the marinade with a slotted spoon and pat the pieces dry with paper towels. Strain the marinade, reserving the liquid and the vegetables separately. Heat the oil in a flameproof casserole or Dutch oven over high heat and add a few pieces of beef. Brown them thoroughly on all sides. Remove them and brown the other pieces, too. It is important to work in batches, because overcrowding the pan will make the beef steam and turn gray instead of the appetizing brown you are after. When the last of the beef chunks are browned, take them out, reduce the heat to medium, and add the reserved vegetables from the marinade. Fry them, stirring often, until lightly browned, 3 to 5 minutes. Stir in the flour and cook, stirring constantly, until well browned. Add the marinade liquid, standing back as it will sputter and splash. Bring it to a boil, stirring until it thickens slightly, then simmer for 2 minutes to reduce the volume somewhat. Stir in the stock with a little salt and pepper. Replace the beef, pushing it well down into the sauce, cover the casserole, and bring to a boil.

Put the casserole into the oven and simmer the beef until it is very tender and falls easily from a two-pronged fork, 2½ to 3 hours. During cooking, give the stew a stir from time to time, and add more stock if necessary to keep the meat covered.

Meanwhile, cook the garnish. Heat the oil in a frying pan and fry the diced bacon until browned, stirring often. Take it out with a slotted spoon, add the onions, brown them also, and set them aside with the bacon. Finally, fry the mushrooms in the same pan, stirring often, until they are lightly browned and all their moisture has evaporated. Add them to the onions and bacon. Deglaze the pan by adding the stock and bringing to a boil. Stir to dissolve the pan juices and pour the liquid over the garnish.

When the beef is tender, remove it from the oven. Lift out the chunks with a slotted spoon and set aside. Strain the sauce through a fine strainer, pressing well to extract flavor from the vegetables. Wipe out the casserole and pour back the sauce—it should be deeply colored and lightly coat a spoon. If it is thin, boil it until reduced and concentrated. Stir in the beef, the onion, bacon, and mushroom garnish, and any accumulated juices. Cover and simmer the bourguignon on top of the stove until the onions are tender and their flavors have been absorbed into the sauce, 10 to 15 minutes. Taste and adjust the seasoning. Boeuf bourguignon improves if kept in the refrigerator at least a day, and it reheats well —that's why I make a lot of it.

Meanwhile, make the croûtes. Trim the crusts from the bread and cut each slice diagonally in half to form a triangle-shaped croûte. For a teardrop or heart-shaped croûte, further trim the triangle by rounding off one side and shaping it into an elongated teardrop or heart. In a frying pan, heat ¼ inch/6 mm of oil over medium heat. Working in batches, fry the croûtes until browned on both sides, 1 to 2 minutes per side. Drain them on paper towels.

To finish, reheat the bourguignon on top of the stove. Serve the stew from the casserole, or transfer it to a serving dish or individual plates. Dip an edge of each croûte first into sauce to moisten it and then into chopped parsley, and set them around the stew as decoration.

Boiled potatoes are the traditional accompaniment to wine-tinged boeuf bourguignon.

Our first meal in the château was postponed for an odd reason: the château had no kitchen. After living in France for seven years, we had learned to expect only a stone sink when a house or apartment changed hands, but it seemed odd that no one cooked in a château this size. I later learned that this is not unusual. Many local châtelains (we call them the château Mafia) come down from Paris only for weekends and summer vacation. For meals, most rely on charcuteries and pastry shops, backed up by the skill of the caretaker's wife. The idea that all Frenchwomen are born cooks is an illusion.

For me, the lack of a kitchen was an advantage. I was only too happy to plan from the floor upward. But there was a catch: in France, the month of August is dedicated to vacation. In the five working days remaining we had to knock down a wall and install plumbing, electricity, and appliances. Though the cabinets consisted mainly of open shelves and the floor tile was partly cement, the temporary kitchen that emerged lasted us twelve busy years. The first meal, enjoyed on the terrace as the sun went down, set the scene for innumerable others.

With total recall, I can see our repast. It was August, and the salad lettuce was already rather tough and past its best but full of flavor. The chicken, raised by Madame Milbert, was lean, juicy, and quite unlike the flabby battery birds we'd grown accustomed to in the United States. With it came spinach and the little fried potatoes we have so often that the children call them Mom's Own. The raspberries had been gathered an hour before, their juiciness a surprise after the hot dry weather we'd been enjoying. Only the accompanying tart crème fraîche and the celebratory bottle of Chablis wine were not from the property.

Butter Roast Chicken with Fresh Herbs

It was a Norman cook who taught me that the key to roast chicken is constant basting with butter. Butter keeps the meat moist, adds flavor, and toasts the skin to that delectable crispy brown. I fill the cavity with whatever aromatic herb is available—rosemary, thyme, sage, tarragon, even parsley—and for good measure sometimes slip a few herb leaves under the skin on the breast. A large roasting chicken makes a splendid dinner for four to six people when accompanied by Mom's Own Fried Potatoes (page 30), mashed potatoes, or your favorite grain.

a 4- to 5-lb/about 2-kg roasting chicken
salt and pepper
a medium bunch of herbs, more for decoration
   (optional)
¼ cup/60g butter, softened
3 cups/750 ml chicken stock

trussing string and trussing needle (optional)

Heat the oven to 425°F/220°C. Wipe the inside of the chicken with paper towels. Fold back the neck skin and use the point of a small knife to scrape free and remove the wishbone—this makes the breast meat easy to carve in neat slices. If you are using soft herb leaves such as sage, tarragon, or parsley, slide your fingers under the breast skin, loosening it from the meat without tearing it, and insert a few herb leaves in a pretty pattern. Season the bird inside and out with salt and pepper, and put a bunch of herbs in the cavity. Truss the bird using a trussing needle, or by simply tying it with string so it holds a neat shape (see the glossary).

Set the bird on its back in a medium roasting pan (not too large or the juices will scorch). Spread the breast and legs with butter. If you have the giblets, add the neck, gizzard, and heart to the pan to flavor the gravy (reserve the liver for another use). Roast the chicken until it sizzles and starts to brown, 12 to 15 minutes. Turn it onto its breast, baste well with the pan drippings, and return it to the oven. (Roasting the breast downward keeps the meat moist.) Lower the heat to 375°F/190°C and continue roasting, basting at least every 10 minutes.

After about 30 more minutes, turn the bird again onto its back so the breast skin crispens. Continue roasting for 15 to 30 minutes longer, basting often, until the leg joint feels pliable when you pull the drumstick and the leg meat starts to shrink from the end of the bone. Pierce the chicken with a two-pronged fork, lift it, and tip the juices from the center cavity into the roasting pan. If they run clear, not pink, the bird is done. If pink, continue cooking until they do run clear. Transfer the chicken to a serving dish or carving board, cover it loosely with foil, and keep it warm.

For the gravy, discard all but a tablespoon or two of fat from the pan (some is needed to emulsify and enrich the sauce). Set the roasting pan on a burner, add the stock, and bring to a boil, scraping to dissolve the pan juices. Boil the gravy rapidly for 10 to 15 minutes, until it thickens slightly and the bubbles break more slowly, showing it is emulsified and concentrated. If it seems thin, continue boiling until reduced and well flavored. Strain the gravy into a saucepan, taste, and adjust the seasoning.

If you are carving the chicken at the table, discard the cooked herbs from the cavity. If carving in the kitchen, arrange the chicken pieces on a serving dish, moisten them with a little gravy, and pass the rest separately.

ABOVE: *I often gather a few leaves of herb from the handy trough (right) outside the kitchen door, tucking them under the skin of a chicken to flavor the meat while roasting.*

Later I became overambitious and bought one of the dark-fleshed, muscular cock birds I had seen in the market, determined to make a real coq au vin. The cooking procedure is straightforward enough, exactly like Traditional Beef Bourguignon (page 26), but the problem was cutting the sizable carcass into pieces. Sharpening my largest knives, I set to and soon realized why butchers are so beefy. Just cutting through the tendons of the legs required considerable force, and when it came to dividing the breast portions through the bones I had, shamefacedly, to call on male assistance. So coq au vin has not entered my regular repertoire, unlike these little Mom's Own Fried Potatoes.

Mom's Own Fried Potatoes

For these potatoes, you'll need generous amounts of fat —vegetable oil, butter, or best of all, fat from the Christmas goose. (The dish of fat can be used over and over again, and I often have one ready at the back of the stove.) If you like, add whole, unpeeled garlic cloves to the potatoes about a half hour before the end of cooking. The garlic will soften enough to be squeezed from the skin and enjoyed on bread or with a bite of potatoes. When I am making the Butter Roast Chicken on page 28, I simply slide a pan of these potatoes on the lower rack of the oven to cook alongside the chicken. It's a perfect side dish for four people.

> 2 lb/1 kg baking potatoes
> 1 cup/250 ml vegetable oil
> 1 cup/250 g butter, or more vegetable oil
> 2 to 3 heads of garlic (optional)
> salt

Heat the oven to 425°F/220°C, or plan to cook the potatoes in the oven with the Butter Roast Chicken. Peel the potatoes and cut them into 2-inch/5-cm chunky pieces. Heat the oil and butter in a shallow flameproof baking dish large enough to hold the potatoes in a single layer, and add the potatoes. They should all touch the bottom of the dish and be half covered with fat. Heat them on top of the stove until bubbling, 3 to 5 minutes.

Transfer the dish to the oven, and roast the potatoes until they are very brown and crisp, 40 to 50 minutes. Stir them from time to time so they brown evenly. If adding garlic, break the heads into individual cloves and add them, unpeeled, to the potatoes after 25 minutes. Cook until the garlic is tender, 20 to 25 minutes more.

Lift out the potatoes and garlic (if added) with a slotted spoon and drain them on paper towels. Keep warm and, just before serving, sprinkle with salt.

ABOVE: *A sprinkling of snow frosts the western facade of the château.*
OPPOSITE: *On sunnier days, Madame Milbert greets visitors from the gatehouse door.*

More difficult to deal with than the raspberries were the buckets of pungent and sour red currants (above) that appeared mysteriously in the kitchen. I knew why. Madame Milbert found them just as recalcitrant as I did. Together we took the only way out—red currant jelly.

Spiced Red Currant Jelly

This jelly recipe is in the British tradition, a lively spiced condiment to serve with hot and cold roast meats and poultry, particularly goose and turkey. Tart little crab apples can be substituted for red currants; simply wash and quarter them—peel, core, and all. This makes 1 quart/1 liter of jelly.

> *4 quarts/2.5 kg red currants, with stems*
> *4 to 6 cups/about 1 kg sugar*
> *1 tablespoon black peppercorns*
> *1 tablespoon coriander seed*
> *2 teaspoons cumin seed*
> *2 to 3 cinnamon sticks*
> *½ bottle (375 ml) red wine*
>
> *jelly bag or cloth*
> *candy thermometer*

Rinse and drain the currants, leaving the stems. Put them in a large pan, bring to a boil, and mash them with a potato masher so they soften more quickly. Simmer until the juice runs, 5 to 7 minutes. (Overcooking destroys the pectin that sets the jelly.) Let the fruit cool to tepid, then transfer it to a jelly bag or scalded cloth set in a colander over a bowl and leave the juice to drain overnight.

Measure the juice and put it in a preserving pan or large saucepan. Add enough sugar to equal three quarters of the volume of juice. Wrap the spices in a piece of cheesecloth, tie securely, and pound them with a rolling pin to crush slightly. Add the spice bag to the fruit juice with the wine. Heat the mixture gently until the sugar dissolves, 4 to 5 minutes, and then bring it to a boil. Skim the jelly often during boiling so it remains clear, and boil it rapidly, stirring often, until it reaches the jell point, 30 to 40 minutes. The temperature should measure 220°F/105°C on a candy thermometer, but the surest test for the jell point is to place a drop of jelly onto a plate chilled in the freezer—the jelly should set right away. Once it has reached the jell point, let it cool slightly, then ladle it into sterilized jars and seal the jars (see the glossary).

Soon I was overwhelmed by red currant jelly, so I froze it as sorbet, which turned out to be both refreshing and a very pretty color. Then the gooseberries arrived, familiar in desserts from my English childhood, but a curiosity to French cooks, who call them "currants for mackerel" and serve them with fish.

Red Currant Jelly Sorbet

For 4 to 6 people, heat 2 cups/500 g red currant jelly with 2 cups/500 ml water until melted. (Any other tart jelly such as raspberry or lemon marmalade does fine, too.) Let the mix cool and, if you like, add 1 to 2 tablespoons kirsch. Freeze in a churn freezer until slushy. Whisk an egg white until frothy, then add just a teaspoonful to the sorbet and continue churning until stiff —this bit of egg white makes the sorbet light and creamy. Serve it in chilled stemmed glasses, topped with bunches of red currants or mint sprigs. Other tart fresh berries, such as raspberries, are a welcome garnish as the sorbet is quite sweet.

Half cake, half pudding, this torte is delicious topped with yogurt mixed with an equal quantity of sour cream.

Almond and Gooseberry Torte

If you don't have gooseberries, try sweet or tart fresh cherries instead, but they will need to be pitted. "Kiss simple," said Alex, the American trainee who tested the torte. One torte serves six.

> 2 cups/250 g gooseberries or pitted cherries
> 1 cup/125 g flour
> 1 1/2 teaspoons baking powder
> 1/2 teaspoon salt
> 2/3 cup/150 g butter
> 3/4 cup/150 g granulated sugar
> 1 egg
> 1 1/4 cups/150 g ground almonds
> confectioners' sugar for sprinkling
>
> an 8-inch/20-cm springform pan

Butter the cake pan, line the base with wax or parchment paper, and then butter and flour it. Wash the gooseberries, dry them on paper towels, and then snip off the blossom ends and stems. Sift together the flour, baking powder, and salt. Heat the oven to 350°F/175°C.

Cream the butter until smooth in an electric mixer. Add the sugar and continue to beat until it is soft and light, 2 to 3 minutes. Beat in the egg until well mixed, about 1 minute. Stir in the ground almonds by hand, followed by the flour mixture. Expect the batter to be quite stiff.

Spread half the batter in the cake pan. Sprinkle the fruit on top and dot with the remaining batter so the fruit is almost covered. Bake until the torte starts to shrink from the sides of the pan and the top is firm when lightly pressed with a fingertip, 45 to 55 minutes. The top will be rustic looking, like a crumble.

Let the torte cool for 10 to 15 minutes in the pan, then loosen the sides and slide the torte onto a rack to cool completely. Sprinkle it with confectioners' sugar, and serve it warm or at room temperature.

Several times I had noticed a shadowy figure moving in the trees near the gate and one day I investigated: Serge Bondat, the honey man. We knew he was accustomed to parking his beehives on the property, paying rent in the form of honey, and we eagerly continued the arrangement —what could be better? Each year in mid-July, Monsieur Bondat delivers a mixed crate of pale, mild colza honey, thicker acacia honey, and best of all, the caramel-colored honey from chestnut and linden flowers, which has a strong bite. Serge is a loner, a modest, retiring bachelor who happily continues his grandfather's business. His neat, somber dress and well-trimmed beard remind me of an Amish farmer. During a good year he reckons to harvest 15 tons of honey by hand: "It's a tough business," he says. "Bad backs are an occupational hazard." Sometimes a friend helps out, but Monsieur Bondat is hesitant. "Even wearing protective gear, I'm stung several times in an average day." He is one of perhaps twenty-five professional beekeepers in the Yonne. Although yields vary, times are getting better. "The 1960s were hard for beekeepers," he says, "but farmers now are more aware of ecology and use less pesticide."

Monsieur Bondat's bees are surprisingly discreet, and we rarely get stung, but wasps are another matter. They are taken seriously in France, so much so that one of the duties of the fire brigade is to destroy wasp and hornet nests. One year the firemen came with their longest ladder to take a nest in our bedroom chimney (we could hear the wasps buzzing as we fell asleep). Clad from head to foot in fireproof gear, the sun blazing down in the midst of a heat wave, the firemen sprayed lethal chemicals on a cloud of angry wasps from the top of a ladder at least 120 feet off the ground. In theory we pay for the service, but we've found that a gift of chilled bottles of *crémant* (the Burgundian term for sparkling wine) is the best form of currency—at least once the firemen are safely back on the ground.

Honey Walnut Bread

I find this large loaf ideal for our pungent chestnut honey as the flavor comes through so clearly, but any good-tasting dark honey will do. The bread improves if you wrap it tightly and store it for a week or two.

> 2¼ cups/275 g flour
> 1 teaspoon ground allspice
> 1 teaspoon baking powder
> 1 teaspoon baking soda
> ½ teaspoon salt
> 2 tablespoons instant coffee granules
> ¾ cup/175 ml warm water
> 3 eggs
> ¾ cup/150 g dark brown sugar
> 3 tablespoons melted butter
> ¾ cup/300 g dark honey
> ¾ cup/100 g chopped walnuts
> grated zest of 1 orange
>
> a 9x5x3-in/23x13x7.5-cm large loaf pan

Heat the oven to 350°F/175°C and set a shelf down low. Butter the pan and line the bottom and sides with strips of wax or parchment paper. Sift together the flour, allspice, baking powder, baking soda, and salt. Stir the coffee with the water until it is dissolved.

Beat the eggs and sugar in a bowl until they are just mixed, then stir in the melted butter and honey. Stir the dry ingredients into the honey mixture in 3 batches, alternating them with the coffee. Lastly stir in the chopped walnuts with the orange zest.

Pour the batter into the prepared pan—it will find its own level in the oven. Bake the bread until a skewer inserted in the center comes out clean, 50 to 60 minutes. The bread will also start to shrink from the sides of the pan and the top will probably crack slightly; this is normal, but if it starts to scorch, cover it loosely with foil. Do not let it overbake and become dry. Leave the bread to cool in the pan so it stays moist.

OPPOSITE: *Like his bees, Monsieur Bondat is constantly on the move. Just keeping up with his 500 scattered hives, each harboring about 70,000 bees at the height of the season, takes 12 hours a day.*

I soon realized that living off a country property is a constant adventure.

As the baskets of produce appeared each morning at Le Feÿ, I became vividly aware of the seasons. We'd already had a tasty bucket of the little golden *mirabelle* plums that are so popular in France. Now purple plums, wasp-nibbled but dripping with juice, were brought in from an ancient tree half-hidden in the dry moat.

Roast Plums in Grape Juice

Plums and grapes ripen together, so it makes sense to combine them in this dessert. Any plums can be used here—purple, green (called Reine Claude after the queen in whose garden they were first grown), or mirabelles. This recipe serves four and is best at room temperature topped with heavy cream or whipped cream.

> 1 lb/500 g black grapes
> ½ cup/100 g sugar, more if needed
> 3 tablespoons/45 g butter
> 1 teaspoon ground cinnamon
> 1½ lb/750 g plums
> ⅓ cup/30 g sliced almonds

Purée the grapes—seeds and all—with half the sugar in a food processor or with a hand-held immersion blender. Bring the purée just to a boil, cover, and let it infuse over very low heat for 15 to 20 minutes. Uncover and leave it to cool.

Meanwhile, heat the oven to 400°F/200°C. Cream the butter in a small bowl and beat in the remaining sugar with the cinnamon. Rinse and dry the plums and set them in a baking dish in a single layer so they all touch the bottom. Top them with spoonfuls of the cinnamon butter. Bake them in the heated oven, basting often with cooking juices, until they are tender and 1 or 2 skins have split, 10 to 15 minutes depending on their size and ripeness. Let the plums cool. Spread the almonds on a baking sheet and toast them in the oven until brown, 5 to 8 minutes.

To finish, strain the grape juice and taste, adding sugar if needed. It should have a slight tang, but not so much as to pucker your mouth. Pour the juice into serving bowls and arrange the plums in them. Spoon the cooking juice over the plums and sprinkle each bowl with toasted almonds.

Soon after the plums a couple of wan tomatoes appeared, followed by glowing bowlfuls that ended equally abruptly with the shortening days of October. In the sun on Madame Milbert's windowsill I noticed a row of half-ripe tomatoes, each one set carefully apart from the next. Like the proverbial rotten apple, a single bad tomato will ruin its neighbors. Madame often saves the life of these stragglers by canning them.

Home-Canned Tomatoes

Simply wipe the tomatoes, scoop out the cores, and pack them whole, skins and all, in quart/liter jars with some thyme sprigs, a couple of bay leaves, and a slice or two of onion. Close the lids and set the jars on a rack in a deep pan. Add enough water to cover them generously and weight them down with a brick if they show signs of floating. Simmer them for an hour and a half, longer for large tomatoes, until the tomatoes lose their shape and collapse. "They start to melt," explains Madame Milbert. Then leave the jars to cool in the water. Once fully cooled, they should have formed a tight seal. Each jar will only be half full of cooked tomatoes—don't worry about it.

Gratinéed Tomato and Orange Soup

In summer I make this soup with fresh tomatoes, and in winter with the few precious cans I've managed to put by from the previous year's crop. The orange flavoring nicely accents the fruit, and the recipe makes enough for six generous bowls.

> *4 lb/1.8 kg fresh tomatoes, cored and peeled, or*
> *   1 quart/1 liter home-canned tomatoes*
> *2 tablespoons olive oil*
> *2 onions, sliced*
> *3 garlic cloves, chopped*
> *a large bouquet garni*
> *1 teaspoon sugar*
> *salt and pepper*
> *a bunch of basil*
> *zest and juice of 2 medium oranges*
>
> FOR TOPPING THE BOWLS
> *1 long thin baguette (ficelle)*
> *3 to 4 tablespoons olive oil*
> *1 cup/100g grated Gruyère cheese*
>
> *6 heatproof soup bowls*

If using canned tomatoes, drain and reserve the juice. Coarsely chop fresh or canned tomatoes. In a soup pot, heat the oil and fry the onions until tender but not browned, 5 to 7 minutes. Stir in the garlic and continue cooking until fragrant, 1 to 2 minutes. Add the chopped tomatoes and juice if using canned or enough water just to cover if you are using fresh. Add the bouquet garni, sugar, salt, and pepper, cover the pan, and bring the soup to a boil. Simmer until the tomatoes are very tender, 30 to 40 minutes.

Meanwhile, heat the oven to 350°F/175°C. Cut the baguette into ½-inch/1.25-cm slices and set them on a baking sheet. Brush with olive oil, turn them, and brush the other side. Bake them until dry and lightly browned, 12 to 15 minutes. Strip the basil leaves from the stems and add the stems to the simmering soup. Shred the leaves and set aside. When the soup is cooked, light the broiler. Discard the bouquet garni and the basil stems, and purée the soup in a food processor. (I don't mind the seeds, but if you want a smoother soup, work it through a food mill or sieve.) Return it to the pan and bring it back to a boil. Stir in the shredded basil, orange zest, and orange juice. Taste and adjust the seasoning.

Without filling them too full, ladle the soup into bowls and set them on a baking sheet. Float a layer of bread toasts on top and sprinkle with grated cheese. Each bowl should get 2 to 3 rounds of bread, depending on the size of the croutons. Brown the cheese under the broiler and serve at once.

OPPOSITE: *Jars of canned tomatoes stand cooling on the windowsill. They are sealed by the vacuum that forms during simmering. Once the jars are cooled, test the seal by loosening the metal snap and lifting the jars by the lid.*

The first green beans, always cause for rejoicing, are followed by such quantities that we can hardly keep pace with blanching and freezing them for the winter. Our family has long been addicted to what we call "burnt beans," but guests are deeply suspicious until they taste them. Another Le Feÿ specialty is roast garlic. One might not think it, but garlic is tricky stuff to grow, demanding specific soil and climatic conditions. Some years Monsieur Milbert brings in generous bundles, other years the garlic rots in the ground so we have to rely on supplies from the market. Connoisseurs prefer purple garlic, plump and sweet, a better keeper than the more common white or pink, but also harder to grow. As fall approaches, tough curly chicory and escarole replace elderly lettuce. I know winter is coming when I see Madame Milbert with a little knife and plastic bag, gathering dandelions after the first frost.

Burnt Beans

Blanch your beans in generous amounts of boiling salted water, cooking them for 5 minutes, then drain and rinse them with cold water. (If the beans are frozen, simply thaw them as they've already been blanched.) Melt a generous lump of butter (yes, butter again!) in a wok and cook the beans over the lowest possible heat for up to an hour, stirring occasionally. They will gradually soften and mellow, absorbing the butter to brown slightly and develop flavor—a revelation to those familiar only with crisp green beans.

Roast Heads of Garlic

To roast garlic, I slice the top off the heads to expose the cloves, then set them in a baking dish, drizzle with oil, and sprinkle them with salt and pepper. If roasted in a 375°F/190°C oven (often alongside a roast), they take 35 to 45 minutes to brown and soften to the center so the pulp can be easily scooped or squeezed out and spread on crusty country bread. Allow one head per person—it sounds like a lot but any leftovers are great for flavoring soups and sauces.

OPPOSITE: *Peach trees mature quickly but, exhausted by bumper crops like this one (right), they tend to be short-lived. Puce ("the flea"), the Milbert's Yorkshire-style terrier, is not adverse to a fruity snack.*

Hot Bacon Salad

The best way to deal with chewy salad greens is to wilt them slightly with a dressing of hot bacon and vinegar. Smoked bacon, cut in a meaty dice that the French call *lardons,* is perfect for this salad, which serves four as a first course or light lunch.

> *a medium head of curly chicory or escarole*
>   *(³/₄ lb/375g)*
> *1 tablespoon vegetable oil*
> *a 4-oz/125-g piece of smoked lean bacon, diced*
> *¹/₃ cup/75 ml red wine vinegar*
> *freshly ground black pepper*

Discard the tough outer green leaves from the chicory or escarole and trim the root end. Separate the pale center leaves and tear any large leaves in 2 or 3 pieces. Wash and dry the leaves thoroughly and put them in a salad bowl.

Just before serving, heat the oil in a frying pan and fry the bacon until lightly browned. Pour off all but about 4 tablespoons of fat from the pan, leaving the bacon in the pan. Then pour the remaining hot fat and bacon over the greens and toss rapidly until slightly wilted, ½ to 1 minute. Add the vinegar to the hot pan (stand back from the fumes) and bring just to a boil, stirring to dissolve the pan juices. Pour the vinegar over the greens and toss again. Sprinkle the salad with freshly ground black pepper and serve at once.

Homegrown produce puts commercial crops to shame. That first year at Le Feÿ I noticed some hard little green fruit. *"Pêches de vigne,"* grunted Milbert, explaining they were the wild, ungrafted peach trees that used to be grown between the rows of grapevines. Like many plants, vines and peaches thrive side by side in symbiotic relationship: "They please each other," he says. Mark and I suspect there was once an economic reason too, a holdover from the days of sharecropping when laborers would furtively plant a crop of their own among the landlord's vines.

Monsieur Milbert had grown our half-dozen wild peach trees, his pride, from cuttings. Most were yellow-fleshed, but one bore astonishing deep crimson fruit, a throwback to some ancestor. (Without grafting to standard root stock, says Milbert, a cutting can revert to earlier generations.) Vineyard peaches ripen a good two months later than cultivars and they are best when cooked. Jam made with them has an intense, rich flavor and the red peaches I used one year produced a startling carmine preserve exactly the color of red currant jelly. Most disconcerting to taste! Thanks to the food processor, our daughter, Emma, learned to make peach crumble (overleaf) at the age of six. The crumble topping comes together at the touch of a button, and whenever possible I leave the fruit unpeeled.

Monsieur Milbert had to admit defeat, however, with the lone fig tree that nestles in the south-facing, sunniest corner of the vegetable garden. He watered it, he gave it compost, he even inserted a flagstone to divide its tap root. The poodle lady, Madame Andrea from down the hill, only made things worse by bringing a great basket of her own tantalizingly fleshy figs. We catch sight of Madame Andrea most days, walking her dog, whose woolly coat almost exactly matches her own rust-colored hair. She has an eye for good produce, having run a restaurant before retiring to the country. She kept Milbert guessing for a week or two about the fig tree, then capitulated: it seems that certain fig trees are "blind" and do not bear fruit. Thanks to a gift of cuttings from her own prolific tree, we now grow fine figs.

Poached Figs with Pistachio Frangipane

A pound of fresh figs makes a splendid warm dessert for four.

> *1 lb/500 g figs*
> *pared zest of 1 orange*
> *2 cinnamon sticks*
> *1 teaspoon black peppercorns*
> *3 whole cloves*
> *2 cups/500 ml red wine*
> *½ cup/100 g sugar*
> *a bunch of green or purple basil*
>
> **FOR THE PISTACHIO FRANGIPANE**
> *¾ cup/90 g pistachio nuts*
> *¼ cup/60 g butter*
> *⅓ cup/60 g sugar*
> *1 egg, beaten to mix*
> *1 tablespoon kirsch*
> *3 tablespoons flour*
>
> *a small piece of cheesecloth*

To poach the figs, tie the orange zest, cinnamon sticks, peppercorns, and cloves in a piece of cheesecloth and put them in a medium saucepan with the wine and sugar. Heat the mixture gently until the sugar is dissolved. Then bring it to a boil and simmer for 5 minutes. Reserve 8 to 10 basil sprigs, and add the remaining leaves and stems to the wine syrup. Prick each fig 2 to 3 times with a fork so the syrup will penetrate. Immerse the figs in the syrup and press a piece of parchment paper on top so they remain submerged. Poach until just tender, 3 to 5 minutes, depending on their ripeness. Let the fruit cool for 5 minutes in the syrup, and then lift them out and set them aside. Boil the poaching syrup until very concentrated and syrupy, 20 to 25 minutes. (If your figs are truly soft and ripe, skip the poaching and just simmer and reduce the syrup as described.)

Meanwhile, heat the oven to 375°F/190°C. For the frangipane, grind the pistachios to a coarse powder in a food processor or using a rotary grater, taking care not to overwork them or they will be heavy. In an electric mixer, cream the butter, beat in the sugar, and continue beating until soft and light, 1 to 2 minutes. Beat in the egg. Add the kirsch and then stir in the ground pistachios and the flour.

Trim the hard stalks off the figs and cut the fruit almost into quarters, leaving them joined at the base. Pull the quarters outward like the petals of a flower and fill the center with a spoonful of frangipane. Set the figs in a baking dish and bake until the frangipane is very hot and set, 7 to 10 minutes. Reheat the red wine syrup if necessary and strain it over the figs, discarding flavorings. Top with basil sprigs and serve figs warm.

Fruit Crumble

The recipe is good for any tart fruit, particularly apples, apricots, plums, and our wild peaches from the garden. Combine ¾ cup/175 g cold butter, cut into pieces, with 2 cups/250 g flour in a food processor and work it to fine crumbs using the pulse button. Alternatively, cut up the butter with a knife and then work it to crumbs with your fingers. Stir in ⅔ cup/125 g sugar. Halve 2 lb/1 kg fresh apricots, plums, or peaches (there's no need to peel them) and discard the pits. Peel, core, and slice apples, if using. If the fruit is very tart, toss it in a little sugar. Spread the fruit in a medium baking dish to form a 1-inch/2.5-cm layer. Cover it evenly with the topping and bake in a 375°F/190°C oven until the crumble is golden and the fruit juice bubbles around the edges, 40 to 50 minutes. It will serve 6 to 8.

If your figs are very ripe, there's no need to poach them in syrup before baking them with frangipane (see recipe at left). Simply simmer and reduce the spiced wine syrup without the figs.

Over the years I've learned a lot from Monsieur Milbert. I relish his folklore: *"Mars aride, avril humide,"* he quotes when it rains nonstop in spring. Following his example, I've come to accept that no two years are alike: this July I saw scarcely a fruit on the trees, but last year was amazing for stone fruit, the branches so weighted down that many of them broke. Our apricots ripened for the first time and the baby peach tree, an ancient variety, was hung with heart-shaped sweet pink fruits. Only the apple trees failed; they flowered too late and were caught by a freak frost. But I will never make a gardener. I will never acquire Milbert's peaceful tolerance of the weather, of slugs, bugs, and roots that won't take. I yearn to discipline plants, to make them flower and bear fruit by rote following my own designs. Nature rampant is not my style.

CHAPTER 2

A Vanishing Life

By the end of our first summer, we'd learned several sharp lessons. From the start, Monsieur Milbert had made it clear he was boss of the garden and determined to remain so. None of us was permitted to pick produce; we were expected to leave a note in the kitchen with the following day's requests. Madame Milbert did the gathering under her husband's eye. If he reckoned a fruit or vegetable was not ripe, we had to wait—and we still do. Leeks are a constant bone of contention, left at least six months to *gonfler* (swell) before lifting. Just last week we had an argument about young green cabbages. *"Non,"* Milbert said firmly. "They dissolve to nothing in the pan." Which is, of course, just why I like them. For a while I thought Monsieur Milbert was simply disobliging until I realized he adheres to a long-standing rural principle: anything edible must be left to grow as large as possible for maximum yield. Tenderness and flavor do not count.

The push and pull of rural life leaves its mark on the landscape, too. At the nearby Château de Bontin, for example, a farmer who had bought the surrounding land took it upon himself to fell a centuries-old *allée* of trees, leaving the house standing stark and bare. It is only now, a generation later, that Arnaud de Bontin has regained the ground and replanted frail trees that will take fifty years to mature. Near Chablis, Bernard and Brigitte Lefebure look over a charming vista, landscaped by a master hand, to the vineyards of Chablis in the distance. But merely the shell remains as the lake and retaining walls that anchored the panorama were destroyed to plant crops with easy access for the tractor. The Lefebures have the old plans, but restoration is a major undertaking.

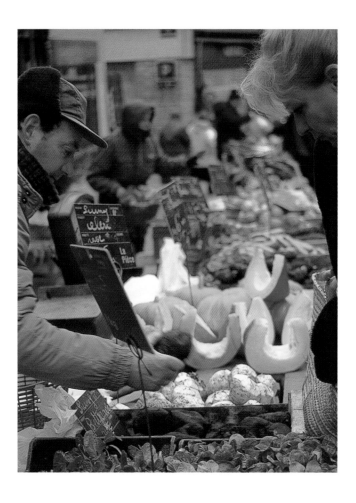

Winter White Vegetables

So many winter roots are white. You could substitute others—artichokes or parsnips—for those suggested here; for color, add carrots or sweet potatoes. The vegetables are simmered in stock, then stirred in bit by bit in the manner of risotto. They make a warming side dish for four.

> ½ lb/250 g small turnips
> ½ lb/250 g celery root
> ½ lb/250 g firm, waxy potatoes
> 1½ cups/375 ml veal or chicken stock
> 3 to 4 tablespoons butter
> ½ cup/60 g grated Parmesan cheese
> salt and ground white pepper

Peel all the vegetables and cut them into ½-inch/1.25-cm dice. Bring the stock to a boil.

Melt half of the butter in a large frying pan and stir in the vegetables. Add half the stock and simmer the vegetables, stirring often, until the stock is absorbed. Add the remaining stock and continue cooking until it is absorbed and the vegetables are tender, 8 to 12 minutes total cooking time. Stir in the remaining butter with the Parmesan cheese, taste, and adjust the seasoning.

PREVIOUS PAGES: *At left, three staples of rural life: an apple tree, cabbages, and logs for the fire. The garden gate at Château du Feÿ, top, is firmly shut at night against wild boar. A local farmhouse embraces an ancient fortified tower.* OPPOSITE: *A bumper crop of wheat shimmers in the sun.* ABOVE: *Among winter vegetables, pumpkin catches the eye.*

Spring Soup

Seasonal vegetables and their verdant green color give this vegetable soup its name. This recipe makes a quick first course or light supper for six people.

> *2 qts/2 liters chicken or well-flavored vegetable stock*
> *¼ cup/30 g flour*
> *the white part of 2 medium leeks, sliced crosswise*
> *the inner stems of a small bunch of celery, sliced*
>   *crosswise*
> *1 cup/150 g fresh green peas*
> *pinch of sugar*
> *salt and white pepper*
> *the inner leaves of a small head of romaine, shredded*
>
> FOR THE CROUTONS
> *3 slices of white bread, ¼ in/6 mm thick*
> *butter or vegetable oil for frying*

Stir about a cup of stock into the flour to make a smooth paste. Bring the remaining stock to a boil, whisk in the flour paste, and continue stirring until the soup thickens. Add the leeks, celery, and peas with the sugar, salt, and pepper. Cover the soup and simmer until the vegetables are tender, 15 to 20 minutes. Five minutes before the end of cooking, stir in the lettuce.

Meanwhile, make the croutons. Trim the crusts from the bread and cut it into ¼-inch/6-mm dice. Heat enough butter or oil in a frying pan so that the croutons will float (I prefer the sweet taste of butter-fried croutons for this delicate soup). Fry the croutons over medium heat until they are evenly browned on all sides. Remove them with a slotted spoon and drain them on paper towels. To serve, taste the soup and adjust the seasoning. Spoon it into bowls and serve the croutons separately.

Spring Soup (above) is a refreshing mix sharpened with romaine lettuce. A local farmer displays infant peas. When grown, they are also a key ingredient in Spring Soup.

Now rising eighty, Roger and Francine Milbert pursue a way of life that is fast disappearing. They rise with the sun and when it sets they retreat into their gatehouse, which year-round is kept in a steamy fog by a wood-burning stove. The cat sits on the dinner table and the television screen flickers in the background. In summer Milbert is in the garden seven days a week weeding, watering, trimming hedges, mowing lawns. In winter he fells trees and cuts logs. Madame Milbert is more housebound but never idle, raising chickens and ducks for their eggs and meat.

Sauté of Chicken with Vinegar, Garlic, and Tomato
Sauté de Poulet au Vinaigre

Cooking meats and poultry with vinegar is an ancient tradition dating from the Middle Ages before lemon was available to add acidity. A Burgundian classic, the recipe calls, of course, for wine vinegar—the older the better—and lots of garlic, which mellows and softens as it cooks to act as a thickener for the sauce. This recipe makes a warming main course for four.

> *a 3½-lb/1.6-kg chicken, cut into 8 pieces*
> *salt and pepper*
> *3 tablespoons/45 g butter*
> *1 large head of garlic*
> *1 cup/250 ml red wine vinegar*
> *1 lb/500 g tomatoes*
> *1 tablespoon tomato purée*
> *a bouquet garni*
> *1 cup/250 ml chicken stock, more if needed*
> *1 tablespoon chopped parsley*

Season the chicken pieces with salt and pepper. Melt half the butter over medium heat in a sauté pan or deep frying pan with lid, and heat until it stops foaming. Add the pieces of chicken, skin-side down, starting with the legs and thighs because they need the longest cooking. When they begin to brown, add the wing pieces and finally the breasts. After about 10 minutes, when all the pieces are brown on one side, turn them over and brown the other side for 1 or 2 minutes.

Divide the garlic cloves and add them, unpeeled, to the pan. Cover and cook over low heat for 10 minutes. Then holding the cover on the pan so the chicken pieces do not fall out, drain off the excess fat. Return the pan to the heat, add the vinegar, and simmer it, uncovered, until very well reduced, 10 to 15 minutes. Chop the tomatoes —there's no need to seed or skin them as the sauce will later be strained. Add them to the chicken with the tomato purée and the bouquet garni. Cover and simmer again until the chicken is tender, 10 to 15 minutes more —the pieces should fall easily from a two-pronged fork. If some pieces are cooked through and tender before others, remove them.

Transfer the chicken pieces to a serving dish and keep them warm. Add the stock to the pan and simmer the sauce, uncovered, until it is concentrated and lightly thickened, 5 to 8 minutes. Work the sauce through a sieve into a saucepan, pressing hard to extract the garlic pulp. Bring the sauce to a boil, take it off the heat, and whisk in the remaining butter in small pieces. Taste it and adjust the seasoning. Spoon the sauce over the chicken and top with chopped parsley.

Make Your Own Vinegar

Vinegar—*vin aigre* or acid wine—is the natural product of any wine region and at home at Le Feÿ, we brew our own in a big crock in the kitchen using leftover red wine. Here's how to do it.

Look in old bottles of vinegar until you find one with a floating, cloudy-looking membrane, rather like a jelly-fish; this is a vinegar mother. Transfer the mother with the vinegar to a crock, preferably with a tap at the base so you can draw off the vinegar easily; a crock is best as the brew should be kept in the dark. Add a bottle or two of fruity red wine and cover the top loosely with cheese-cloth to exclude insects but let in the air. Leave it for 6 months before tasting. The vinegar should be mellow with a good backing of acid. If thin tasting, let it mellow another month. Once the vinegar is established, keep the crock topped up with leftovers of red wine.

At one time Madame Milbert tended upward of 100 rabbits (yes, they do breed with astonishing rapidity every six weeks), though now the brood is reduced to a dozen or so. It is her pride never to have lost a tooth, though she has never used a toothbrush. She has mellowed over the years, but when younger she was a prime source of sneaky information guaranteed to annoy. "Did you know the school chef left the storeroom door open so the cat got in?" she would say, or "There's a poacher with a gun in the woods but of course I didn't interfere." She herself was—and still is—constantly guilty of feeding sweet biscuits to our dogs while swearing to the contrary.

Madame Milbert's Rabbit Terrine

Some of our guests find Madame Milbert's rabbits too much like pets to put them in the pot, so I bone the meat to make a terrine, one way of disguising its origin. The recipe assumes you can buy a whole rabbit. If it is in pieces, simply cut the meat from the bone and divide it as described below. This terrine is crunchy with hazelnuts, which grow wild in our hedgerows. One makes a delicious appetizer for ten to twelve.

> *a 3-lb/1.4-kg rabbit, with the liver if possible*
> *1 tablespoon butter*
> *2 tablespoons Cognac*
> *2 tablespoons Madeira or sherry*
> *1 cup/130 g shelled hazelnuts*
> *2 to 3 chicken livers*
> *salt and pepper*
> *½ lb/250 g barding fat or thinly sliced fat bacon*
>
> **FOR THE STUFFING**
>
> *1 lb/500 g lean pork, ground*
> *½ lb/250 g pork fat, ground*
> *2 garlic cloves, chopped*
> *½ teaspoon ground allspice*
> *pinch of ground cloves*
> *pinch of grated nutmeg*
> *1 tablespoon salt, or to taste*
> *1½ teaspoons black pepper, or to taste*
> *2 eggs, whisked to mix*
> *2 thyme sprigs*
> *2 bay leaves*
>
> *a 2-quart/2-liter terrine mold*

With a pointed knife, cut the dark meat from the legs of the rabbit, discarding the sinews. Cut the white saddle meat from the backbone, lifting each side off in one piece, and remove the fillets from under the ribs. Slice the fillets and half the saddle meat lengthwise into ½-inch-/1.25-cm-wide strips. Reserve the leg meat and remaining saddle meat for the stuffing. Heat the butter in a frying pan and cook the strips of meat gently until firm and white, 2 to 3 minutes (this later prevents the meat from shrinking and making hollows in the terrine). Put the strips in a dish with the Cognac and Madeira or sherry and mix well. Cover and leave to marinate for about an hour.

Heat the oven to 350°F/175°C. Spread the hazelnuts on a baking sheet and toast them in the oven until brown, 12 to 15 minutes. Let the nuts cool slightly, then if they are not already peeled, rub them in a rough cloth to remove the skins. Leave the oven on.

Trim the rabbit and chicken livers of membrane, sprinkle them with salt and pepper, and roll them up in a wide strip of barding fat or 2 to 3 strips of bacon to form a cylinder as long as the terrine. When you roll the barding fat or bacon into a cylinder, it should overlap just enough to encase the livers. Set it aside. Line the bottom, sides, and ends of the terrine with the remaining barding fat or bacon, saving a piece or two for the top.

For the stuffing, work the reserved uncooked rabbit leg and saddle meat with the ground fat and ground pork through the fine blade of a grinder. Drain the marinated strips and set them aside. Beat the marinade into the ground meat with the garlic, allspice, cloves, nutmeg, salt, and pepper. Add the eggs, and then stir in the hazelnuts. Fry a small piece of the mixture, taste, and adjust the seasoning; it should be quite spicy since the flavors mellow as the terrine cooks.

Spread a quarter of the stuffing in the lined terrine,

arrange half the rabbit strips on top, and cover with a quarter more stuffing. The terrine should be about half full. Set the cylinder of wrapped livers down the center, cover with more stuffing, and then add the remaining rabbit strips and stuffing. Cut the reserved barding fat or bacon in narrow strips and arrange them in a diagonal lattice pattern on top of the meat. Set the thyme sprigs and bay leaf on top and add the lid.

Set the terrine in a bain-marie and bring it to a boil on top of the stove. Then transfer it to the oven and cook until the terrine is firm to the touch, 1 to 1¼ hours; a skewer inserted in the center of the terrine should be hot to the touch when withdrawn after 30 seconds.

Lift the terrine from the bain-marie and let it cool to tepid, then remove the lid and set a 2-lb/1-kg weight on top (a brick wrapped in plastic is ideal). Cover the terrine, weight and all, and refrigerate it for at least 2 days and up to a week so the flavor mellows. Serve the terrine either straight from the mold, or unmold it if you prefer, cutting it into thick slices and discarding the barding fat. All terrines taste best if allowed to come to room temperature before serving.

For any meat or game terrine, olives and gherkin pickles are the classic accompaniment, with lots of country bread.

Madame Milbert's poultry and rabbits are not for personal consumption, but for sale. There's no sentiment attached; it is simply a question of economic value. By tradition, the income a country wife can generate is hers to keep. At Château du Feÿ a constant stream of customers calls at the gatehouse, conspicuous among them the local gendarmes who enjoy a break from patrolling the fast-running highway in the valley below us. Near Christmas they come more often—a generous contribution to police funds is mandatory—and I suspect another incentive is the prospect of a warming tot of Monsieur Milbert's home-brewed Calvados. He is self-supporting not only in vegetables, but in pick-me-ups as well.

Somewhere near Le Feÿ in a location deliberately undisclosed, Monsieur Milbert grows cider apples. Come October, he transports them in plastic sacks to our side courtyard, where he leaves them to mature and ferment slightly. In November the crusher arrives, an antique, clanking contraption run on water hydraulics. The juice is hosed into casks hidden in one of the château's many cellars, and after a week or so the rooms above become permeated with the heady, pungent smell of fermentation. A spell of warm weather often hits around this time—the French call it St. Martin's summer as it often coincides with the saint's feast day on November 11—so the cider ferments all the faster. As the juice bubbles, it racks and cleans itself, with some sediment frothing out of the top bung hole and the rest falling to the bottom of the barrel to form the *lit* or bed. "It's all natural, you know," smiles Milbert. "This is my fiftieth year for cider, not bad, not bad." In a good season, his cider is full-bodied and sweet, but if not he doctors it with sugar on the sly. One disastrous year, when the apple blossom was nipped by frost, there was no cider at all. Meals in the gatehouse were glum affairs.

I would never have associated apples with Burgundy, but in fact Le Feÿ is on the border of cider country. The Pays d'Othe area just behind us is cool and damp, too rugged for vines but perfect for fruit trees. "They feel at home here," says Louisette Frottier, proud owner of the sole traditional cider press still in operation. There were once a hundred or more, one for each village or hamlet.

As well as making his own cider, Monsieur Milbert is a *bouilleur de cru*, the proud possessor of a license to distill 18 liters of Calvados apple brandy annually, free of tax. No new licenses have been issued since the 1950s, and his is one of the few that remains. Once a year he takes 200 liters of year-old cider (the older the better) to the traveling still that calls close by in St. Julien du Sault. The resulting Calvados (always shortened to Calva) is a legend in our family, a primitive firewater at 110 proof, which clears the head and wards off the meanest bronchitis. It could be used at a pinch to power the lawn mower, quips Mark. No wonder Milbert calls it *eau de vie*, water of life.

OPPOSITE: *This traveling still transforms Monsieur Milbert's cider into fiery Calvados.*

Roast Duck with Apples and Calvados

I may hesitate to drink Monsieur Milbert's Calvados but it makes a fine show when flaming on the stove. I picked up the taste for apples in savory dishes when we lived in Normandy, and this recipe has remained a favorite. Marc or Cognac can be substituted for Calvados—all that matters is that the alcohol be sharp enough to cut the richness of the duck. How well done you like roast duck is a matter of taste—for once I differ with French chefs and opt for well-done meat. It's your call. One good-sized duck serves three to four.

> *a 4- to 5-lb/about 2-kg duck*
> *salt and pepper*
> *1 to 2 tablespoons vegetable oil*
> *1 to 2 tablespoons Calvados*
> *1½ cups/375 ml chicken stock*
> *½ cup/125 ml crème fraîche or more chicken stock*
> *a bunch of watercress or salad greens for decoration*
>
> FOR THE SAUTÉED APPLES
>
> *2 tablespoons/30 g butter*
> *4 tart apples, peeled, cored, and sliced in eighths*
> *2 to 3 tablespoons sugar*
> *¼ cup/60 ml Calvados*
>
> *trussing needle and string*

Heat the oven to 425°F/220°C. Wipe the inside of the duck with paper towels and pull away any loose pieces of fat. Lift the neck skin and cut out the wishbone—this makes the breast meat easy to carve in neat slices. Season the bird inside and out with salt and pepper and truss it so it holds a neat shape (see the glossary).

Set the bird on its back in a medium roasting pan and spoon over the oil. If you have the giblets, add the neck, gizzard, and heart to the roasting pan (reserve the liver for another use). Roast the duck until it just starts to sizzle, 15 to 20 minutes. Baste it with pan juices and prick the skin all over with a fork to let the melted fat escape. Continue roasting for 30 more minutes, basting

often. Remove the duck from the oven, prick the skin again, and discard the excess fat from the pan (pouring off the fat as it accumulates helps render the skin crisp and brown). Turn the bird onto its breast and return it to the oven (cooking it breast downward keeps the meat moist). Lower the heat to 375°F/190°C and continue roasting, basting often, and discarding the fat from the pan. After about 30 more minutes, turn the bird again onto its back so the breast skin crispens.

Meanwhile, cook the apples. Melt the butter in a frying pan over medium-high heat, add the apples, and sprinkle with about a tablespoon of the sugar. Turn them, sprinkle with more sugar, and fry briskly until caramelized and tender, turning them so that they brown evenly and thoroughly, 8 to 12 minutes.

If you like your duck breast to be pink, after 1½ hours total cooking time, lift the bird on a two-pronged fork and pour the juices from the cavity—they should run pink but not red. If you like well-done duck, as I do, continue cooking for at least 15 minutes longer until the juices from the cavity run clear and the leg joint feels pliable when you pull the drumstick. When done to your taste, transfer the duck to a carving board or platter, cover it with foil, and keep it warm.

For the gravy, pour off all but 1 to 2 tablespoons of fat from the roasting pan. Set the roasting pan over high heat and boil the remaining pan juices until reduced to a glaze. Add the Calvados, stand back, and ignite it with a match. Add the stock and bring to a boil, scraping to dissolve the pan juices. Boil the gravy rapidly for 5 to 10 minutes, or until it is reduced by half. Add the crème fraîche or more stock, bring the gravy just to a boil, and strain it into a small saucepan. Bring it back to a boil—if the gravy seems thin, continue boiling to reduce it. Taste it, adjust the seasoning, and keep it warm.

Discard the trussing strings from the duck. If you are carving at the table, fill the cavity with watercress or some other pretty fresh greens; if carving in the kitchen, arrange the pieces on a warm serving dish. Reheat the apples over medium heat. Add the Calvados and flame it, standing back as the flames may rise high. Spoon apples beside the duck and serve the gravy separately.

The arrival of the cider-apple crusher marks the end of autumn at Château du Feÿ. In a good year, the plastic sacks of apples are piled high. With the apple crusher comes its master, Bernard Gionnet, clad for business in fisherman's waterproofs, high boots, and a peaked cap. The machine shudders to life and the pockmarked little red, green, and yellow apples mount by a chain of buckets to be pulped, wrapped in burlap, and then pressed into a stream of cloudy, aromatic juice. From time to time a glass is passed around, and everyone pronounces on the vintage.

For more than a year after we arrived at Le Feÿ, Madame Milbert's poultry kept a treasure from our eyes. Then one day I ducked into the chicken house and in the corner caught sight of a half-moon metal door, telltale sign of a wood-fired bread oven. Inside was a shallow domed roof some two yards across, its base made of special bricks to withstand high temperatures. The chimney flue was outside the baking chamber, a mysterious arrangement until we looked in *L'Art du Boulanger* of 1767, wherein exactly such an oven is described. In the largest ovens, 12 feet in diameter, 600 pounds of bread could be baked in a single batch according to the *Boulanger;* ours is scarcely smaller, a reflection of the number of Le Feÿ inhabitants and the importance of bread at that time. The first time we fired up the oven, we did so with such enthusiasm that flames roared out of its mouth like a dragon and we scorched the mantle beam almost to tinder. Now, under the tutelage of an expert baker, we are more circumspect.

Our oven is the common rounded shape, a *pomme* (apple). "But you'll find a few oval *poires* (pears) too," explains Robert Haumonté, white-haired and chatty, who has been a baker all his life, starting with apprenticeship at age fourteen. A visit by Monsieur Haumonté is an all-day affair. It takes three hours or more to bring the oven to the right temperature, a searing 550°F/270°C or more. For that, there's an age-old test: if too cool the dome of the oven will be dark with carbon, but at high temperatures the carbon burns off to reveal the underlying pale bricks. Once this happens, Monsieur Haumonté rakes out the remaining glowing ashes and wipes the oven floor with a quick swirl of wet rag on the end of a long pole—the first of many *tours de main* (turns of the hand) of the professional baker.

The dough, meanwhile, has been rising nicely in the warmth behind the chimney. Monsieur Haumonté will have begun the day by vigorously kneading the four ingredients for baguette bread dough— flour, water, salt, and yeast—in the form of levain, a soft fluffy sponge of dough reserved from the previous day's batch. He leaves the dough to rise in an inelegant plastic bucket (modern materials do have their place) and after about five hours, when the dough has doubled in bulk, he knocks out the air, cuts the dough in chunks, and weighs each one to be sure it checks in at the legal 400 grams or 13 ounces. Amazingly, this very same measure was used in 1415 when King Charles VI fixed prices for breads of this weight: "Thirteen *onces* of white bread will be sold for three *deniers* (a small coin), dark bread for two *deniers,* and bread mixed with barley for two *deniers tournois.*" Today the price of plain white bread is still subsidized so a baguette costs only 4 francs (about 75 cents).

Robert Haumonté's true skill comes into play once the dough has risen. He takes a chunk and with gestures almost too swift to follow he pats, folds, rolls, and seals the loaves with an underseam (the *clef* or key), elongating the dough for a baguette or flattening and folding it for a *fendu* or broken shape. Sometimes for fun he plaits a complex braid that is intriguingly identical on all four sides. He lays the loaves, seam up, on a dish towel, pleating the towel to separate each loaf.

After a long slow rising of at least 3 hours (important in developing flavor as well as even, open texture), each loaf is rolled onto the peel, the long-handled wooden shovel for transporting the bread to the oven. As a final gesture, Robert slashes the dough with a razor so the bread puffs up evenly in the oven. Or he will cut and pull open the sides for an *épi* (an ear of wheat), or snip the top for hedgehog spines. It all looks so easy but just a small slip and a loaf can be ruined.

As a young man, Robert knew his pay would be docked for each loaf that was misshapen or that "kissed" (i.e., touched) its neighbor. Using the peel to deposit the bread inside the oven with a rapid, expert jerk in just the right place is in itself a challenge. It is the baking hot bricks, plus steam from a drenched cloth set to one side of the oven, that gives wood-fired bread its inimitable crisp crust.

Baking is not only physically trying—a traditional bakehouse is routinely over 100°F/38°C—but many bakers are forced to retire early because of eczema or asthma caused by constant contact with flour. The hours are crippling too: for most of his life, Monsieur Haumonté worked from midnight until midday, sleeping in the afternoons. Social life? Robert looks surprised. *"C'est un beau métier* (it's a great calling)." Clearly that is enough. Just down the hill from us in Villevallier I'm glad to say we still have an artisanal baker, the third to take over in seven years. Conditions are better today, of course— the ovens are electric, the bread is kneaded by machine—but I wonder how long he will last.

Baker Robert Haumonté sweeps glowing ashes from the floor of our wood-fired bread oven.

Ear of Wheat Bread
Epi de Pain

One of Monsieur Haumonté's favorite loaves is shaped like an ear of wheat, perfect for breaking into individual crispy rolls. He uses plain white dough, but I like to add some whole wheat flour for a nutty flavor. This recipe makes two long loaves.

> ¼ cup/60 g butter
> 1 heaping tablespoon honey
> 1 tablespoon salt
> 2 cups/500 ml lukewarm water
> 1 tablespoon/10 g active dry yeast
> 3 cups/375 g stone-ground whole wheat flour
> 3½ cups/425 g all-purpose flour, more if needed

Melt the butter in a saucepan. Stir in the honey, salt, and 3 to 4 tablespoons of the warm water and let cool to tepid. Put 3 to 4 more tablespoons of the warm water in a small bowl, sprinkle over the yeast, and leave it until dissolved, about 5 minutes.

Pour the whole wheat and all-purpose flours onto a work surface and make a large well in the center. Add the honey mixture, the dissolved yeast, and the remaining warm water to the well. Mix the ingredients in the well with the fingertips of one hand. With a pastry scraper in your other hand, gradually draw in the flour and mix it with the liquid ingredients to form a soft and slightly sticky dough; if the dough is very sticky, work in more all-purpose flour.

Sprinkle the work surface with flour and knead the dough, pushing it away from you with one hand and holding the near side with the other. Peel the dough from the work surface, give it a quarter turn, and continue kneading—repeating the rhythm of pushing, peeling it up, and turning—until it is very smooth and elastic, 5 to 7 minutes. Add more flour sparingly; the dough will naturally become less sticky during kneading. It should be soft and pliable; too much flour will make it dry and tough. (You can also knead the dough in an

electric mixer using the dough hook; allow 4 to 5 minutes.) Shape the dough into a ball, transfer it to an oiled bowl, and flip it so the top is oiled. Cover the bowl tightly with plastic wrap and leave the dough to rise in a warm place until doubled in bulk, 1 to 1½ hours.

Turn the dough onto a lightly floured work surface and knead just to knock out the air, 15 to 20 seconds. Cut the dough with a knife into 2 equal pieces. Flour your hands and pat one piece of dough into a 6 x 12-inch/15 x 30-cm rectangle. Starting with a long side, roll the rectangle into a cylinder. Pinch the overlap to seal it and form a seam. With your palms, roll the cylinder, stretching it to a 20-inch/50-cm stick. Very generously flour a large dish towel and set the loaf, seam upward, parallel with one long side. The towel should be large enough so the loaf barely extends, if at all, over the ends. Pleat the towel along the side of the loaf. Shape the other loaf and set it, also seam-side up, on the towel against the pleat. Cover the loaves with a second dry dish towel and let them rise in a warm place until doubled in bulk, about an hour.

Heat the oven to 425°F/220°C. Roll a loaf onto a large oiled baking sheet so the seam is downward. To shape the wheat ear, use a large scissors to make a deep cut (⅔ of the way through the loaf) at a 45° angle about 2 to 3 inches/5 to 7 cm from one end. Pull the point of dough above the cut outward from the loaf. Make a second cut, 2 to 3 inches/5 to 7 cm from the first, on the other side of the loaf and pull out a second point so there are points of dough extended from both sides of the narrow loaf. Repeat the cuts down the length of the loaf and you will see the wheat ear take shape. There should be 7 to 9 points of dough in all. Repeat with the other loaf. Bake the loaves until well browned and the bottoms sound hollow when tapped with your fist, 20 to 25 minutes. Eat the bread as soon as possible, preferably warm from the oven.

ABOVE: *A pile of finished loaves, including the classic baguette and Ear of Wheat.* OPPOSITE: *Monsieur Haumonté brushes loaves with water for a crisp crust.*

For croissants, Monsieur Haumonté kneads cold butter so it is malleable but keeps its shape (top left). Then he rolls and folds his dough in layers and cuts it in triangles. Finally he shapes each piece of dough loosely so the croissant has room to rise. His baked croissants puff up to at least double their original size.

It all looks easy, but croissants are the greatest test of a baker's skill. They pose a contradiction: yeast works best at around $110°F/38°C$—blood heat—but this temperature would melt the butter that is used to interleave the dough and create those irresistible crumbling flakes. So croissants involve a compromise. The butter is chilled before use and the finished croissants are left to rise slowly in a cool place, often overnight. Another key is to work the dough gently so as not to develop gluten in the flour, which would render the dough elastic and the croissants misshapen and tough.

I take pride in restricting ourselves as much as possible to homegrown produce, but the Milberts truly live off the land. In summer a dozen vegetables may be on their table, but once the winter frost sets in and the spinach leaves freeze, they are limited to their beloved leeks with pumpkin, potatoes, carrots, and any other roots that can be stored in a cold, dark cellar. In early summer, Madame Milbert strips the flowers from lime tree branches to dry for herb tea, and in the fall she goes into the woods to hunt black *trompettes de mort* mushrooms, a type of chanterelle. Her source is a secret that will die with her—even her husband does not know where she goes.

We are also well supplied with nuts. Volunteer walnut trees grow happily and when the crop is plentiful, Madame Milbert may give us a treasure—a bottle of home-pressed walnut oil so concentrated that it seems just a spoonful perfumes a whole bowl of salad. Walnut oil and a somewhat sticky walnut liqueur are regional specialties, and in one of our barns stands a stone wheel, high as a man, once used for extracting oil from a variety of nuts and seeds as well as for crushing apples for cider. Just outside the gate a centuries-old avenue, marked on a map of 1751, provides the wild chestnuts (*châtaignes*) Madame Milbert peels with diligence, kindly handing a bag or two to me for Christmas dinner. They are smaller than cultivated chestnuts (*marrons*), aromatic and lighter in texture. The skin tends to cling to the nut meat, so I find they do best as purée, which I like to spice with musty coriander and allspice.

The last warmth of summer seems to glow from a hefty pumpkin, pride of Monsieur Milbert's vegetable garden.

Chestnut Purée

For 4 people, allow about a pound/500 grams of chestnuts. Various tricks are suggested for peeling them—soaking in boiling water or broiling briefly, for instance —but I find the simplest is to take a comfortable seat, turn on some music, and tackle them raw, one by one, stripping off the peel with a small sharp knife and cutting off as much of the inner skin as possible at the same time. Cover the peeled chestnuts with water in a saucepan, add a little salt, and simmer them for 30 to 40 minutes, covered, until they are very tender and almost falling apart. (For more flavor you can cook the nuts in half veal or chicken stock and half water.) Drain the nuts, reserving the liquid, then work them through a potato ricer or purée them briefly in a food processor with a little of the cooking liquid. Return the chestnuts to the pan, and for every 2 cups of purée, beat in a teaspoon each of ground coriander and allspice, salt and pepper to taste, and enough cooking liquid for the purée to fall easily from the spoon. Heat the purée, beating constantly, to make it light and fluffy, and taste it for seasoning. The consistency of the finished purée, stiff or soft, is up to you, but be sure it is not sticky.

On some winter weekends we feel under siege. The woodlands fill with hunters and their dogs on the march, all excitable and notoriously liable to shoot at anything that moves. The warning to wear red is no joke and we keep our own dogs indoors. Nonetheless, culling is controlled and in 1997, for instance, our village hunting club was permitted to shoot four deer and unlimited wild boar (sanglier), though young ones under three months (marcassin) had to be spared. Two derelict buses (top left) have been cobbled together to form a cozy retreat in the woods for hunters and dogs.

61

You might think the woodlands that surround Le Feÿ would afford us protection and privacy. For part of the year, perhaps, but not once the hunting season opens. The forest still abounds with game—wild boar from the forests routinely root at night in our garden and we sometimes glimpse roe deer cantering through the front field. As late as the 1850s, Burgundian huntsmen were accustomed to sound six blasts of the horn to warn of a wolf, five for a stag, four for a wild boar, three for a deer, and two for a fox, though wolves had not been seen for a hundred years. French hunters are a belligerent lot. Just recently a quarter million of them turned out in Paris to protest a European Union directive that would curb their rights to trample over other people's land. So open is hunting that one morning from our bedroom window I spotted a poacher, bold as brass, strolling in our bit of woodland, dog at his heels and gun at the ready. To my lasting regret, I was stark naked at the time or I would have gone after him!

During hunting season, this drive through our woodlands is off limits to walkers and dogs.

Venison Stew with Black Mushrooms and Ratafia

Claude, the genial giant who looks after the village water supply and who rescues us when the pump fails, is a crack marksman, and his quarry is the perfect partner to Madame Milbert's mushrooms. One day I was in a rush to cook a venison stew—no time to give the meat a traditional 2- to 3-day soak in marinade—since guests were due that evening. So I decided on something stronger—a quick soak in ratafia, the grape-juice liqueur laced with marc that is produced by many Burgundian wine makers (you'll find our recipe on page 75). After all, a touch of sweetness is good with venison. With Madame Milbert's black mushrooms and some crème fraîche, it proved a memorable combination. As a substitute for ratafia, I'd suggest a really rich sweet muscat or late-picked Riesling; port wine is also acceptable. This recipe makes a hearty meal for six to eight.

a 2-lb/1-kg boned shoulder or haunch of venison

FOR THE MARINADE
½ bottle (375 ml) ratafia
3 garlic cloves, sliced
3 shallots, sliced

FOR COOKING THE VENISON
1 tablespoon butter
1 tablespoon vegetable oil
1 onion, sliced
a large bouquet garni
salt and pepper
3 cups/750 ml veal stock, more if needed
½ lb/250 g fresh or 2 oz/60 g dried black trumpet
  mushrooms or chanterelles

FOR THE SAUCE
3 tablespoons butter
3 tablespoons flour
1 cup/250 ml crème fraîche or heavy cream

Trim the sinew and any fat from the venison and cut it into 2-inch/5-cm chunks. In a nonreactive bowl, mix the ratafia, garlic, and shallots, add the venison, and toss to mix. Cover the bowl and refrigerate the meat for 4 to 8 hours.

Heat the oven to 350°F/175°C. Lift the venison from the marinade and dry the pieces on paper towels, reserving the liquid and the vegetables. In a heavy casserole, heat half the butter and oil. Fry the pieces of venison over high heat a few at a time, browning them very thoroughly on all sides and adding more butter and oil when the pan gets dry. Set the venison aside. When all the meat is browned, lower the heat to medium, add the onion, and sauté it, stirring often, until lightly browned, 7 to 10 minutes.

Add the marinade to the casserole, bring it to a boil, and simmer for 2 to 3 minutes, stirring to deglaze the pan juices. Replace the meat and add the bouquet garni with a little salt and pepper. Pour in enough stock to just cover and push the meat well down into the liquid. Cover the pan and bring it to a boil. Transfer the casserole to the oven and cook until the venison is fairly tender when pierced with a two-pronged fork, 1½ to 2½ hours depending on whether the venison is wild or farmed (wild venison needs more time to become truly tender). Stir the stew from time to time during cooking and add more stock if at any time the sauce starts to stick.

Meanwhile, trim the stems of the fresh mushrooms, discarding any earth; wash them only if they are very sandy, draining them thoroughly. If using dried mushrooms, pour over warm water to cover them generously and leave them to soak until they are swollen and soft.

When the venison is fairly tender, stir in the fresh mushrooms. If using dried mushrooms, lift them out of the soaking water, leaving the sediment behind, and add them to the venison. If you like a more intense mushroom flavor, strain the soaking water through a coffee filter and add it to the stew. Continue cooking until the venison is very tender and the mushrooms are cooked, 15 to 30 minutes.

Transfer the casserole to the stovetop and bring the stew to a boil. To thicken the sauce, crush the butter and flour with a fork to form a paste called beurre manié. Add this to the boiling sauce in small pieces, stirring so it softens and thickens the sauce evenly. Stir in the cream, bring the sauce back to a boil, and simmer for 2 to 3 minutes, or longer if it seems thin. The sauce will continue to thicken somewhat as it simmers. Taste and adjust the seasoning. Venison stew reheats well and the flavor mellows on keeping.

63

To better understand the Milberts, you should know their background. Both were born in this *pays* (neighborhood). Much more than a geographical concept, the *pays* evokes its inhabitants and their way of life. The Yonne *département* in which we live embraces dozens of *pays,* and longtime residents think small, almost treating another *pays* as an unfamiliar land. By local standards the Milberts have done well. When they married during World War II, for lack of a permanent home they lived in a barn, sleeping on straw. What they earned, they saved. For the last twenty-five years they have been at Château du Feÿ, their lifestyle settled and confident. On the face of it, Monsieur Milbert is the widely respected patriarch of a family with thriving grandchildren.

But there is a dark side to such apparent rustic bliss. Of the four Milbert children, one developed a muscular disease in childhood, dying several years ago in her forties after devoted nursing by her mother. One son, a baker by trade, disappeared three months after his sister's death—his wife had left him, taking their two small children. Another son, a plumber in a nearby village, is never seen and his name is not even mentioned. Only the daughter, Françoise, and her brood of three children are regular visitors, chasing our dogs with cheerful shouts. Her husband, Daniel, takes potshots at the few pheasants and helps with heavy jobs such as lifting Milbert's potato crop and dismembering a windfall tree.

Françoise and her family sometime come to her parents for Sunday lunch. This is the main meal of the week and the centerpiece is always red meat—a chunk of braising beef or possibly a leg of lamb—supplied by the butcher in exchange for a rabbit or two. First course is likely to be radishes, tomatoes, red beets, root celery, whatever the garden yields, with a slice or two of ham or dried saucisson. Our globe artichokes are so tender that the Milberts eat them raw, pulling off the leaves and chewing them almost like candy. We are less resolute, simmering them to tenderness before serving them with this walnut vinaigrette, a fragrant accompaniment to many vegetable salads.

Walnut Vinaigrette

Put a teaspoonful of mild Dijon mustard, a large pinch of salt, and a good sprinkling of fresh black pepper in a small bowl with 3 tablespoons of vinegar—personally I like the flavor of sherry or balsamic with walnut. Wrap a cloth around the base of the bowl so it does not shift as you whisk, and then gradually add ½ cup/125 ml walnut oil, whisking constantly with one hand and drizzling in the oil with the other. Be sure to start slowly so that, thanks to the mustard, the dressing forms a light emulsion, thickening slightly so it coats food evenly. Chopped garlic, shallot, and herbs are optional extras in the dressing—tarragon has a particular affinity for artichokes—but for freshness add them just before serving. Lastly, taste and adjust the seasoning of the dressing, not forgetting to taste again after it is mixed with the salad ingredients; often you'll need more salt and pepper. If serving with warm vegetables such as artichokes, set the bowl of dressing in a simmering bain-marie to warm it before serving.

ABOVE: *Hand-picked walnuts and chestnuts await buyers in the market.*
OPPOSITE: *The green of early summer is full of promise for autumn. From left are rows of carrots, cabbage, leeks; in the background are tomatoes not yet ripe.*

Pot au feu bubbles in an ancient open fireplace, in a pot suspended from the original pothook. In her day, Madame Milbert was a noted cook, simmering pot au feu, braising rabbit, and roasting legs of lamb like a professional. Supper each evening is truly souper, consisting of vegetable soup with plenty of bread—between the two of them, the Milberts consume a couple of baguettes each day. Ironically, Madame Milbert's greatest treat is a tin of commercial cookies, the more synthetic, the better. Home cooking simply reminds her of hard work.

Pot au Feu with a Twist

I've always found pot au feu to be terribly plain—the classic accompaniments of sea salt, mustard, and gherkin pickles are simply not my style. So one day, I added a touch of Italy by sprinkling my boiled meats with gremolata, the aromatic mixture of chopped parsley, garlic, and lemon zest that is served on osso buco. *Squisito!* The accompanying vegetables were vastly improved as well. The right ingredients for pot au feu are crucial. Meats must include lean beef such as chuck, and flank or brisket for gelatin to enrich the broth, plus one marrow bone per person. For vegetables, carrots, leeks, and celery stalks or roots are mandatory, with an onion or two stuck with a clove for flavor, and an option on turnips and rutabaga. The hallmark of successful pot au feu is a limpid broth, slowly simmered so maximum flavor is extracted from each ingredient. The cooking time of the vegetables, for instance, must be carefully judged so all arrive just right at the table. The broth is usually served as a first course, simmered for a few minutes with a handful of angel hair pasta. Then follows a lavish platter of sliced meats, which are piled in the center of the dish, surrounded by the vegetables, each in a small pile or *bouquet*. Pot au feu forms an entire, substantial, meal. This recipe serves eight.

> *a 3-lb/1.4-kg piece of beef or veal shank, with bone, tied with string*
> *a 2-lb/1-kg piece of beef chuck or brisket, tied with string*
> *2 lb/1 kg beef short ribs, tied with string*
> *8 quarts/8 liters water, more if needed*
> *1 onion studded with 4 cloves*
> *1 celery stalk*
> *a large bouquet garni*
> *1 cinnamon stick*
> *1 tablespoon salt, more to taste*
> *1 tablespoon black peppercorns*
> *8 beef marrow bones*
> *2 lb/1 kg medium carrots, quartered and cut into 3-inch/7.5-cm sticks*
> *3 lb/1.4 kg leeks, trimmed, halved lengthwise, and cut into 3-inch/7.5-cm pieces*
> *1½ lb/750 g medium turnips, cut in eighths*

> FOR THE GREMOLATA
> *5 garlic cloves*
> *a large bunch of flat-leaf parsley*
> *3 lemons*

> FOR SERVING
> *4 oz/125 g angel hair pasta*
> *sea salt, mustard, and gherkin pickles*
>
> *cheesecloth for wrapping bones and vegetables*

Put the beef shank, chuck, and short ribs in the stockpot with enough water to cover the meat generously. Bring slowly to a boil, skimming often. Add the studded onion, celery, bouquet garni, cinnamon stick, salt, and peppercorns. Wrap and tie each bone in cheesecloth so the marrow stays in place and add them to the pot. Simmer very gently, uncovered, skimming occasionally, for 3 hours. The secret to a clear broth is to maintain a gentle simmer with no threat of boiling.

Wrap and tie the carrots, leeks, and turnips in separate bundles in cheesecloth. Add these to the pot, pushing the vegetables down into the broth and adding more water if needed to cover them. Continue simmering for another hour, or until the meats and vegetables are very tender. The meats should fall easily from a two-pronged fork. If some ingredients are done before others, remove them to a platter. Be sure there is always enough broth to cover the meats and vegetables during cooking, so add hot water if needed.

Transfer the bones, meats, and vegetables to a board. Strain the broth to remove the flavorings, then boil the broth until it is reduced by about half, or until it is concentrated and well flavored. Taste and adjust the seasoning. If preparing the pot au feu ahead, replace the meats and vegetables in the broth and refrigerate them.

Shortly before serving, make the gremolata. Finely chop the garlic. Strip the leaves from the parsley stems and chop the leaves together with the garlic. Grate the zest from the lemons, taking care to leave behind the bitter white pith. Mix the zest with the garlic and parsley.

If necessary, reheat the meat and vegetables in the broth by simmering until heated through. Discard the cheesecloth from the bones and arrange them on a very large platter. Slice the meats and arrange them overlapping on the platter. Unwrap the vegetables and pile them in mounds around the meat. Cover everything with foil and keep warm.

For the first course, bring the broth back to a boil, add the pasta, and simmer until tender, about 2 minutes. Serve the broth and pasta very hot in shallow bowls. For the main course, sprinkle some of the gremolata over the meats just before serving. Pass the remaining gremolata with the sea salt, mustard, and pickles in separate bowls.

A glass of Calva rounds out every Milbert family repast, with Madame's homemade cassis for the women. The concentration of this potion is astonishing, a purple-black essence of black currants and sugar married with Monsieur's 110-proof Calvados (rather than the 80- to 90-proof white alcohol that appears on grocery shelves here during the harvest season). At Christmas I am feted with a dusky bottle of the house cassis, and there's a manly liter of Calvados for Mark. Madame once gave me her cassis recipe, which proved to be a high-risk procedure involving boiling the alcohol. My toned-down adaptation is based on vodka.

Madame Milbert's Cassis Liqueur

Just a teaspoon of cassis will perfume a glass of sparkling or still white wine to make kir. Cassis is also delicious spooned over white wine sorbet or the Spice Bread Ice Cream on page 115. Raspberries can be used the same way to make raspberry liqueur (framboise). Follow this recipe to make 1½ quarts/1½ liters of liqueur.

> 2 lb/1 kg black currants
> 1 bottle (750 ml) vodka, more if needed
> 2 cups/400 g sugar, or to taste

Remove the black currants from their stems by pulling the stems gently through the tines of a fork. Wash and drain the berries in a colander. Put them in a 2-quart/2-liter preserving jar. Pour over the vodka, adding more if needed to cover the currants completely. Cover tightly and leave in a cool place for at least 4, and up to 6, months. From time to time, open the jars and crush the currants with a potato masher.

After 4 to 6 months, put the currants and vodka in a saucepan and mash thoroughly again with a potato masher. Heat gently without boiling, stirring often, until the currants soften and their juice is loosened, 10 to 15 minutes. Work the mixture through a food mill or sieve, pressing well to extract all the juice.

Return the juice to the pan, add the sugar, and heat gently, stirring occasionally, until the sugar has dissolved, 10 to 15 minutes. Take care not to let the juice

boil hard or it may flame. Remove the liqueur from the heat and taste it, adding more sugar if needed. It should be rich and slightly tart or sweet, depending on your taste. Let it cool, then bottle and seal tightly. Store for at least 3 months so the flavor mellows. Cassis liqueur keeps well for years.

Pear in a Bottle

Wash and thoroughly dry a large empty bottle, choosing a broad, squat shape as an ordinary wine bottle is too narrow. When a pear is well formed on the tree and about the size of a hazelnut, insert it into the bottle. Fasten the bottle to the tree branch, supporting it with a forked stick. Shroud the bottle in rags so the pear does not scorch. Note that if the pear touches the side of the bottle as it grows, it will rot. Leave until the pear is fully ripe and one day it will fall into the bottom of the bottle. The pear may not be very large, but it is certainly a curiosity. Detach the bottle from the tree and fill the bottle with white alcohol.

Monsieur Milbert used Calvados, but eau de vie made from pears is more correct. Such a treasure must be preserved, so top the bottle up regularly with alcohol to keep the pear covered.

ABOVE: *Cassis is left to mellow in a sealed jar.* OPPOSITE: *One notable year, Monsieur Milbert slid a special bottle in our direction. Inside was imprisoned not one, but two whole pears that he had persuaded to grow from flower. The directions are above, but don't be too optimistic, as he had three failures for each fully grown pear.*

Monsieur Milbert may rule outdoors at Château du Feÿ, but it is Portuguese-born Madame Maria who has left her mark within. Maria is a phenomenon, a powerhouse of strength who at forty-eight took over the cleaning and much of the management of the twenty-five-room main house as well as the farmhouse and cottage. Within a month she had cleaned the place from top to bottom; two weeks later she asked permission to take over washing the sheets as she was not happy with the local laundry. Little escapes Maria's notice; she has an amazing memory, remarking at once when a towel is missing or an ornament misplaced.

It was a year before I realized that she could not read or write, having never had the opportunity to learn. She started work in a household at the age of eight, standing on a stool to reach the sink. In her early teens she peddled breakfast rolls in the streets of Lisbon, toting a flat wicker tray on her head. She learned to cook the best way, by practice. Even now, after twenty years of life in France, her cooking remains Portuguese. She describes feasts of cuttlefish in its ink, suckling pig, salt cod with fried potatoes, and onions, and soups of kale, potatoes, and chorizo sausage.

Like the Milberts, Maria does her best to live off the land. In the fall she buys cheap fowls that have reached the end of their egg-laying life, and cleans and plucks them by the dozen for the freezer. Pork shoulder, bought at wholesale price, is boned, diced, and marinated in red wine, onion, and garlic to make sausage that is smoked almost black in the attic above her kitchen. She raises rabbits in the backyard. Come October when the field corn is dry and hard, the kernels are ground for flour. Like others in the Portuguese community, Maria has an electric grinder for the purpose. She adds yeast, salt, and warm water to make a slightly sticky dough that she bakes in large round loaves, the bigger the better, in the style of her hometown.

Portuguese Corn Bread
Broa de Maria

Broa is one of the staples of life in Portugal, a chewy bread made with finely ground yellow cornmeal that keeps for weeks at a time. I've never forgotten the slice Maria gave me from the giant loaf brought back from her annual August vacation near Oporto, still regarded as home despite the many years she has lived in France. I've found that Italian polenta stands in well for the cornmeal, and I like to use whole wheat instead of white flour in echo of Maria's original loaf. My version makes one 2½-lb/1.2-kg loaf—not as grand as Maria's but certainly substantial (see photo on page 89).

> 1 cup/175 g yellow cornmeal, more for sprinkling
> 1 tablespoon salt
> 3 cups/750 ml boiling water
> 1 tablespoon/10 g active dry yeast
> ¼ cup/60 ml warm water
> 2 tablespoons olive oil
> 4 cups/500 g whole wheat flour, more if needed

Put the cornmeal in a bowl, stir in the salt, and make a well in the center. Add the boiling water to the well and stir to mix the cornmeal to a paste. Leave it to cool. When the cornmeal is cool, sprinkle the yeast over the warm water and leave until dissolved and starting to bubble, at least 5 minutes.

Add the yeast mixture and olive oil to the cornmeal paste and work until smooth, using your hand or the paddle of a heavy-duty electric mixer. Sprinkle some of the flour over the dough and work it in until mixed. Continue working in more flour until you have a smooth dough that is soft but not sticky.

Knead the dough, either working it by hand on a generously floured work surface or continuing to work it in the mixer. Add more flour if the dough seems sticky and continue kneading until it is elastic and pulls away from the work surface or sides of the bowl in a ball, about 10 minutes by hand or 5 to 7 minutes in the mixer.

Transfer the dough to an oiled bowl and flip it so the top is oiled also. Cover the bowl with a damp cloth and leave the dough to rise in a warm place until doubled in bulk, 1½ to 2 hours.

Oil a baking sheet and sprinkle it generously with cornmeal. Turn the dough onto a floured work surface and shape it into one round loaf, keeping it as high and plump as possible. Be careful not to overwork the dough

at this stage or it may collapse and become very sticky, lacking in gluten. Transfer the loaf to the baking sheet and sprinkle it with more cornmeal. Leave it to rise in a warm place until almost doubled in bulk, 30 to 40 minutes. Meanwhile, heat the oven to 400°F/200°C.

Using a razor blade or the point of a sharp knife, slash the top of the loaf in a wide crosshatch pattern. Bake the loaf for 10 minutes. then lower the heat to 350°F/175°F and continue baking until the bread is well browned and sounds hollow when tapped on the bottom, 30 to 40 minutes longer. Transfer it to a rack to cool.

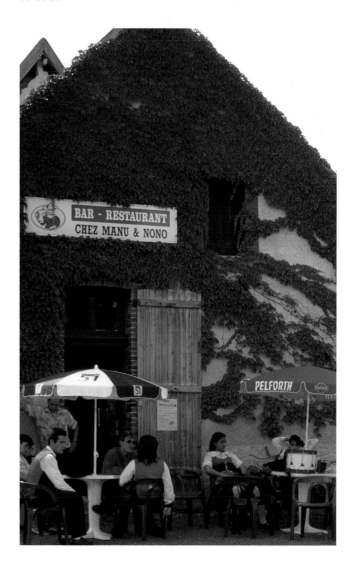

OPPOSITE: *The little church of Béon stands isolated in fields. Legend has it that the inhabitants of the surrounding village were killed by the plague.* ABOVE: *In summer, the Portuguese community goes "on the road," performing their national dances in costumes at fêtes which move from village to village.*

Like many people in France, Maria does not have a garden where she lives. Her rented allotment, as it is called, on the fertile soil near the river yields grapes for wine, bushels of tomatoes, peppers, pumpkins and squash, pears and quince. She exchanges brisk words and cooking tips with Michel Lorain, who has the next-door plot, totally unfazed by the fact that he is chef/owner of the Côte St. Jacques, one of the top restaurants in all of France. She has tried in vain to pass on her expertise to her daughter-in-law, a determined young woman with red hair and a sharp tongue.

Maria's Christmas Turkey

"Plain meat has no taste," says Maria, so she marinates poultry and meat at least a day before cooking. At Christmas, when she permits herself and the family a roast turkey, hers is aromatic with lemon, garlic, and hot red pepper. She serves the bird with potatoes and onions roasted in the pan juices, plus a salad of mâche (lamb's lettuce), all of course from her garden. In France, big is not beautiful as far as turkey is concerned —a plump female bird of 8 to 10 pounds/about 4 kg is the ideal and serves eight to ten. This is also an excellent way to roast a large chicken.

> *an 8- to 10-lb/about 4-kg turkey, with giblets*
> *2 lemons, halved*
> *3 garlic cloves, chopped*
> *2 teaspoons salt*
> *1½ teaspoons ground red chili pepper*
> *½ teaspoon grated nutmeg*
> *1 cup/250 ml dry white wine*
> *¾ cup/175 ml olive oil, more for basting*
> *ground black pepper*
> *4 lb/1.8 kg medium potatoes, peeled*
> *6 medium onions, peeled*
> *2 cups/500 ml chicken or veal stock*
>
> *trussing needle and string*

A day ahead, wipe the turkey inside and out with damp paper towels. Rub the skin thoroughly with the cut lemons. Make the marinade in a bowl by combining the garlic, salt, chili pepper, and nutmeg and whisking in the white wine. Gradually whisk in the olive oil. Use your hands to rub the marinade over the turkey inside and out; reserve the remaining marinade. Sprinkle ground black pepper all over the bird and truss it with a trussing needle (see the glossary). Set the turkey in a nonreactive dish, cover it loosely with plastic wrap, and refrigerate it

for a day. After 12 hours, turn the turkey so it marinates evenly.

Heat the oven to 350°F/175°C. Transfer the turkey to a roasting pan, breast-side down, and leave the marinade in the dish. Cut each potato into 2 to 3 chunks and quarter the onions. Toss the vegetables in the remaining marinade and add them to the roasting pan. They should be tightly packed around the bird so that they don't overcook. Pour any remaining marinade over the turkey. Roast it for 2 to 2½ hours. When the back (upper) side of the bird has browned well, after about 30 minutes, turn it breast-side up. Maria insists that, thanks to the marinade, there's no need to baste the turkey, but all the same I keep a close eye and moisten it with a pastry brush dipped in olive oil from time to time.

The turkey is done when no pink juice runs out when the thigh is pierced with a skewer and when a meat thermometer inserted in the thigh registers 185°F/90°C. After this long cooking, the potatoes and onions will be tender and brown. We take everything out at this stage, but Maria leaves it longer as she likes her turkey very well done, almost falling from the bone with crisp dark skin. Transfer the turkey, potatoes, and onions to a platter for serving and keep warm.

For the gravy, spoon off all but 2 to 3 tablespoons of fat from the pan. Heat the roasting pan on top of the stove until the pan juices are sticky and brown, 2 to 3 minutes. Pour in the stock, scraping the pan to dissolve the juices. Simmer the gravy until it is reduced by half, 10 to 15 minutes. Strain the gravy into a saucepan and taste it for seasoning. Serve it very hot.

OPPOSITE: *In Burgundy, free-range birds are truly raised outdoors. Here a flock of turkeys pecks in a field of corn.*

Maria's neighbor in nearby Joigny is Claude Simon and both live in the medieval

heart of the town. The ancient Simon cellars are hollowed in the hillside, a maze of vaulted stone roofs and steps that once led down to the river Yonne. One day Monsieur Simon dug into a blocked-up arch and a pile of human bones fell out: he had stumbled on the church graveyard above. "I put the bones back at once," he confided, as if I thought he was a grave robber. Monsieur Simon seems to us an eighteenth-century character like the age-old tools in his forge. His work is built to last, with none of today's deliberate obsolescence. He has a quick eye for contemporary design, though, and recently made us a resplendent weather cock with an impish, Cocteau look about it. His massive shoulders tilt distinctly to the left. I assumed this was due to rheumatism until I saw him in action, right hand raised high as he beat the red-hot metal with a hammer and realized that fifty years in his trade (which he inherited from his father) have given him a permanent list.

Monsieur Simon has little bits of garden and vineyard scattered all over town to indulge his passion for growing vegetables, fruits, and ancient varieties of vine such as the Noah, which, he tells me, is fragrant like Muscat. If he takes a fancy to you, he will open the trapdoor to his cellar. This leads to an Aladdin's cave of homemade wines, white alcohols, and bottled preserves. The walls are lined with jars of indeterminate age, many of the contents faded to nondescript beige. There is even a funky bar where Claude Simon holds court and tells you how his sister learned English—and perhaps other things— from American soldiers in 1944. The drink on offer is always Monsieur Simon's mellow home-brewed ratafia. Most ratafia is white, but Monsieur Simon makes an unusual red version with red grape juice.

Most wine and cider growers in Burgundy make a bit of ratafia for home consumption. The concept is simple: Mix enough marc or other distilled alcohol with fresh fruit juice to keep the juice from fermenting, then leave it to mature for six months or so. The result is fruity and fragrant, about the strength of port.

ABOVE: *My decanters of ratafia.* OPPOSITE: *Though mostly retired now, master smith Claude Simon still keeps his hand at the forge. In his spare time, he brews wine and cans huge quantities of preserves, stocking them in the ancient vaulted cellars which run under his house.*

Ratafia

To make 2 bottles of ratafia, stir together 1 quart/1 liter freshly pressed apple or grape juice with 2 cups/500 ml Calvados (for apples) or Cognac or marc (for grapes). Pour this fortified juice into 2 bottles (750 ml each) and seal each with a cork. Leave the bottles in a cool, dark place for 6 months. The ratafia will cloud at first, but eventually a deposit will collect in a mat at the bottom of the bottle, leaving the ratafia sparkling clear. Decant it into a carafe or another bottle, leaving the sediment behind—if you like, make sure by pouring the ratafia through a coffee filter. Seal and store it—the flavor improves on keeping.

Ratafia Ice Cream

Ratafia can be drunk as an apéritif, or it can be poured over fruit or used to flavor ice cream. If you don't make your own ratafia, you may find it in some wine shops. Muscat wine or a sweet port is a good substitute.

To make nearly 1 quart/1 liter of pleasantly alcoholic but creamy ice cream, first make an egg custard with 1 cup/250 ml milk, 1/3 cup/60 g sugar, 3 egg yolks, and a vanilla bean. Strain and let it cool. Mix in 1 cup/250 ml heavy cream and 2/3 cup/150 ml ratafia. Freeze the ice cream in a churn freezer until set.

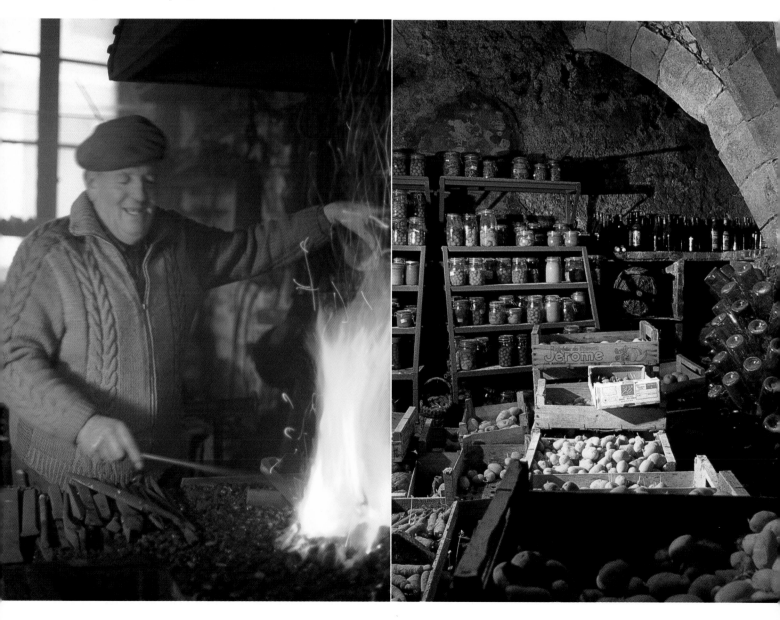

It is now four years since Maria retired, an eternity in the struggle to keep a big old house clean. Her potential replacement, the acid-tongued daughter-in-law, dropped out when she ran away with a salesman, taking Maria's two grandchildren with her. Only two candidates held fast after seeing the two dozen rooms with their parquet floors to polish and lofty ceilings constantly draped with cobwebs (we keep a special long-handled feather duster to detach them). Couloudine's name somehow did not imply a serious approach to housework and I mistrusted her two-inch spike heels, so we settled on wild-eyed Pauline with the missing teeth and bone-thin physique.

It was a mistake for us all. Life had treated Pauline hard and her eagerness to succeed in a task beyond her strength could not compensate. She was a chain-smoker, and after her departure I found bottles of beer hidden behind the washing machine. It seemed inevitable when she called one morning to say she had been diagnosed with lung cancer, that slow but inexorable killer. I've had cancer myself, mercifully a more treatable kind, and have some small understanding of the pressure it must place on a modest family; their teenage son is the light of Pauline's life. At least, you will be glad to know, the French state is generous with health care and sick pay—social benefits (and taxes) here are among the very highest in Europe.

As it happened, another former cancer patient would take Pauline's place. Luisa is Portuguese, from the same tightly knit community as Maria, and with her daughter Rosa (sometimes accompanied by pert little Victoria) she organizes our lives with similar dispatch. She herself is a skilled seamstress, professionally trained. Moreover, we have the benefit of her whole family. Her sons do odd jobs of painting and moving furniture; her husband is a mason with the perfectionist's approach to setting a neat stone and replacing the tiles on our constantly sagging roofs. Luisa is not an instinctive cook like Maria, but she has a welcome green thumb with our potted plants and herbs like those used in this green sauce.

Green Sauce

I take a relaxed approach to this cold sauce, adding whatever herbs happen to be plentiful but always hoping to include some chives. Tarragon, mint, and dill are my other favorites, and I sometimes add a few capers or green peppercorns. Green sauce is good with many foods—hot or cold fish, cold roast chicken, vegetable salads, even cold roast meats.

In a small bowl, mix together 1 chopped shallot, 1 chopped garlic clove, a teaspoon of white wine vinegar, and the juice and grated zest of half a small lemon. Stir in ½ cup/125 ml plain yogurt and a couple of tablespoonfuls of heavy cream. Last of all, add 3 to 4 tablespoons of your choice of chopped herbs and 2 tablespoons chopped chives with some salt and pepper. Taste and adjust the seasoning. This makes 1 cup/250 ml sauce, enough for 4 people.

OPPOSITE: *My kitchen is never complete without a bunch of herbs at the ready. The tiles, in soft Burgundian grays and greens, are locally made.*

CHAPTER 3

The Wider Scene

If you asked where, geographically, Château du Feÿ is situated, Mark and I can truthfully reply: in Burgundy. Joigny, just three miles/five kilometers from Le Feÿ, boasts that Burgundy begins on its stretch of the Yonne River and has posted a sign embellished with grapes to let the whole world know. If we keyed Le Feÿ to a food map, we might say it lies between Brie (on the borders of Champagne) and Chablis, which is the northernmost of the famous Burgundy wine towns. The Milberts' *pays* may be only the five or six villages easily reached by *vélo,* or bike, from Le Feÿ. But we of the automobile generation tend to range wider and faster. Route Nationale 6, which has grown from the old stagecoach road from Paris to Lyon that skirted Château du Feÿ, connects us speedily to the main Autoroute du Soleil heading south. Within an hour or two we can be buying mustards in Dijon, or sampling hams in the Morvan mountains or goat cheeses at Sancerre on the Loire. But there is so much to discover in our own backyard.

"Almost all the inhabitants of the region have blond hair and round faces and later in life, through drinking, their bodies round out like their cheeks," remarked an Italian priest, Friar Sebastiano Locatelli, when traveling here in 1665. Things haven't changed much and I can easily pick out that rotund Burgundian prototype in our nearest open market held twice a week in Joigny. Vendors have gathered here since Roman times—Joigny was then Jovinium. I like to imagine that today's Joviniens, as the townspeople call themselves, live up to their namesake, the jovial god Jove.

Like any good market, the Saturday gathering in Joigny is pure theater. Anticipation mounts as I see the laden baskets of returning shoppers. Pushing open the entrance doors, I'm enveloped at once by a flood of sound and sunlight that beams down through the nineteenth-century arched glass roof, to my mind a utilitarian, elegant design that has never been bettered. A group of perhaps seventy vendors pay a small quarterly fee for the right to display goods on wooden trestles or, better still, to set up a stand against the wall under an awning. The hall is packed and a plan of campaign is clearly necessary.

First to Madame Durville, poulterer extraordinaire. She sells out rapidly and today I want a couple of her plump white farm-raised ducks, double the supermarket price but worth every centime. They come with their heads and feet as proof of authenticity and I ask her to clean and truss them for me—it is thanks to such quality and personal service that the market thrives. Thanks to that, and to the chance to see the neighbors. I often run into Madame Maria (she arrives early to snap up bargains) and Chef Jean-Michel Lorain, who comes, I think, mainly to sniff the air of his hometown. For years now, the crowd has been multinational, with Arabic, Turkish, Portuguese, and a sprinkling of Italian permeating the French. A Tunisian displays his native wares. I've counted fourteen different olives in addition to nuts, dried legumes and fruits, and the rust-colored harissa to set fire to couscous. At the door, Romanian gypsies sell baskets.

On to the tables laden with produce. Late spring means bushy-topped baby carrots, and early fall brings bulging golden pumpkins. But I mustn't be distracted from less showy treasures such as little boxes of hand-picked wild strawberries or the first fresh flageolets, green kidney beans of incomparable flavor that are traditional with roast lamb. I'm always on the lookout for golden and black chanterelles (alarmingly called trumpets of death because of their color). Ours is a fertile area for wild mushrooms and most are locally picked, small and scruffy with leaves (clean mushrooms are suspect, usually cultivated and lacking in taste). Each year in early fall an exhibition of regional mushrooms is held at nearby Migennes, up to sixty and all of them fresh. A mushroom hunt is a telling lesson in prudence. At least a dozen are labeled *mortel* (deadly), among them the Death's Cap, which I myself have found in our woodland.

Warm Wild Mushroom Mousse

A mixture of mushrooms is best here. As well as golden and black *chanterelles,* I aim for *cèpes* (boletus) and craggy *pieds de mouton* (sheep's feet), depending on the season. The mousse makes an elegant first course for six.

> 2 tablespoons olive oil
> ¾ lb/375 g mixed wild mushrooms
> 1 shallot, finely chopped
> 1 garlic clove, finely chopped
> salt and pepper
> 2 eggs
> juice of half a lemon
> 2 cups/500 ml heavy cream
> a small bunch of chervil or parsley
> 1 cup/250 ml chicken stock
>
> a 3-cup/750-ml ring mold

Heat the oven to 350°F/175°C. Brush the mold with a little olive oil. Pick over the mushrooms and trim the stems. Wash them quickly in a bowl of cold water and lift them out into a colander, leaving the grit behind. (Never let fresh mushrooms sit in water for long as they quickly become waterlogged.) Dry them on paper towels and cut any larger mushrooms in 2 to 3 pieces. Heat the olive oil in a frying pan over quite high heat, add the mushrooms with the shallot, garlic, salt, and pepper, and sauté them until tender and any liquid has evaporated, 5 to 7 minutes.

Pick out about a third of the prettiest sautéed mushrooms and set them aside for the sauce and garnish. Put the remaining mushrooms in a food processor with the eggs, the lemon juice, half the cream, salt, and pepper. Work the mixture to quite a fine purée. Taste it for seasoning and pour it into the prepared mold. Set the mold in a bain-marie and bring it to a boil on top of the stove. Transfer the bain-marie to the oven and cook the mousse until just set, 25 to 30 minutes.

Meanwhile, make the sauce. Reserve 2 to 3 chervil sprigs for decoration and chop the rest. Boil the stock until it is reduced by half, 3 to 5 minutes. Add the reserved mushrooms and remaining cream. Bring the sauce to a boil and simmer until it is somewhat reduced and full of flavor, 10 to 15 minutes. Take from the heat, add the chervil, and taste, adjusting the seasoning. Set the sauce aside

When the mousse is cooked, remove it from the bain-marie and let it cool for 2 to 3 minutes. Run a knife around the edge and turn it onto a warm serving plate. Reheat the mushrooms and sauce and spoon them over the mousse to coat it lightly. Decorate with the chervil sprigs and serve it at once.

PREVIOUS PAGES: *The rural wealth of Burgundy is on display. At top left the vineyards of the Côte St. Jacques in Joigny, which date to medieval times, slope almost to the riverside. Sens market scenes frame photographs of a specialty grocer in Dijon and of a pasture filled with Charolais cattle, source of the famous Burgundian beef. The great church of St. Jean (page 79) towers above the Yonne River at Joigny.* OPPOSITE AND ABOVE: *Girolle mushrooms from the market are delicious fried with garlic or used as the basis of a sauce for Warm Wild Mushroom Mousse.*

On this June morning I pass stout, dusty Madame Fillot, one of a disappearing breed of truly local farmers who plant, gather, and sell whatever happens to be ready. Today it's not much—potatoes, baby carrots, mint, and seedling lettuces for transplanting—all in contrast to the nearby stands laden with imported produce obtainable in any supermarket. Better news comes from the watercress lady. She's doing so well that her new line of green and red oak leaf lettuce is already gone by 10:30 in the morning. I can tell with my eyes shut when it is strawberry season—the aroma of freshly picked berries hits my nostrils the instant I enter the market. They are easy to choose, just head for the darkest berries with the strongest smell and small pointed shape that indicate the prized *sans rivale* variety.

Summer Fresh Fruit Tart

The joy of summer fruits is their juice, but this same juice can rapidly soak and ruin a crisp pastry case. The traditional precaution is to add a layer of pastry cream, but I prefer to bake almond frangipane in the bottom of the tart as insulation—it holds up longer and tastes delicious. I like to select a colorful mix of the best seasonal berries and stone fruits as suggested here, or you can settle on just one favorite fruit, if you prefer. One tart serves six to eight.

FOR THE PÂTE SUCRÉE
1 ½ cups/175 g flour
½ teaspoon salt
½ cup/100 g sugar
3 egg yolks
1 teaspoon vanilla extract
7 tablespoons/100 g butter

FOR THE FRANGIPANE
¼ cup/60 g butter
⅓ cup/60 g sugar
1 egg, beaten to mix
½ teaspoon vanilla extract
½ cup/60 g ground almonds

FOR THE FRUIT
2 cups/375 g mixed berries (strawberries, raspberries, or blackberries)
3 to 4 stone fruits (apricots, peaches, or plums)
juice of 1 lemon
½ cup/125 g apricot jam (for glaze)
a few mint sprigs or other herb (for decoration)

a 10-inch/25-cm pie pan with removable base

Heat the oven to 375°F/190°C and put a baking sheet to heat low down in the oven. Prepare and blind-bake the pâte sucrée tart shell using the ingredients listed above and the technique as described in the glossary (page 299).

To make the frangipane, cream the butter and beat in the sugar until light, about 2 minutes. Beat in the egg, then stir in the vanilla and ground almonds. Spread the frangipane in the blind-baked tart shell. If the pastry edge is already very brown, protect it by folding over a strip of foil. Bake the tart until the frangipane is firm and browned, 12 to 15 minutes. Set it aside to cool.

To prepare the fruit, hull the strawberries, rinsing them only if sandy, and halve them if they are especially large. Sort through the blackberries or raspberries. Halve the apricots, plums, or peaches, discarding the pits, and cut any large halves in crescents—some people like to peel peaches, but I don't bother. Sprinkle the peaches and apricots with the juice from half a lemon to prevent browning.

For the apricot glaze, melt the apricot jam with the juice from the remaining lemon half and 1 to 2 tablespoons water. Work the glaze through a sieve into a small saucepan.

To finish the tart, reheat the apricot glaze and brush the baked frangipane base of the tart with it. Arrange the fruit in the shell, either in concentric circles or in a contemporary free-form design like a vase of flowers. Brush the fruits lightly with more glaze, decorate the top with a mint sprig or two, and serve the tart at room temperature. It will hold for 2 to 3 hours without spoiling.

The sweet pie pastry that I use for fruit tarts also makes great cookies the French call *sablés* (sandy) because they are so crumbly. At Le Feÿ we've re-launched the medieval habit of adding herbs to flavor them as an unusual tea cookie or a distinctive accompaniment to sorbet and ice cream.

Herb Sablés

Make pâte sucrée as for Summer Fresh Fruit Tart opposite, adding 3 to 4 tablespoons chopped herb with the egg yolks—I particularly like lemon balm, rose geranium, or mint. Roll the dough to a ¼-inch/6-mm thickness and stamp out large or small rounds. Transfer the cookies to a baking sheet, brush them with an egg beaten with a pinch of salt, and press a whole herb leaf in the center of each one. Bake them in a 375°F/190°C oven until lightly browned, 10 to 15 minutes depending on their size. Transfer them to a rack to cool. The recipe makes 16 to 20 medium cookies.

I favor the freeform designs of contemporary fruit tarts rather than the more traditional arrangement of stiff concentric circles.

The aspic for parsleyed ham should be only just set so the full flavor of white wine, herb, and garlic is apparent. Don't worry if it looks ragged when unmolded.

Next door to the fruit stands, butchers gaze at their seasonal haul of pale, skinny baby goats. These are the billy goats, culled at six to eight weeks because, as males, they can provide no lucrative milk for cheese. Here's Georges Clopin, artisan charcutier, leaning over tubs of country pâté and *rillettes* (a rich purée of pork), with *boudin noir* (blood sausage) and *andouillettes* (sausages of pigs' intestines). He is framed by garlands of half a dozen dried sausages—Burgundian rosette de Lyon is world renowned. The permanent line of customers at the Clopin stall is proof that his charcuterie is truly artisanal as it is freshly made at home without the fancy decor and preservative sticky layers of aspic that betray a more commercial origin. Despite his obvious prosperity, Monsieur Clopin casts a pessimistic eye from his commanding position in the center of the market. "Bad times, these," he grumbles, shaking his head. "As we say in France, this won't put butter in the spinach!"

Parsleyed Ham in Aspic
Jambon Persillé

Half the charm of parsleyed ham is its color, a brilliant mosaic of pink meat set in a glittering green aspic of white wine. Monsieur Clopin adds lots of finely chopped shallot and a touch of garlic to the mold, so that's what I've done here. Traditional parsleyed ham is a perfectionist exercise, calling for 5 to 6 hours' simmering to fully cook raw ham and pigs' feet (which add vital gelatin). In this shorter version to make at home, I'm using cooked country ham with powdered gelatin to set the aspic. Try serving parsleyed ham with a vegetable salad such as ratatouille or celery remoulade as a splendid lunch or buffet for eight to ten guests. I think you'll like the piquant contrast of salty ham with the wine, shallot, and garlic.

> *a 2-lb/1-kg piece of cooked country ham*
> *1 bottle (750 ml) dry white Chardonnay wine*
> *¾ cup/175 ml veal stock*
> *2 bay leaves*
> *2 to 3 thyme sprigs*
> *1 teaspoon peppercorns*
> *a large bunch (2 oz/60 g) of curly parsley*
> *¼ cup/125 ml boiling water*
> *2 tablespoons/15 g powdered gelatin*
> *salt and pepper*
> *4 shallots (about 2 oz/60 g), finely chopped*
> *1 to 2 garlic cloves, chopped*
>
> *a 2-quart/2-liter deep glass bowl or terrine mold*

Combine the wine, half the stock, bay leaves, thyme, and peppercorns in a saucepan. Cover the pan, bring to a boil, and reduce to a simmer. Strip the parsley leaves from the stems and add the stems to the simmering wine mixture. Let it simmer for about 30 minutes. Wash and dry the parsley leaves, chop them, and place them in a small bowl. Pour the boiling water over the leaves to set the color and leave to cool. Divide the ham into uneven chunks, discarding the fat and any sinew; I find that the finished aspic is prettiest if I pull the ham apart into big slivers with my fingers rather than cutting into cubes with a knife.

Pour the remaining stock into a medium bowl, sprinkle the gelatin on top, and leave it until spongy, about 5 minutes. Strain the wine mixture into a measuring cup —there should be 3 cups/750 ml; if necessary add a little water. Bring the wine mixture just back to a boil and pour it over the gelatin. Let it stand for 1 minute, and then stir to melt and mix in the gelatin. Taste the aspic, season it with salt and pepper (remember that the ham is salty), and leave it to cool until tepid. Aspic will thicken quite suddenly when cold, so do not chill it.

To mold the ham, add a shallow layer of aspic to the glass bowl or terrine mold and chill it in the refrigerator or over ice water until set. Mix the ham with the shallots, garlic, and parsley (along with its liquid) in a large bowl. Add the remaining tepid aspic, mix well, and transfer the entire mix to the mold. Press the pieces of ham well below the surface of the aspic and make sure no air bubbles are trapped beneath the ham. Cover the mold and chill it until set, at least 6 hours. It keeps well for up to a week, but once cut open should be eaten within a day.

To serve the ham, dip the mold in hot water for 15 to 30 seconds to loosen the aspic. Run a knife around the edge, unmold the ham onto a platter, and cut it in wedges or slices. Alternatively, if you like, serve the aspic directly from the mold.

By the end of that first summer in Burgundy, we had grown more adventurous, assured of the enormous pleasure of coming home again to Château du Feÿ. We began by exploring the area formed by a triangle of the two cathedral cities of Sens and Auxerre, flanked by the abbey town of Tonnerre. Sens casts a stately shadow, the southern approach still dominated by the massive cathedral built in the late twelfth century by one William, who also masterminded the construction of Canterbury cathedral in England. It's amazing to think that eight centuries ago architecture was already an international profession. Sens has a cosmopolitan history as a stop on the great highway south from Paris to the Mediterranean, whether traveling overland or by river barge. The main street was once lined with coaching inns, and at the Hôtel Paris et Poste you can still see the open courtyard where teams of horses were changed for the next stage.

Sens is Gilbert Parret's center of business. As a cheese affineur who ages cheeses in his own cellars, he is two cuts above a mere cheese merchant. When I ask about the legendary 365 French cheeses, one for every day of the year, Monsieur Parret looks askance. "There are many more than that!" he says. We plunge into a heated discussion on the culinary merits of dry versus medium-dry goat cheese. We agree that the former is best for flavoring stuffings and sauce, the latter for broiling on toasts or pizza. Gilbert is in touch with cheese makers all over France, buying Camembert, Pont l'Evêque, and Livarot from Normandy, aged cheeses such as tôme from Savoy, blues from the Auvergne, and goat cheeses from the Loire. From Burgundy itself comes Epoisses, the rind washed with marc and water so the curd ages to a redolent, some think reeking, cream. Monsieur Parret is looking for "artisan producers, *des sérieux.* I like to visit them, see how the cows are doing, how the grass is growing, how the family thrives," he explains. He believes in developing local cheeses and has organized a group of goat cheese farmers as a cooperative, controlling quality and helping to market their products.

The cellars where Gilbert Parret ages his cheese are kept at 90% humidity and a chill 43°F/7°C, but despite the low temperature, the nutty, sour smell of fermention is strong. "Cheese is nourished on water," explains Gilbert, pointing to a 20-inch/50-cm wheel of cheese. "Look at this Brie, you see the *fleur* (bloom)." From floor to ceiling, the rooms are stacked with great 100-pound/45-kg wheels of Comté (the best French Gruyère), neat chipboard boxes of Camembert, flats of little goat cheeses laid on straw to aid evaporation. When I ask how many cheeses he is guarding with such care, he says "perhaps 4,000." He sells over 60 Brie wheels alone in an average week, around 500 pounds of cheese.

ABOVE: *Artisan cheeses are sold throughout Burgundy.* OPPOSITE: *Gilbert Parret, cheese expert extraordinaire, manhandles one of his wheels of aged Gruyère.*

Brie Cheese and Walnut Brioche

The name *brioche* may originate from the habit of adding creamy Brie cheese to enrich bread dough, a possible precursor of the butter-flavored brioche we know today. Although the flavor of Brie is muted after baking, it does lend a distinct savory character. The bread is a bit denser than ordinary brioche. This recipe makes two medium loaves, and thick slices make a fine accompaniment to pâtés and terrines. The Brie and walnut dough also makes great rolls.

> *1 tablespoon/10 g active dry yeast*
> *¼ cup/60 ml lukewarm water*
> *4 cups/500 g flour, more if needed*
> *2 tablespoons sugar*
> *1½ teaspoons salt*
> *6 eggs, beaten to mix*
> *1 cup/125 g walnut pieces*
> *½ lb/250 g ripe Brie cheese*
> *½ cup/125 g butter*
> *1 egg beaten to mix with ½ teaspoon salt (for glaze)*
>
> *2 loaf pans (each 8½x4½x2½ in/30x11x6 cm)*

Sprinkle the yeast over the water and let it stand until dissolved, about 5 minutes. Sift the flour onto a work surface and make a large well in the center. Sprinkle the sugar and salt onto the flour. Add the beaten eggs and yeast mixture to the well. With your hand, gradually work in the flour to form a smooth dough—it will be quite sticky. Alternatively, use a heavy-duty electric mixer with a dough hook.

To knead the dough by hand, lift it up and throw it down on a floured work surface until it is very elastic and resembles the texture of chamois leather, about 5 minutes. Work in more flour if necessary, so that at the end of kneading the dough is sticky but holds together in one piece. You can also knead the dough in the mixer, taking 3 to 4 minutes. Transfer the dough to a buttered bowl, turn it over so the top is buttered, and cover the bowl with a damp cloth. Leave it in a warm place until doubled in bulk, about an hour.

Heat the oven to 400°F/200°C. Spread the walnut pieces on a baking sheet and toast them in the oven until browned, 7 to 10 minutes. Set them aside to cool and leave the oven on. Butter the loaf pans, line them with wax or parchment paper, and butter the paper. Cut the cheese into cubes, discarding the rind—without rind, it should weigh about 6 oz/175 g. Put the butter between 2 sheets of wax or parchment paper and pound it with a rolling pin until it is as soft as the cheese.

When risen, knead the dough lightly to knock out the air. Work in the soft cheese and butter, squeezing with your fist until they are completely incorporated, or use the mixer. Work in the walnut pieces. Divide the dough in half and shape it into 2 loaves. Lower the loaves into the pans, cover with a cloth, and let them rise in a warm place until the pans are almost full, ½ to 1 hour.

Brush the loaves with the egg glaze and score the tops with a razor blade or the point of a sharp knife. Bake them for 30 to 40 minutes, until they start to shrink from the sides of the pan and sound hollow when tapped on the bottom. Unmold and cool them on a rack. To serve, cut the bread in thick slices, brown them in a toaster, and serve warm.

Brie Cheese and Walnut Brioche toasts so well that I usually make it in a loaf pan, ready to slice. Above it are two loaves of Broa (recipe page 71).

Madame Parret never lets leftover cheese go to waste. For her Cheese Toasts, she often uses Morbier, a creamy aged cheese that melts nicely, but other cheeses, such as Gruyère, Brie, soft goat cheese, even Cheddar, do equally well. Monsieur Parret, for his part, has a nice little trick with goat cheese that you might like to try: baking cheese wrapped in bacon.

Cheese Toasts

Heat the oven to 400°F/200°C. Set thick slices of country bread in an oiled baking dish and sprinkle each one with a tablespoon or two of dry white wine. Top them with thinly sliced cheese, covering the bread completely. Scatter a thinly sliced onion on the cheese and sprinkle with salt and pepper. Bake the toasts until the bread is toasted and the cheese is browned and bubbly, 20 to 25 minutes. The onions may char, but this adds to the flavor. Serve them very hot.

Goat Cheese in Bacon

Wraps small goat cheeses—the fresher the better—in thinly sliced regular bacon, overlapping it as little as possible. Then set the cheese in a heatproof dish and bakes it in a 350°F/175°C oven for 10 to 15 minutes, until the bacon is crisp and the cheese starts to melt. Perfect with a green salad.

Sens, for us, has become a source of exotica beyond the range of Joigny and we go the few extra miles for mangoes or pomegranates, fresh cilantro or dry martini vermouth (I'm an addict). Fish is far fresher and more varied here, though it remains a disappointment. We are still a good few hours by autoroute from the nearest sea coast. The traditional recipes of Burgundy call for river fish such as pike, trout, and perch and Henri the local carpenter, an avid fisherman, assures me that the Yonne just down the hill is once again *"très poissoneuse* (very fishy)" thanks to tight controls on pollution and fishing. Indeed, the regional newspaper reports pike of up to a yard long winning the yearly competition. Those are big fish, yet I've never actually seen anyone catch other than a minnow. When I ask Henri, he looks shifty. Like so many matters in France, I suspect the contest is "arranged."

Poached Trout in White Wine with Spinach

Look for pink-fleshed trout to provide maximum contrast with this lively green spinach stuffing. Count on two small fillets per person—the recipe serves six.

FOR THE STUFFING

1 lb/500 g fresh spinach
2 tablespoons butter
2 shallots, chopped
1 garlic clove, chopped
½ cup/125 ml crème fraîche or heavy cream
the leaves of a medium bunch of parsley, chopped
grated zest of 1 lemon
large pinch of grated nutmeg
salt and pepper
2 slices of stale white bread, cut in pieces

FOR COOKING THE TROUT

12 small trout fillets (about 2 lb/1 kg total), with
  skin
2 shallots, sliced
½ bottle (375 ml) dry white Burgundy wine
½ cup/125 g cold butter, cut in small pieces
salt and pepper

Make the stuffing. Tear the stems from the spinach, and thoroughly wash and drain the leaves. Coarsely shred the leaves. Melt the butter in a deep frying pan over medium heat, add the shallots and garlic, and sauté until soft and fragrant, 1 to 2 minutes. Pack the spinach on top, cover, and cook until wilted, stirring often, 2 to 3 minutes. Stir in the cream, parsley, lemon zest, nutmeg, salt, and pepper and cook without a lid, stirring occasionally, until all the cream is absorbed, 3 to 5 minutes. Meanwhile, work the bread to crumbs in a food processor or blender. Stir the crumbs into the spinach, taste, and adjust the seasoning. Set the stuffing aside to cool. (You'll find this a handy stuffing for meats and vegetables, too. I use it often.)

Heat the oven to 350°F/175°C. On the work surface, curl each fillet in a circle, skin-side outward, and fill the center with a generous spoonful of cooled spinach stuffing. Spread the sliced shallots in a medium baking dish and set the stuffed fillets upright in the dish, which should be large enough to accommodate the fish without crowding. Pour over the wine. Cover the dish with foil and bake until the fish is no longer transparent when flaked with a fork, 15 to 20 minutes.

Transfer the fish to individual serving plates (2 fillets per plate) and keep them warm. Strain the cooking liquid into a saucepan and boil it until it is reduced to about 2 tablespoons of glaze, 8 to 12 minutes. Whisk in the cold butter a piece at a time, working on and off the heat so the butter softens and thickens the sauce creamily without melting to oil. Taste and adjust the seasoning. Spoon the sauce over the fish and serve at once.

OPPOSITE: *Two optimistic young fishermen try their luck on the sunlit banks of the Yonne River in Joigny.*

Burgundians like to consolidate their wealth in stone. Clockwise from top left: the cathedral of St. Étienne dominates the Yonne in Auxerre; the two sides of the Auxerre clock tower; medieval gables, one reflected in the window opposite; and, carved into a street facade, two medieval companions share a jug of wine, the Burgundian way to relax.

Château du Feÿ lies an equal distance from Sens and Auxerre, but it has taken us longer to appreciate the city of Auxerre, the departmental capital of the Yonne. The towers of the cathedral and abbey of St. Germain ride high above the river, imposing but remote. The one-way traffic system would deflect an invading army. Surprises such as the terraced vegetable gardens huddled down behind the abbey are easy to miss and for years, I walked straight past medieval carvings of angels and snails above my head in the streets. Houses are equally secretive, hidden behind high stone walls and carved Renaissance facades. A doctor friend lives in one of them, the graceful seventeenth-century Hôtel Deschamps de Charmelieu, its wings enclosing a generous garden. That such mansions should be inhabited by working professionals rather than princes or even rich merchants is surely a sign of the times.

But a modern amenity also draws us to Auxerre. Metro is a wholesale supermarket chain that caters to *les métiers de bouche* (mouth professions), which is the picturesque French moniker for the hotel and restaurant trade. The meats and produce are the best in the area, rivaling those from Rungis, the great wholesale market for Paris. Metro stocks industrial-strength cleansers (invaluable in an old château) and oddities like giant toilet rolls that last five times as long as the regular size. At Metro you can track current fashions in food from the items on offer. One year it will be rabbit, corn on the cob, and figs, another year persimmons and butternut squash. Rather than stocking perishables in individual refrigerated cases, Metro climate controls each department, supplying clients with igloo jackets for the coldest, meat and cheese. Peak hours revolve around a restaurant schedule, with early mornings busy, particularly Thursday, Friday, and Saturday, together with a quick midafternoon flurry for forgotten items. It's amusing to see top local chefs pushing their carts (outsize like everything else) and lugging crates of bottles with the rest of us.

Auxerre borders on wine country. To the south winds the river Yonne, warming vineyards originally planted by the Romans. In the mid-seventeenth century, on his way from Sens, Friar Locatelli stopped for a meal here, lunching "gaily off omelettes and vegetable pie that we found excellent. . . . They eat out of huge wooden platters on which everything—salt, soup, meat, etc.—is all jumbled up together, and when they are empty they drink wine or beer out of them." This same habit of rinsing the soup bowl with a dash of wine, called *faire chabrol,* is still found in country districts. The Auxerrois vins de table run the gamut of whites and reds, and it's encouraging that a bottle still costs little more than a fast-food hamburger and chips. We use these wines on the stove almost as often as in the glass.

Peppered Pears and Prunes in Irancy Wine

We have a single, ancient moss-encrusted pear tree of the poire du curé variety. Each year I think it is dying, and each year without fail (unless nipped by late frost) it produces baskets of firm juicy fruit, perfect for poaching. (Bosc and Anjou also poach well.) Marinating the pears in wine syrup overnight colors them to a spectacular deep purple, which is highlighted by the black prunes. Peaches and plums are good poached in red wine, too, though I'd leave out the prunes. Serve the fruits, chilled or at room temperature, with vanilla ice cream and a sugar cookie—a memorable dessert for six.

> *6 firm pears, with stems*
> *½ cup/100 g sugar*
> *1 bottle (750 ml) red wine*
> *1 cup/250 ml water, more if needed*
> *1 tablespoon coriander seed*
> *1 teaspoon black peppercorns*
> *2 cinnamon sticks*
> *1 vanilla bean, split*
> *4 oz/125 g pitted prunes*
>
> *a small piece of cheesecloth*

Choose a medium saucepan just large enough to fit the 6 pears. Combine the sugar, wine, and water in the saucepan and heat gently, stirring occasionally, until the sugar dissolves, 7 to 10 minutes. Wrap the coriander seed, peppercorns, and cinnamon sticks in cheesecloth and tie them securely into a little bundle. Crush the spices by pounding the bag with a rolling pin or heavy saucepan. Add the bag to the red wine syrup with the vanilla bean, cover, and leave over low heat to infuse, 15 to 20 minutes.

Peel the pears, leaving the stems both for appearance and to make handling easy. Using a sharp teaspoon, scoop out the cores by digging deep inside the pears from the bottom so as to leave the outside intact. Cut a thin slice from the base of the pears so they will stand upright when serving.

Immerse them at once in the hot wine syrup, packing them as tightly as possible. If not completely covered they will appear blotchy when cooked, so if necessary add some more water. Set a heatproof plate on top to keep the pears submerged. Let the syrup cool, then refrigerate the pears in the syrup for 12 hours—this long maceration not only flavors them, it also helps color them a deep purple.

Transfer the pan of pears to the stove, remove the plate, and bring the syrup just to a boil over gentle heat. Be sure not to let the syrup remain at a boil or you risk breaking up the pears. Poach them for 15 minutes, or up to 30 minutes if they are very firm. Add the prunes and continue poaching until the pears look translucent and are very tender when pierced with a skewer, 10 to 15 minutes more; the timing will depend on the ripeness of the fruit. Leave them to cool to tepid in the syrup.

With a slotted spoon, transfer the fruit to a bowl. Boil the syrup until reduced by about half and the flavor is concentrated, 10 to 12 minutes—it should be slightly sticky in consistency. Strain the hot syrup over the pears and prunes, discard the spice bag and vanilla bean, and cover and chill the fruit. The flavors will mellow if you keep the fruit refrigerated for a day or two. Serve the fruit in bowls, with a scoop of ice cream if you like, and spoon the syrup on top.

Wine Sauce for Fruit

For fruits that need no cooking such as peaches, strawberries, and mangoes, this recipe is even simpler than Peppered Pears and Prunes in Irancy Wine.

For 4 people, combine a bottle (750 ml) of red wine and ½ cup/100g sugar in a saucepan. Split a vanilla bean to loosen the seeds, add it to the pan, and heat gently, stirring often, until the sugar dissolves. Bring the syrup to a boil and boil it until syrupy and reduced by about half, 10 to 15 minutes. Let the syrup cool to tepid while peeling, slicing, hulling, or otherwise preparing the fruit. When cool, pour the syrup over the fruit, reserving the vanilla bean to use again. The flavors will improve if you leave the fruit to macerate 3 to 4 hours in the refrigerator.

Peppered Pears and Prunes in Irancy Wine, simmered in a heavy copper pot, are set out on an old charcoal stove.

The town of Tonnerre completes the triangle of territory that we think of as home ground (Chablis falls in the middle and I'll return there shortly). At first blush, Tonnerre didn't seem to have much to say for itself until we heard of its most notorious citizen, the transvestite Chevalier d'Eon. In the permissive eighteenth century, the Chevalier led a bisexual life, spying for King Louis XV. He was successively a Captain of Dragoons, an advocate to the High Court in Paris, an emissary to the British court of St. James, and a brilliant duellist in the golden age of fencing. Posing as a woman under the title Chevalière d'Eon, he dallied as fiancée of Beaumarchais, one of the wittiest playwrights of the time, and as a man, he caught the fancy of Catherine the Great of Russia as well as the English Queen Charlotte. So classic was his case of double sexual identity that sexologists coined a new word: eonism. Tonnerre has never witnessed such a flamboyant character since.

Tonnerre is at the eastern end of the Yonne. Given the fame of the Côte d'Or and its wines such as Clos de Vougeot, it comes as a surprise to learn that Tonnerre, and particularly the outlying village of Epineuil, once produced some of Burgundy's most popular wines (a modest revival is now under way). In fact, in 1850 the Yonne department as a whole was by far the most prolific wine-growing area in Burgundy; in the entire country, only the Gironde (Bordeaux) earned more from wine. What gave our department its edge was not the climate or the soil, but the natural highway to Paris—the river Yonne.

Nonetheless, in the wine region just south of Auxerre, vineyard villages still cluster along the river Yonne. For me, the very names are an invitation to pull a cork. Bailly is famous for sparkling Crémant de Bourgogne; St. Bris-le-Vineux makes the only sauvignon blanc in Burgundy; Coulanges-la-Vineuse is known for its light pinot noir. But by common consent the best reds come from plain-sounding Irancy. Meet Jean-Pierre Colinot, wine maker, raconteur, and live wire. Round and vigorous, he epitomizes the Burgundian character and physique (remember Friar Locatelli's description?). He is totally immersed in his trade, producing powerful, well-rounded wines in the old style. "Cooks do their cooking, and vignerons make wine according to their characters," he observes. "Here in Irancy we divide into two camps. Me, I'm a romantic, I go for tradition. The others are the brains—I call them the Cartesians."

Monsieur Colinot likes to mix his pinot noir with small amounts of the César grape, which is unique to the region and according to legend was brought here by the Romans. "It's full of tannin," he says, "so let a bottle age and then it will be perfect with game—in a wine sauce of course!" Before we continue, a glass must be sampled, and Jean-Pierre mentions a zesty little cocktail he had just last week, a combination of three favorite Burgundian products: cider, ratafia, and cassis.

OPPOSITE: *An engraving of the transvestite Chevalier d'Eon.* ABOVE:
*Jean-Pierre and Anita Colinot are proud of their vines, some of the best in
Irancy—a key village in the Auxerrois wine-growing region. For the better
vintages, grapes are picked by hand.*

Once gathered, grapes are dumped into the back of a rather large truck and transported later to be pressed.

Monsieur Colinot explains that, like all wine districts, even little Irancy with a total area of only 100 hectares (250 acres) is composed of microclimates, the best with names such as Les Mazelots, Côte des Moutiers, and the sought-after Le Palotte. The territory was originally mapped by monks in the Middle Ages—the vineyards were owned by the Bishop of Auxerre—and Jean-Pierre Colinot is proud to own some of the best of it: "I'm lucky, my family has made wine here for centuries." He's just come to an agreement with his sister over inheritance ("she's a tough one, that") and how to share the stone-built bourgeois house, the cellars sprawling half a block under the street, and the bits of vineyard scattered around the village. These subdivisions reflect French law, which gives equal rights to all children, girls as well as boys, legitimate or *naturel,* in contrast to the Anglo-Saxon custom of favoring the eldest son.

As you can imagine, the social consequences of equal inheritance rights have been incalculable in France, sometimes more desirable in theory than in practice. Land, particularly valuable ground such as vineyards, has been divided into smaller and smaller plots. For instance, the wooded slopes we own around Château du Feÿ, once vineyard, are to this day still intersected by minuscule strips under multiple ownership. These strips of scrub are virtually worthless—there is a ban on replanting because Europe has a vast surplus of wine—and you might think the owners would want to sell. Forget it! Indeed, family disputes can cause property to be abandoned and you'll occasionally see apparently valuable houses empty and neglected because *indivision* prevails and the owners cannot agree on who shall take what. These laws date back a long time and were codified under Napoleon, who is normally revered in France. But "he got a lot wrong," flatly declares Jean-Pierre.

During the thirty-five years he has worked his vineyards, Monsieur Colinot has made many improvements. He has replaced the old wooden barriques with resin tanks for fermenting and aging the wine ("much easier to clean than stainless steel"). He doesn't believe in oak barrels for the lighter Irancy red wines, which are among the most northern reds made in Europe: "There's scarcely a vintage that would not be overwhelmed." Some of his wines are *tête de cuvée,* made from the first and most gentle pressing of the finest grapes. He now makes a *vin de garde,* left to ferment naturally with the seasons instead of being artificially incubated with heat. Starting in 1999, Irancy has been given permission to give a more specific label to some of its wines, always a sign of moving up in the ranks. This is a triumph for growers like Jean-Pierre Colinot, whose sales will rise accordingly.

As we leave, Monsieur Colinot takes us on a tour of the narrow streets, lined everywhere with cellars. "British, are you?" he says. "One of your famous politicians has a house here—Monsieur Paddy Ashdown—I believe you people call him Mr. Pants Down." Not much escapes Jean-Pierre Colinot, not with two nubile daughters around.

Quail with Grapes on a Potato Cake

You won't see many quail in Irancy vineyards now, but they were once so common that one area is called Les Cailles (the quail). The birds would run around happily in the shade of the leaves—being poor fliers, they prefer the ground—so to roast them in vine leaves and serve them with a sauce of white wine and grapes seems the most natural of marriages. Eight quail perched on crispy potato cakes makes a fine dinner for four.

> *8 medium quail*
> *salt and pepper*
> *16 fresh vine leaves or a small jar (8-ounce)*
>   *of vine leaves, drained and rinsed*
> *8 slices of bacon*
> *2 tablespoons butter*
> *2 tablespoons marc or Cognac*
> *1 cup/250 ml dry white wine*
> *1 cup/250 ml veal or chicken stock*
> *½ lb/250 g seedless green grapes*
>
> **FOR THE POTATO CAKES**
> *1 lb/500 g baking potatoes*
> *¼ cup/60 ml heavy cream*

Heat the oven to 400°F/200°C. If using fresh vine leaves, soften them by plunging them in boiling water 1 to 2 minutes, then draining and rinsing them in cold water to set their color.

Prepare the quail. Sprinkle the birds inside and out with salt and pepper and wrap each in 2 vine leaves, then a strip of bacon. Secure the vine leaves and bacon by tying each quail with a bit of kitchen string as you would a small package. Tie another string around the leg knuckles. Put the birds in a roasting pan, dot them with butter, and roast them, basting often, until the legs feel loose, 25 to 30 minutes. Another way to check if they are done is to lift one on a two-pronged fork; the juice should run clear, not pink. (I like quail well done, though in France they are served rare.)

Meanwhile, make the potato cakes. Generously oil a baking sheet and set it aside. Peel the potatoes and coarsely grate them, using a food processor or hand grater. Squeeze them in a cloth to remove as much water as possible and put them in a large bowl. Stir in the cream, salt, and pepper. (Work quickly so the potatoes do not discolor.) Spoon the potatoes onto the baking sheet in 4 mounds and flatten them with a spatula into

¼-inch/6-mm cakes; I don't worry about getting the cakes terribly neat, since any loose edges become even crispier. Bake them in the same oven as the quail until well browned on the bottom, 12 to 15 minutes, then flip the cakes and continue baking until crisp, 12 to 15 minutes more. Don't be surprised if the cakes tend to stick until they are fully browned.

When the quail are done, set the roasting pan on top of the stove over high heat. Add the marc, stand back, and flame it. When the flames die down, remove the birds and keep them warm while finishing the sauce. Discard the fat from the pan, add the white wine, and boil it, stirring to dissolve the pan juices, until it is well reduced, 8 to 10 minutes. Add the stock and simmer until it becomes a well-flavored jus, 4 to 5 minutes. Strain this jus into a saucepan, add the grapes, swirling the pan gently to distribute the heat, and warm them over low heat for 2 to 3 minutes. Taste and adjust the seasoning of the jus.

Set the potato cakes on warm serving plates. Discard the strings from the quail and set 2 side by side on each potato cake. Spoon the jus and grapes over the birds and serve.

ABOVE AND OPPOSITE: *Grapes, bacon, and vine leaves add sweet, salt, and a touch of bitterness to quail.* OVERLEAF: *Little maisons de vigne dot the vineyards of Chablis, each with its own character. In the days before motor transport, these houses were home to pickers who slept among the vines; now they shelter tools.*

Drive up the hill from Irancy to the plateau and the vineyards quickly give way to commonplace farmland. A few kilometers later, just as abruptly, the landscape reverts to dense, tightly packed vines rolling to the horizon. Chablis! The Chablis vineyards are extensive, 4,000 hectares/10,000 acres or forty times the size of Irancy. By an accident of geology, a stratum of Kimmeridgian clay laden with seashell fossils emerges here (the same clay that gives an enviable bouquet to the wines of Champagne) and the Chardonnay grape, which 10 kilometers away in the Auxerrois yields whites of little depth, is transformed. "Bone dry, but by no means thin," says wine writer Hugh Johnson of the best Chablis. "They have a remarkably powerful scent, and a flavor which I can only describe as slightly mineral, rather than fruity." (It is surely no coincidence that Chablis pairs wonderfully with shellfish.) These wines are no relation of the so-called Chablis produced in other countries. The French have managed to curb other growers calling their sparkling wine "Champagne," but they have not been so successful in forcing the "Chablis" label off cheap bulk whites from California and elsewhere.

I dodge a leggy tractor, built high to work the vines, as it bounds through the main street of the town at alarming speed, looking like a giant grasshopper. I am bound for Domaine Laroche at the corner of the square, one of the top five wine houses in Chablis. We bring friends and students here to sample wine, chilled to perfection straight from the cellar. ENGLISH SPOKEN, RATHER WELL reads the sign in the window. Yes, indeed. Brendan Moore is one of the many British to be found in the international wine trade and he treads the fine line between camaraderie and salesmanship with zest. If you venture to suggest that a bottle of his Chablis may be disappointing, he grins in appreciation, admitting he's tasted better. "Let's try another," he says.

I find it mind-boggling that an experienced wine taster can distinguish not just the four grades of Chablis (Petit Chablis, Chablis, Premier Cru, and the top-flight Grand Cru) but can also make an informed stab at identifying the wine maker and the specific vineyard. (Chablis has seven grand cru vineyards and thirty of premier cru quality, representing about a fifth of the total area under production.) Not so long ago in Australia, I was corralled into joining a panel of experts evaluating several hundred wines side by side with food. I rapidly learned to spit side by side with the pros, though without their elegance and accuracy. I admired the stamina of these Masters of Wine, then remembered that when teaching a class of students, my own taste buds take a similar load. It's partly a question of training, and habit. And of imagination. Brendan tells me that a good Chablis will age over the years "from fruity and fresh to woodsy, with hints of mushroom and truffle." Well, possibly.

An archetypal wine town, Chablis is warm, wealthy, and ever-so-slightly smug. The winding streets and stone-built houses are deceptively modest, the growers' signs discreet. Property rarely changes hands and time is measured in generations rather than years. Even so, Chablis is different, more adventurous, more freewheeling than the Côte d'Or, the fabulous "Gold Coast" to the south. The region recovered more slowly from the devastation of phylloxera a century ago and as a result the vignerons are less entrenched. "Many of us are young by wine-making standards," says Laurent Camu, owner of La Cave du Connaisseur. "My family came back in the late 1960s when Chablis began to expand." And expand it did, from 600 hectares/1,500 acres in 1965 to 3,500 hectares/8,750 acres in 1992. (The expansion continues, but only in the lower categories of Chablis and Petit Chablis.) Monsieur Camu is the sixth generation of a wine-growing family owning some 30 acres of vines, considered a medium-

Chablis is a warren of vaulted stone cellars, the damp earthen floors and constant temperature providing the perfect environs for aging wine. At left, a map of the vineyards orients the viewer from a nearby hillside. The mighty medieval pressoir (right) turns once a year in celebration of the harvest.

sized holding. "We are regarded as dangerously rash by growers of the Côte d'Or, but we've made great strides. Now we are starting to challenge Meursault in international markets." Everyone is into marketing gimmicks—a few growers in the Fourchaume Premier Cru vineyard cull their grapes from a plot named Homme Mort (dead man), site of the former public gibbet. The bones add a certain spice to the wine, or so it is said.

Domaine Laroche is one of the largest wine businesses in Chablis, and owner Michel Laroche was among the first growers to learn English and look worldwide. First and foremost, Michel is a businessman, but after investigating investments in South Africa and Chile, he opted for his native France and bought vineyards in Languedoc. "It makes sense," says Brendan, "Michel is very much le patron, he does it all himself so he needs to be within cracking distance to keep control."

Michel Laroche and Jean-Pierre Colinot, the Cartesian and the romantic, the world traveler and the Bourguignon, the new and the old. Yet these two men share many ideals; both are dedicated to making fine wine, and to exploring new ways to improve it; both come from a long line of vintners and both are proud to have family following in their footsteps. Despite the new international focus, wine is still at base a personal business, depending on individuals, on entrepreneurship, and on the land handed down from generation to generation.

No visit to Chablis is complete without a glass at the café, downed beside the locals placing lottery bets. If I'm lucky there'll be a basket of *gougères* on the counter, the perfect accompaniment.

Cheese Puffs
Gougères

Gougères are held to have originated here in the Yonne and you'll find large, rather woolly versions in the pastry shops. Bake them at home and the fragrant cheese-laden puffs are best-sellers every time. This recipe makes twelve good-size *gougères*.

> ¾ cup/100 g flour
> ¾ cup/175 ml water
> ⅓ cup/75 g butter
> ½ teaspoon salt
> 4 eggs
> ¾ cup/75 g coarsely grated Gruyère cheese
> 1 egg beaten to mix with ½ teaspoon of salt (for glaze)
>
> piping bag and ½-inch/1.25-cm plain tube

Heat the oven to 375°F/190°F and butter a baking sheet. For the choux pastry, sift the flour onto a piece of paper. In a small saucepan, heat the water, butter, and the salt until the butter is melted, then bring everything to a boil. Immediately remove the pan from the heat, add the flour all at once, and beat vigorously with a wooden spoon until the mixture is smooth and pulls away from the sides of the pan to form a ball, 30 to 60 seconds. Beat the mixture over low heat for 30 to 60 seconds more to dry it.

Whisk one of the eggs in a bowl until mixed and set it aside. With a wooden spoon or an electric mixer, beat the remaining eggs into the dough one by one, beating thoroughly after each addition. Beat enough of the fourth reserved egg into the dough so it is shiny and just falls from the spoon; you may not need all of the reserved egg. Beat in the grated Gruyère cheese. Put the dough into the pastry bag and pipe 12 mounds about 2 inches/5 cm in diameter on the baking sheet. Brush the puffs with the egg glaze.

Bake the *gougères* until puffed and golden, 25 to 30 minutes. Take one puff from the baking sheet and let it cool for a minute. If it remains crisp on the outside, it is done. If not, replace it and continue cooking for 5 to 10 minutes longer. When done, let the puffs cool slightly, then remove them from the baking sheet. Serve them warm—they should be slightly soft in the center.

Goat Cheese Puffs
Gougères au Fromage de Chèvre

Make the dough for plain *gougères* (opposite), omitting the Gruyère cheese. For the filling, soften 6 oz/175 g goat cheese with a fork, if necessary working in a little milk so the cheese is easy to shape, and stir in 2 tablespoons chopped chives. Put the plain dough into the pastry bag and, using about half of the dough, pipe 12 shallow mounds about 2 inches/5 cm in diameter on the buttered baking sheet. Dip the back of a teaspoon into egg glaze and flatten the mounds to form rounds. Set a teaspoon of goat cheese filling on each round. Do not press down on the filling and be sure that it does not reach over the edge of the dough or touch the baking sheet. Using the piping bag with the remaining dough, cover the goat cheese filling completely—it should be sandwiched between two layers of plain dough. Brush the puffs with egg glaze and bake like plain *gougères*. The tops will crack open during baking to expose the filling. The recipe makes 12 *gougères*. Serve them warm with a lettuce or vegetable salad.

LEFT: *Over the years I've developed several variations of* gougères—*big puffs, little ones, a flat one looking like a fluffy pizza, and now this new one stuffed before baking with a nugget of soft goat cheese.* ABOVE LEFT: *A platter of classic plain* gougères *is set out for a winter party.*

Chablis is also known for a minor specialty, andouillettes, the pungent sausages made from pigs' intestines. "Everything is done by hand, the cleaning, scalding, stuffing, everything," explains Madame Soulié, who makes these delicacies, thus earning the seal of approval of L'Association Amicale des Amateurs d'Authentiques Andouillettes (AAAAA). Only in France could sausages of pigs' guts arouse such frenzy, and I willingly join in. Rich, earthy, with a touch of the farmyard, *andouillettes* can be so rank as to be inedible; the uncertainty of what you're getting is part of the appeal. They are invariably grilled to serve with *frites* and the local mustard from Dijon.

Ham with Juniper and White Wine
Jambon Chablisien

The nature park of the wild Morvan region, famous for wild pigs, is south of Chablis, hence this local dish of thinly sliced cooked ham baked in a pungent white wine sauce. It is great for leftover ham, providing a quick supper for four people.

> *1 lb/500 g sliced cooked ham*
> *1 teaspoon juniper berries*
> *1 teaspoon black peppercorns*
> *¼ cup/60 ml white wine vinegar*
> *1 cup/250 ml Chablis or other dry white wine*
> *3 tablespoons/45 g butter*
> *5 shallots, finely chopped*
> *2 tablespoons flour*
> *1 cup/250 ml veal or chicken stock*
> *2 teaspoons tomato purée*
> *3 to 4 tablespoons heavy cream*
> *salt and pepper*

Heat the oven to 350°/175°F. Put the juniper berries and peppercorns in a plastic bag and crush them thoroughly with a heavy pan or rolling pin. Put the crushed spices in a small saucepan, add the vinegar, and boil until reduced by half, 3 to 5 minutes. Add the wine and boil until reduced again by half, 7 to 10 minutes.

Meanwhile, melt the butter in a saucepan, add the shallots, and sauté until soft but not brown, 2 to 3 minutes. Stir in the flour and cook until it begins to foam. Whisk in the stock and bring to a boil, whisking constantly until the sauce thickens. Add the reduced wine mixture, and stir in the tomato purée, cream, salt, and pepper. Bring the sauce to a boil, taste, and adjust the seasoning.

Pour a layer of sauce into a shallow baking dish. Arrange the ham slices on top and coat them with the remaining sauce. Bake until very hot and bubbling around the edges, 10 to 15 minutes. Serve the ham hot.

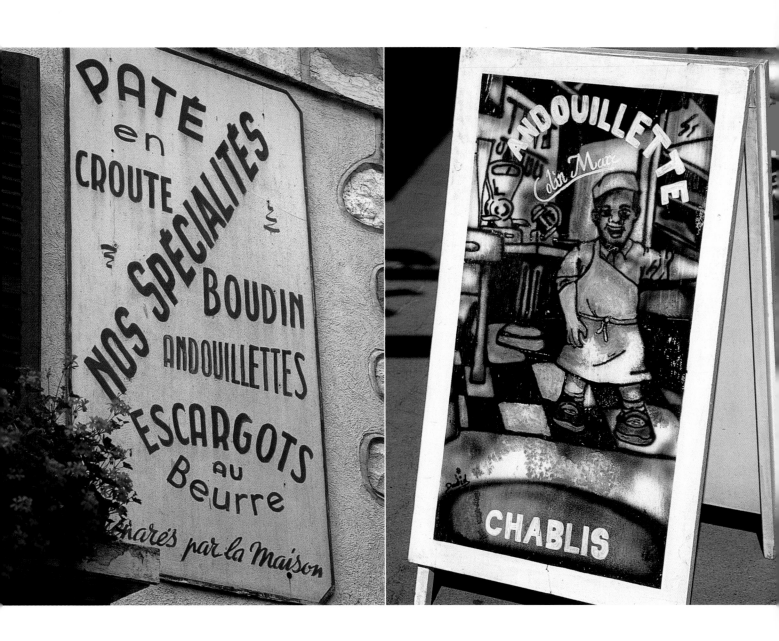

OPPOSITE AND ABOVE: *Burgundians relish all parts of the pig as well as snails, hence these eye-catching signs.* OVERLEAF: *Only the car and the trousered woman date this timeless scene in Dijon.*

Dijon, the capital of Burgundy, seems remote from our home ground, as indeed it must always have been, nearly two hours distant by car even today. We go there for more good food—a couple of restaurants earn one star in the *Guide Michelin*—and to play the tourist, visiting the splendid museum and cathedral and buying loaves of spice bread and pots of mustard to take home. At ground level, Dijon could be just another old town. But when you look upward, past the curly wrought-iron balconies, past the carved facades of creamy stone to the soaring roofs and pinnacles, the historic splendor of the city becomes apparent. In the fourteenth century when Philip the Bold married Marguerite of Flanders, the court at Dijon became a center for all the arts, notably good living. In fact, for a brief, glorious hundred years ending in 1477, the dukes of Burgundy outgunned the kings of France, ruling from Macon in the south, up through Champagne and Luxembourg to Holland and the North Sea. But for a turn of battle, France might now be part of Burgundy, not the reverse.

Hidden behind the imposing facade of the ducal palace is the even more grandiose fifteenth-century kitchen, flanked by six giant hearths, each eight paces wide with a mantel high enough for a cook to walk upright (though with no allowance for starched toques, which were invented in the early nineteenth century). The size of the kitchens gives an indication of the vast scale on which a feudal lord entertained, on the lines of a modern army mess. The contemporary King Richard II of England was said to employ 2,000 cooks, and according to one account, his court consumed in a week a staggering 496 sheep, 70 cattle, 63 hogs, 17 salt hogs, 1,511 goats, 14,900 chicken, 12,390 pigeons, and 1,511 goslings. Although stripped and aseptic now, 600 years ago the duke's kitchen must have bustled with noise and, above all, smells. On most days only two or three hearths would be lit, the choice depending on the direction of the wind, but when all the fires were kindled for a banquet, the smoke and steam must have been stifling.

Good food and wines remain a Burgundian priority. The observation of television guru Bernard Pivot that "even the water in Burgundy tastes delicious" now extends in Dijon to another lowly staple, bread. In the tangle of streets surrounding the covered market of Dijon, I discovered Au Pain d'Autrefois (Bread of Yesteryear). Here the aroma of fresh bread eddies into the street from the great cast-iron oven that is fired into the early morning, a heartening sight for commuters. The bread is *biologique*— whatever this buzzword means—and multigrain mixes and flavored breads like walnut and olive are a specialty. Such artisanal bakeries are few. Only recently has the French public come to appreciate such breads and been prepared to pay double, even triple, the price of the standardized, subsidized white baguette.

Further along the street a glance in the shop window of pâtissier Fabrice Gillotte shows why he has made *meilleur ouvrier de France,* the prestigious award for outstanding craftsmanship. It is the culinary competitions that are best known overseas, but in fact these MOF awards exist for about 200 artisan trades. To compete can be a distraction, almost a full-time business as the awards run on a four-year cycle, but undoubtedly the system has played its part in ensuring that France has not only fine chefs and pastry cooks, but also the best stonemasons, cabinetmakers, and roofers.

Monsieur Gillotte's chocolates are extraordinarily tempting. Made with a minimum of sugar and a maximum of dark chocolate, they are just my style. To say he limits his talents to chocolate would be a contradiction: his filled chocolates alone run to over fifty flavors, many of them novelties such as

Szechuan pepper or nougatine flavored with tea and lime. Ganache is his specialty and each year he develops a new flavor; last year's was blackberry, with a year 2000 special "still in the planning stage." A dozen meticulously crafted chocolate cakes and pastries line the counter, with a three-foot chocolate sculpture dominating the window.

"Fabrice is always seeking perfection," declares his wife proudly as she offers me a *mendiant* (beggar). This is a coin of dark chocolate, embedded with a single pistachio in its purple skin, a brown unblanched almond, a white hazelnut, and a beige cube of candied fruit, their violet, brown, white, and beige colors echoing the robes of the Franciscan, Carmelite, Dominican, and Augustinian monastic orders that once dominated the city.

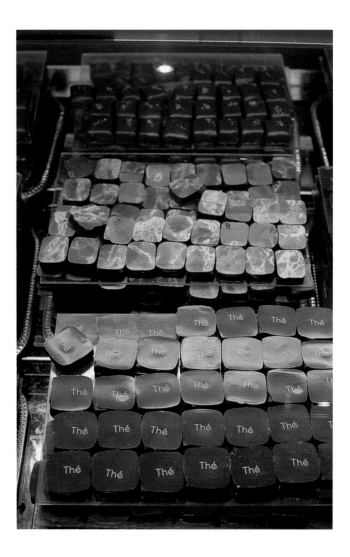

Chocolate Beggars
Mendiants au Chocolat

For about 4 dozen beggars, heat the oven to 350°F/175°C. Spread ¾ cup/90 g peeled hazelnuts on a baking sheet and toast them in the oven until browned, 12 to 15 minutes; let them cool. Prepare and set aside an equal amount of unblanched almonds. Measure ½ cup/60 g unpeeled pistachios and set them aside also. Pour boiling water over ⅓ cup/60 g diced candied peel —citron or lemon peel is the most appropriate color, but I think orange tastes best. Drain the peel and dry it on paper towels—this removes any sugar crystals.

Chop ¾ lb/375 g of your favorite dark chocolate and set it in a metal bowl over a pan of hot but not boiling water. Heat gently, stirring with a wooden spoon until the chocolate is melted. Professional chocolatiers would temper the chocolate at this stage to give it more gloss, but I don't bother. Line 2 baking sheets or trays with wax or parchment paper. Drop teaspoonfuls of warm chocolate onto the paper to make 1¼-in/3-cm rounds. If the chocolate runs too much, wait a few minutes until it cools and thickens a bit. After shaping a dozen rounds and before the chocolate sets, add a hazelnut, almond, pistachio, and cube of candied peel to each one. Continue with the remaining chocolate. Leave the beggars to set in a cool place (they will lose their gloss in the refrigerator), then peel them from the paper. Store them, layered with paper, in an airtight container.

OPPOSITE AND ABOVE: *The dazzling display of fresh chocolates testifies
to the artistry of* meilleur ouvrier de France *Fabrice Gillotte. At top is
his novelty autumn chocolate box; above is the enrobing machine, which keeps
tempered chocolate at the perfect temperature and consistency for coating.*

In their heyday, the Burgundian dukes controlled the oriental spice trade, and a taste for the warmth of nutmeg, cinnamon, cloves, anise, and ginger lingers in the province, notably in the famous spice bread, a honey-laden version of our gingerbread. Spice bread adapts well to additions such as ground almonds and chopped candied peel, and in the windows of Dijon bakers you'll see snails, chickens, even bottles of wine crafted from the obliging batter. Spice bread deserves to be better known —Simon and Emma are long past their schooldays, but this is still the first treat they look for when they come home.

Burgundian Spice Bread
Pain d'Epices

Good spice bread is moist with honey and aromatic with spices, notably anise, and making it is a leisurely process. The batter must be left to stand for eight hours before baking to develop the starch in the flour so the bread is moist and tender. At Le Feÿ, the aroma of baking spice bread wafts up the stairs and along the corridor—a feast in itself. Once baked and cooled, the loaves should be enclosed tightly in plastic wrap and kept at least three days, and up to two weeks, so the honey permeates the bread, moistening and mellowing the spices. One batch makes two medium loaves.

> 1 ¼ cups/300 ml milk
> 1 cup/200 g dark brown sugar, packed
> 1 ½ cups/500 g honey
> 4 cups/500 g flour
> 2 tablespoons/30 g finely chopped candied orange peel
> 1 teaspoon ground aniseed
> ½ teaspoon ground cinnamon
> ½ teaspoon ground cloves
> ½ teaspoon salt
> 2 egg yolks
> 2 teaspoons baking soda
> 1 tablespoon water
>
> 2 medium loaf pans (8x3x3 in/20x8x8 cm)

Heat the milk, sugar, and honey in a saucepan, stirring until the sugar dissolves. Bring it just to a boil, and then set aside until tepid. Sift the flour into a bowl and make a well in the center. Add three quarters of the cooled honey mixture and stir with a wooden spoon, gradually drawing in the flour to make a smooth batter. In a small bowl, mix the candied peel, spices, and salt. Stir in the remaining honey mixture and add it to the batter, stirring until smooth. Cover and refrigerate the batter for 8 to 12 hours.

Heat the oven to 250°F/120°C. Butter the loaf pans, line them with wax or parchment paper, and butter the paper. To complete the batter, mix the egg yolks and baking soda with the water in a small bowl. Stir this mixture into the batter.

Spoon the batter into the pans, filling them half full —the batter rises quite a bit during baking—and cover them loosely with foil. Bake them for 30 minutes, and then remove the foil. Continue baking until a skewer inserted near the center comes out clean, 1½ to 1¾ hours more. Note that spice bread should be slightly underbaked so it is soft in the center and has not started to shrink from the sides of the pan. Let the breads cool to tepid, then turn them out, remove the paper, and wrap them tightly in plastic wrap.

Spice bread batter is also used to make gimblette cookies, which resemble biscotti, and for little cakes called *nonnettes,* after the nuns who would serve them to visitors. Traditionally they are topped with thin white icing, but I recently came across this attractive variant with chocolate ganache. Here I butterfly the tops, like the cupcakes I had as a child.

Nonnettes

For 24 little cakes, make the batter for Burgundian Spice Bread (opposite) and keep it 8 hours. Heat the oven to 350°/175°C and line 24 medium muffin cups with paper cases. Finish the batter by adding the egg yolks, baking soda, and water and spoon it into the cases and smooth the tops. Bake until a skewer inserted near the center of a cake comes out clean, 20 to 25 minutes. Let them cool to tepid, then transfer to a rack and cool them completely. To make the ganache, chop ¾ lb/375 g dark chocolate, put it in a medium bowl, and pour over 1 cup/250 ml boiling heavy cream. Let the ganache cool for 4 to 5 minutes and then stir it until smooth. Leave it to cool until almost set. Cut a shallow cone from the top of each *nonnette,* halve the cone, and reverse the halves to form butterfly wings. Drop a spoonful of chocolate into the hollow left in each nonnette and stick the wings at an angle in the chocolate. Leave the chocolate for a few minutes to set.

Spice bread comes in a multitude of shapes and sizes in the bakeries of Dijon. Novelty shapes can include frogs, snails, champagne bottles, and the more appropriate form of the honey bee.

Spice Bread Ice Cream

Leftover spice bread is excellent toasted, as the heat develops the spices. Local chefs add the dried crumbs to this ice cream, delicious with apple pie.

Make the dried spice bread crumbs by breaking ½ lb/250 g spice bread to coarse crumbs with your fingers or a food processor. Spread them on a baking sheet and toast in a 350°F/175°C oven until they are dry and crisp, 10 to 15 minutes. Let them cool. Meanwhile, make a quart/a liter of vanilla ice cream and freeze it until almost firm, or let commercial ice cream soften until you can stir it. Then stir the spice bread crumbs into the ice cream and taste, adding more spice such as ground ginger or cinnamon if you wish. Freeze the ice cream until firm. It will serve 6 to 8.

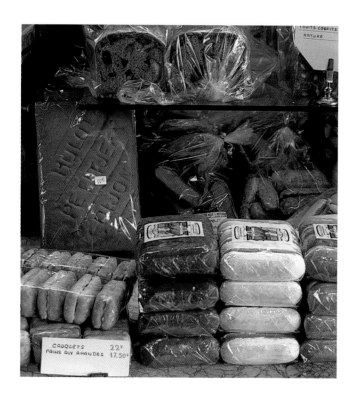

Even older than the Burgundian taste for spices is the love of mustard, a favorite of the Romans. The great dukes of Burgundy liked to speed parting guests with the gift of a barrel of mustard. Legend has it that the name derives from 1382, when Duke Philip the Bold of Burgundy granted the city of Dijon a coat of arms bearing the motto "*Moulte Me Tarde* (Much Awaits Me)," a trademark adopted by today's mustard makers. A more likely derivation is equally picturesque: *moulte ardre* means "much burning." No matter what the origins, the name refers to a type of mustard, not to the place where it is made. Dijon mustard must contain only black mustard seeds (the strongest and most expensive), which are stripped of their skin before grinding. Mustard from Meaux, just east of Paris, is more coarsely ground and includes the skins, giving a rougher texture, darker color, and less intense taste. As for the mustard from Bordeaux, smooth, mild, and often flavored with herbs, Burgundians dismiss it as effeminate.

It is no accident that the traditional centers of French mustard production are famous for their wines (Meaux borders Champagne). Good French mustard needs wine vinegar or verjuice (the juice of sour grapes), and often wine itself to develop characteristic flavors that vary from region to region. Recipes of the top Dijon manufacturers—Maille, Grey Poupon, and the like—are secret and all are subject to appellation controlée quality standards. Most Dijon mustard has a clean, sharp taste, designed to be a condiment though it is also perfect for cooking. Do not, however, overheat mustard as this destroys the enzymes that contribute much to its taste—mustard in a sauce should always be added toward the end of cooking or it will turn bitter.

Pork Chops with Mustard and Bacon

This modest little dish is a mainstay of many a Burgundian bistro where it is served with boiled or panfried potatoes. The few ingredients complement each other just right. Choose thick pork chops so they serve four people generously.

> *4 thick pork chops*
> *2 to 3 tablespoons flour*
> *salt and pepper*
> *1 tablespoon vegetable oil*
> *a 4-oz/125-g piece of lean bacon, diced*
> *¾ cup/175 ml dry white wine*
> *1 cup/250 ml veal or chicken stock, more if needed*
> *a bouquet garni*
> *½ cup/125 ml crème fraîche or heavy cream*
> *1 tablespoon Dijon-style mustard, or to taste*
> *1 tablespoon chopped parsley*

Heat the oven to 350°F/175°C. Put the flour in a shallow bowl and season it with salt and pepper. Coat the pork chops with the flour, patting to remove any excess, and set them aside. Heat the oil in a sauté pan or deep frying pan with an ovenproof handle and fry the bacon until browned. Remove the bacon and set it aside. Add the chops to the pan and brown them well, 2 to 3 minutes on each side. Pour in the wine and simmer with the chops for 2 minutes. Add the stock and the bouquet garni, and replace the bacon. Cover the pan, transfer it to the oven, and cook until the chops are very tender when pierced with a two-pronged fork, 1 to 1¼ hours. Turn them from time to time, and add more stock if at any time the pan seems dry.

Transfer the chops to a warm serving dish or individual plates and keep them warm. Add the cream to the pan and bring the sauce to a boil, stirring to dissolve the pan juices. After 3 to 5 minutes, take the pan from the heat, discard the bouquet garni, and whisk in the mustard, parsley, salt, and pepper. Taste and adjust the seasoning, adding more mustard to your taste; don't let the sauce come back to a boil once you've added the mustard. Spoon the sauce over the chops and serve them right away.

OPPOSITE: *Made to a strict formula, the mustard of Dijon is like no other. Old mustard pots are displayed in the windows of the Grey Poupon/ Maille shop on the main street of the city.*

On the way home from Dijon

I like to take country roads through medieval villages like Montréal and Noyers, stopping finally at the abbey of Pontigny, all the more attractive because it is a bit off the tourist map. Following the Cistercian rule, this austere gothic monument is stripped of all decoration, even of stained glass, but for a single statue of the Virgin in one transept. Often I have the church to myself, the tranquility absolute. So it must have seemed to Thomas à Beckett who in the twelfth century took refuge here for six years before returning to England and martyrdom at the hands of King Henry II. As I wander the abbey, I ponder what makes a vineyard owner, or a chef, successful (never mind that I'm on monastic ground; even Cistercian abbots were keen on food and drink).

How much of good food and fine wines are owed to the place, and how much to the person? How much to technology and how much to tradition? Mark and I debate this chicken-and-egg question all the time. How glad I am that he shares my passion for food. Indeed, in the days when I was dating I remember that a new relationship never got beyond the social niceties unless we shared an interest in cooking. Mark passed the test with flying colors by asking me to a Michelin-starred restaurant first time around. In many ways we've made our life together around this common excitement. Are you surprised that eating out is our favorite pastime?

CHAPTER 4

On Burgundian Tables

Moving to Burgundy opened a whole new *pays* of restaurants and we soon marked every page of the red *Guide Michelin* listing the towns in our region. Other guides have challenged Michelin's preeminence but none has such ancient authority (it was founded in 1898) and, conservative that I am, I've always found it the best place to start. Around Château du Feÿ there was an encouraging cluster of restaurants rated one, two, and three stars. Clearly there was food for investigation and I was eager to find out just what makes a restaurant outstanding, and what gives a chef the passion and dedication to reach the top. I'm still learning. Every restaurant has a different personal story, and in this small, warm world I've made many good friends.

We started at the top. Back then, in 1982, the Côte St. Jacques in Joigny had two stars ("worth a detour" in Michelinese) and it was soon to become one of some twenty restaurants in France that earn the highest three-star rating, meriting "a special trip." For us no special trip is needed as ten minutes brings us to the restaurant door. *"Bonjour, bonjour,"* greets Chef Michel Lorain, a cheerful, gap-toothed figure in impeccable chef's whites—no toque, though; this was the freewheeling eighties. We have a little chat about wild mushrooms, and then are ushered to our table by Madame, Parisian in approach and very much in charge. Looking back, I realize that Michel has always had a keen sense of style, of creating dishes with just that touch of novelty which compels attention, earning praise from restaurant critic Patricia Wells, for "thoroughly modern, classic French cuisine that displays a rare sense of equilibrium and sophistication."

After dinner Michel comes around for a chat. Socializing in the dining room now forms an important—often too important—part of a chef's public relations, and with his engaging manner and shock of gray hair (now almost white), Michel is very good at it. He told me he had ambitious plans for the property, which had been a posting inn but was now being ruined by the trucks thundering past on the *route nationale* outside. The chef hoped to tunnel under the road and gain access to the river Yonne, never mind the cost. "Then we will have a garden, a pool, suites of very elegant rooms, and of course a bar." One hitch was the trailer park just across the river. "I may need to buy it," says Michel, and later he does. Over the years we've seen Chef Lorain acquire a boat dock and launch to go with it, a helicopter pad, and a miniature golf course. He has planted 7 hectares/18 acres of vineyard high above Joigny, and is bravely making the best he can of its Pinot Gris, perhaps more as a gesture of solidarity with the town than as a pleasure for his guests. He has also constructed an excruciatingly modern budget hotel on the opposite side of the river, the roof picked out in green neon. Michel's tastes in decoration do not accord with mine, but otherwise we are the best of friends!

When our son, Simon, was sixteen, Chef Lorain kindly offered him a summer job as *bagagiste*. Clad in prickly black regulation trousers and a white shirt, the tails invariably flopping, Simon would hump suitcases through the tunnel and up to the famous suites of rooms overlooking the river, each decorated in a different, ever more eclectic style. When the regular bellman took over during the more lucrative mornings and late afternoons, Simon was put to washing up, scoffing leftovers of the remarkable petits fours. He did his best, but at a puppylike 6 feet 4 with hands to match, the damage to the house crystal was scary. "I only broke three glasses and a window," Simon confided cheerfully one day and, seeing me wince, added, "It's all right, Mum, they don't know who did it!"

Simon worked at the Côte in 1986, the banner year when the restaurant received its third star. By then, young Jean-Michel Lorain was thoroughly into his stride after ten years of culinary training, first as an apprentice with his father, then as a commis and sous-chef in the kitchens of Troisgros in Roanne, Girardet near Lausanne, and finally at Taillevent in Paris, all legendary kitchens, all rating three Michelin stars. Such initiation, almost a pilgrimage, can be crucial in forming the taste and the techniques of a gifted young cook. It is the contemporary approach, the little touches of presentation, and above all the philosophy of a master chef that his young acolytes seek to discover.

At the Côte St. Jacques, much praise was given to the light freshness of the cooking, to little touches like smoking cod before poaching it to serve with a caviar cream sauce, or floating zucchini and cream quenelles on a chilled gazpacho of langoustines. Let me say at once that all of the recipes in this chapter such as Lobster in a Parcel (opposite) are my version of the originals—there's no way to recreate the finest restaurant cuisine at home and I'd never try to do so.

Lobster in a Parcel

These crispy packages moistened with a lobster jus are an ideal dinner appetizer for four deserving guests, an inspiration of Jean-Michel Lorain. Given the luxury of the lobster, it's worth using a good Chardonnay wine.

> *a medium live lobster (about 1½ lb/750 g)*
> *2 tablespoons butter*
> *salt and pepper*
> *3 tablespoons Cognac*
> *2 shallots, finely chopped*
> *1 garlic clove, finely chopped*
> *½ small carrot, finely chopped*
> *1 cup/250 ml Chardonnay white wine*
> *1 cup/250 ml fish stock*
> *2 to 3 tablespoons crème fraîche or heavy cream*
>
> FOR THE PASTRY CASES
> *4 sheets of phyllo pastry dough*
> *3 tablespoons melted butter*

Set the lobster on a chopping board and cover the tail with a cloth. Hold the lobster firmly by the tail. Using the point of a large knife, pierce the shell at the center of the head all the way down to the chopping board. Continue cutting to split the head. Turn the lobster around and, holding the head, cut it in half lengthwise through the tail. Crack the claw shells by striking them with the back of the knife to break the shell without cutting through the claw meat; this allows the heat to penetrate during cooking. Pull out and discard the stomach sac located just behind the eyes on each half. Remove the green liver (tomalley) and any greenish black coral, chop them coarsely, and reserve them.

To cook the lobster, melt the butter in a sauté pan. Set the lobster halves, cut-side up, in the pan and season the exposed flesh with salt and pepper. Cover the pan and cook over medium heat until the lobster shell is bright red and the meat is no longer transparent, 5 to 7 minutes. Add the Cognac and flame it either with a lighted match or by tilting the pan to catch the gas flame. (Stand back as the flames will rise high.) Remove the lobster halves from the pan and let them cool.

For the jus, sauté the shallots, garlic, and carrot in the same pan that was used to cook the lobster, stirring often until well browned, 5 to 7 minutes. Add the wine and boil until reduced to a glaze, 6 to 8 minutes. Add the fish stock and boil again until well reduced with con-centrated flavor, 8 to 10 minutes. Whisk in the reserved liver and coral (the coral turns red when cooked). Simmer the jus for 2 minutes and then strain it into a small pan, reserving the vegetables and setting them aside in a bowl. Taste the jus and adjust the seasoning.

When the lobster is cool enough to handle, pull out the tail meat and slice it on the diagonal. Remove the body meat, picking it out in pieces with a sharp skewer or knife point. Add the lobster meat to the vegetables along with the cream and a couple of spoonfuls of jus. Extract the claw meat in one piece and halve each claw horizontally, making 4 pieces for garnish.

To assemble the parcels, unwrap the phyllo dough and lay one sheet on the work surface. Cover the remaining sheets with a slightly damp towel. Brush the single sheet of dough lightly with melted butter, add another sheet, and brush it also. Continue until you have 4 layers, keeping the stack covered while you work so it doesn't dry out. Butter a baking sheet. (Rewrap the leftover dough and keep it for another use.)

Cut four 6-in/15-cm squares from the buttered sheets of phyllo. Spoon a quarter of the lobster filling in the center of each square. Pull in the corners of the squares to cover the filling completely. Flip the parcels so they are seam-side down and flatten them, shaping them in rounds like a hamburger. Poke an air hole in the center of each package so steam can escape, set them on the baking sheet, and brush the tops with butter. Cut the trimmings into 4 strips and loosely roll them, pinching together on one side, to resemble roses. Set them also on the baking sheet. The parcels and jus can be prepared up to 8 hours ahead and stored in the refrigerator.

To finish, heat the oven to 375°F/190°C. Bake the packages until crisp and brown, 20 to 25 minutes. (Remove the roses after 10 to 12 minutes, or as soon as they are brown.) A skewer inserted in the center of each parcel should be hot to the touch when withdrawn after 30 seconds. Reheat the lobster jus and spoon it on 4 individual plates. Add the packages, top each with a rose and a piece of claw meat, and serve at once.

PREVIOUS PAGES, TOP LEFT: *Wine fuels the Burgundian restaurant scene.* RIGHT: *Father and son, Michel and Jean-Michel Lorain, are genial hosts of the top-rated Côte St. Jacques restaurant in Joigny. Bacchus, god of wine, presides appropriately over their garden. At bottom and on page 119 are two of their signature dishes: my version of Lobster in a Parcel and the masters' hûitres de Marennes en petite terrine océane.*

But an economic cloud dimmed the brilliance of the Côte St. Jacques' third star. *"Etoile d'immobilier* (a real estate star)," carped one critic. Some people blame the *Guide Michelin* for sending the wrong signal to the three-star restaurants, and others think the chef-owners were too compliant. Either way, among the top restaurants in France during the glitzy 1980s there was a reckless over-investment in infrastructure—top-of-the-line Baccarat crystal, Limoges china, Porthault linens, flashy paintings, and decorator-distressed paint work—fun to look at but nothing to do with cuisine. "Great chefs have no taste," quips Mark, looking around at some dining rooms of that period with their brassy chandeliers, purple felt on the walls, gazebos and grass cloth, knickknacks and nudes, financed essentially by piling up debt. Those like Michel Lorain who expanded early have survived, but the 1990s economic downturn has hurt more recent debutants and ruined a few.

Among the chefs who feel at risk in the fickle restaurant business is Bernard Loiseau at the Côte d'Or in Saulieu. Chef Loiseau (his name means "the bird") is a bit of a loudmouth who expounds his difficulties on television. "How can I create great food when I have to worry about finding 50,000 francs ($8,000 or more) every single day of the week to pay back the bank," he trumpeted just recently. He underestimates himself. Bernard Loiseau is a brilliant, creative chef who loves to push invention to the limit. "The table is a festival, every meal should offer a dream," he declares. Remembering that as a child he gathered snails among the stinging nettles, he put them together in the pan. For several years he banished butter, cream, and egg yolks from the kitchen. Well before the current phobia of animal fats, Loiseau was using nonstick pans and a minimum of oil. He abandoned the use of stock, regarded as the basis of much French cuisine (the French word for stock, *fond,* also means "foundation") and turned to water for extracting fresher, purer essences of taste. He thickened sauces with vegetable purées, for example replacing the usual garlic butter on frogs' legs with a jus of parsley. Lentils give body to mussel soup (overleaf), testament to what can be done without a roux.

OPPOSITE: *Bernard Loiseau sets a welcoming table of hors d'oeuvre beside the fire at the Côte d'Or restaurant in Saulieu.* ABOVE: *A basket of dried fruit and nuts awaits the cheese course.*

Lentil Soup with Mussels

I'd not heard of combining lentils and shellfish, but the salty mussels add intriguing depth to the rather flat taste of the average lentil. Bernard Loiseau uses the famous lentils from the volcanic soil of Le Puy in central France—green when raw, they cook to a rich brown —but more common brown or red lentils will do, too. Some cooks like to soak lentils overnight, but personally I think there's no need. This makes enough soup for six hearty bowls.

> *½ lb/250 g lentils (about 2½ cups/600 ml)*
> *1½ quarts/1.5 liters water, more if needed*
> *salt and pepper*
> *2 quarts/1 kg mussels*
> *2 shallots, chopped*
> *juice of ½ lemon, more to taste*
> *1 cup/250 ml dry white wine*
> *chervil or snipped chives (for decoration)—optional*

Put the lentils in a soup pan with the water and a little salt. Cover, bring to a boil, and simmer until the lentils are very soft and falling apart, 2 to 2½ hours. If you are used to cooking lentils as a side dish or salad, you may be tempted to stop cooking too soon; the lentils should be falling apart as you stir them so they are soft enough to purée smoothly.

Meanwhile, scrub the mussels under running water, scraping to remove any barnacles and weed. Pull off the stringy beard with a small knife. Discard any mussels that are damaged or do not close when tapped, as they may be dead.

Combine the shallots, lemon juice, and white wine in a large pan and simmer until the shallots are tender, about 2 minutes. Add the mussels, cover the pan, and cook over high heat until the mussels open, stirring once, about 5 minutes. Reserve 8 to 12 mussels in their shells for garnish. Let the remaining mussels cool slightly, then shell them, discarding any that are still closed. Pour the cooking liquid from the mussels into a bowl, leaving any grit behind in the pan. Stir the liquid into the simmering lentils and continue simmering, stirring often toward the end of cooking to prevent sticking and adding more water if the soup gets very thick. Add only enough water to keep the lentils from sticking—otherwise the soup will be too watery.

When the lentils are very tender, purée them in a food processor or using a hand-held immersion blender. The soup will lighten in color and become quite creamy and smooth. Stir in the shelled mussels. Bring the soup just back to a boil—the mussels will be tough if overcooked. If the soup is too thick, stir in a little water—it should be moderately thick but not pasty. Taste and adjust the seasoning with lemon juice, salt, and pepper. Serve the soup in bowls, each topped with 2 or 3 mussels in their shells and, if you like, a sprig of chervil or a sprinkling of snipped chives.

ABOVE: *The original dining room of the Côte d'Or, with diplomas and photos of the famous on the walls, dates to the 1930s reign of Alexandre Dumaine, master chef of his generation.* OPPOSITE: *Chef Loiseau is famous for game, roasted rare and served cloaked in a wine sauce thickened with blood and with a simple garniture.*

By sautéing celery julienne,

then simmering it briefly in water, Chef Loiseau concentrates a maximum of flavor. In his instructions, the chef is precise: "Don't wait to finish cutting the celery root, but to stop it discoloring, toss it with lemon juice as you work." His original recipe uses truffle juice but I've substituted walnut oil.

Celery Root Ragoût

Peel a large celery root (about 1½ lb/750 g), cut it in half, and rub it with a cut lemon to prevent the bright white flesh from discoloring. Cut each half into ¼-inch/6-mm slices, stack the slices, and cut the celery root into sticks a little thicker than julienne. Alternatively, cut the sticks using a mandoline. Squeeze more lemon juice over the celery sticks and toss to coat them. Put the celery in a pan of cold salted water, bring to a boil, and simmer until tender but still firm, 5 to 6 minutes. Drain the celery in a colander. Heat ½ cup/125 ml walnut oil in the saucepan, add the celery, and toss it for 1 to 2 minutes over low heat until the oil is absorbed. Remove from the heat, squeeze in the juice of a half lemon, taste, and adjust the seasoning. Serve for 4 as a side dish with beef and game. The celery is good cool, too, as a salad.

Part of the mystique

of a top restaurant is generosity, the overflowing warmth and welcome that can be conveyed in many ways. In France, add-ons are important—little *amuse-bouches* (literally "amuse the mouth"), the little extras that punctuate the beginning, end, and sometimes the middle of a fine meal. Tiny gougères (page 106) are a Burgundian favorite and the other day we were offered this cheese wafer with the invitation to "Please eat it with your fingers," an added incentive to relax.

Parmesan Fricco

Finely grate 4 oz/125 g Parmesan cheese. Put about 2 tablespoons of the cheese in a nonstick pan and spread it to a 3-in/7.5-cm round. Set the pan over low heat and cook until the cheese melts and starts to brown underneath, 2 to 3 minutes. It will smell temptingly of toasted cheese. Let the wafer cool for 30 seconds, then loosen it with a metal spatula and transfer it to a rack to cool and stiffen, making sure it lies flat. Run cold water on the underside of the pan to cool it quickly, then fry more wafers. (It is essential to start each time with a cool pan.) If you like, sprinkle them lightly with paprika before serving. This makes 12 to 16 wafers and I'll nibble several without a second thought.

In summer, Bernard Loiseau

serves a little cup of chilled melon soup as the refreshing opening to a meal. Here I suggest scooping the melon into balls, adding Chef Loiseau's flavoring of tarragon. As far as the French are concerned, only one variety of melon deserves attention and that is the orange-fleshed Charentais, but any fragrant, juicy melon will do.

Melon Soup

For 4 people, thoroughly chill 2 medium or 1 large melon. Halve the melons, discard the seeds, and with a ball cutter, scoop the melon flesh into balls. Scoop out the remaining flesh with a sharp spoon and purée it in a food processor with 3 tablespoons port and 1½ tablespoons sherry vinegar. Mix 2 to 3 tablespoons chopped tarragon into the purée. Taste, and if the flavor lacks intensity, add a little sugar. Chill both the purée and the melon balls. To serve, pour the purée into chilled cups, pile the melon balls on the center, and top each one with a tarragon sprig. Serve very cold.

ABOVE: *My version of chilled melon soup strikes a cooling note.* OPPOSITE: *At L'Espérance, an extraordinary dessert as well as tiny madeleines, candied fruits, and berries in season offer an elegant end to a fine meal.*

The third member of the triumvirate of top chefs in our area is Marc Meneau of L'Espérance at St. Père-sous-Vézelay. Like Lorain and Loiseau, Meneau has a strong sense of style as well as a keen nose for contemporary trends. Unusually for a top chef, he did not follow the usual path of apprenticeship and *stages* all over France, as he only started to cook professionally in his mid-twenties. Monsieur Meneau's natural talent was honed by talking and working with nearby chefs, and by study. "I learned to cook by reading books," he says. "Life has taught me discipline. From my mother I inherited the café–grocery of St. Père, a fine legacy, and the knowledge that money does not come easily." His cuisine displays a strong sense of place, of *terroir*. He loves dark, earthy flavors and each year gives a Fête du Saint-Cochon (Feast of the Sacred Pig) with long-forgotten dishes such as couée with pork lungs, liver, and heart seethed in red wine and thickened with blood. "My food is full of flavor; appearance, for me, has always come second to taste," he says.

Marc Meneau also has an exceptional hand with pastry. With Julia Child and Patricia Wells, I once took a group of culinary professionals on a gastronomic odyssey, visiting a trio of three-star restaurants in twenty-four hours. Knowing the chef's brilliance with desserts, we asked him to cover the sweet end of things. He protested—no chef likes to be restricted to pastry—then created an unforgettable repast. Each table was set in eighteenth-century style with a galaxy of pastries and petits fours, including homemade marshmallows, miniature pound cakes, almond tiles, fondant-coated fruits, little fruit tartlets, fruit bonbons, and filled chocolates.

Course followed course, first a bowl of hot drinking chocolate made with whole, unpasteurized milk and whisked, we were told, for two hours over the lowest possible heat. Ethereal toasted brioche came separately for dunking. Then came a tart of dark rose petals in fresh cheese, the perfume of rose harking back to the Renaissance. And the pièce de résistance, Chef Meneau's grandmother's apple gâteau, baked overnight to achieve the requisite essence of apple with a hint of orange and butter. I couldn't wait to try it at home, and you'll find our simplified Le Feÿ version on the next page.

Apple Gâteau Le Feÿ

Very thinly sliced apples (preferably Granny Smith) are layered with a suspicion of sugar and grated orange zest, then baked overnight in the lowest possible oven. (The first time you make it, you'll need to keep an eye out as your oven may be too warm even at the lowest setting.) One small cake serves six, and I'd suggest adding one of the caramel sauces below.

> *4 lb/1.8 kg tart apples*
> *1 to 2 tablespoons butter, for the mold*
> *5 to 6 large lumps of sugar*
> *2 oranges, for zest*
>
> *1½-quart/1.5-liter tall soufflé dish*

Heat the oven to 150°F/66°C. Generously butter the soufflé dish and butter a wide strip of wax or parchment paper to form a collar extending at least 3 inches/7.5 cm above the rim of the dish. Press the collar, buttered side inward, against the inside of the dish and chill until the butter is set and the paper sticks to the dish.

To extract the zest from the skins of the oranges, rub them with the sugar cubes so the cubes soften and turn bright orange. Wrap the orange-flavored cubes in plastic wrap and crush them with a rolling pin.

Peel the apples and scoop out the stem and flower ends. Halve them and scoop out the core with a melon baller or the point of a knife. Set a half, cut-side down, on a board and cut it crosswise into the thinnest possible slices. Alternatively, slice the apple halves on a mandoline. Arrange a layer of apple slices in a flower pattern in the bottom of the mold. Top this first layer of apple with more apple slices arranged across the others like ripples in a pond. (This crossed pattern of slices ensures that the cake holds together when unmolded.) Sprinkle the second layer with the crushed orange sugar. Continue filling the mold until the apples, held in place by the paper collar, extend at least 2 inches/5 cm above the rim. (They will shrink down into the mold during cooking.) Cover them with a round of buttered paper.

Bake until the apples are much reduced and meltingly soft when pierced with a skewer, 12 to 14 hours. Tear off the top of the paper collar and let the cake cool to tepid. Unmold it onto a warm platter—the top should be lightly caramelized with a little syrupy juice running down the sides. Serve it warm, with a caramel sauce.

Caramel Salt Butter Sauce

Caramel, of course, is simply toasted sugar. It took a master chef like Marc Meneau to think of making caramel sauce, not just with the usual cream, but with salted butter to add an inimitable bite to the sweetness. The resulting butterscotch sauce is great with ice cream as well as fruit desserts like apple gâteau.

Heat 1 cup/200 g sugar with ½ cup/125 ml water and a squeeze of lemon juice over low heat until the sugar dissolves—be sure to use a heavy pan as caramel is one of the hottest ingredients in the kitchen. (The lemon juice helps stop the sugar from crystallizing.) Boil the syrup rapidly without stirring until it starts to turn golden around the edges. Do not stir—if you do, the syrup may crystallize. Meanwhile, melt ½ cup/125 g salted butter with ¾ cup/175 ml heavy cream. When the syrup begins to color, lower the heat a bit and continue boiling to a deep golden color—it will darken rapidly. Remove the pan from the heat and let it cool for 30 seconds. Add the butter and cream, standing back as the sauce will sputter and bubble up in the pan. Put it back over the heat, stirring until the caramel is completely dissolved. Let the sauce cool, then taste it and add a pinch of salt to sharpen the flavor if necessary. Serve hot or chilled. It makes enough to top 4 to 6 desserts.

Honey Caramel Sauce

I found out how to make a honey caramel sauce quite by accident. One day my caramel was starting to cloud, and I'd read somewhere that honey would cut the crystals. Magic—not only did the syrup clarify, it tasted strongly, deliciously, of honey.

Follow the recipe above for Caramel Salt Butter Sauce without adding the butter and cream. When the caramel has reached a golden brown, remove the pan from the heat and add 2 tablespoons honey. Swirl the pan to mix in the honey, then add ½ cup/125 ml water, or cream if you prefer a cream sauce. Heat the sauce, stirring until the caramel has dissolved. Serves 4, warm or cold.

Lightly caramelized, translucent Apple Gâteau Le Feÿ—confit in the sense of preserved—is astonishingly mellow and concentrated.

Somewhere during Marc Meneau's memorable spread of desserts we tasted his famous dried fig and marc ice cream. Here's my reconstruction.

Dried Fig and Marc Ice Cream

Marc is the French grappa, a spirit distilled from grape crushings with a powerful, earthy flavor much favored in Burgundy. It blends just right with figs in this recipe, which makes a potent ice cream to serve six to eight.

> 1 cup/250 g dried figs
> ½ cup/125 ml marc
> 2 cups/500 ml milk
> 2 cups/500 ml heavy cream
> a vanilla bean, split
> 6 egg yolks
> ¾ cup/150 g sugar
>
> ice cream churn

Cut the figs into 2 to 3 pieces, put them in a jar, and pour over the marc. Cover the jar tightly and leave the figs to macerate for 24 hours, longer if possible.

For the vanilla custard, bring the milk and cream just to a boil with the vanilla bean. Cover and leave them to infuse over low heat for 10 to 15 minutes. Whisk the egg yolks and sugar together until light and thickened, 2 to 3 minutes. Stir the hot milk and cream into the egg yolk mixture and return this custard to the pan. Cook the custard over medium heat, stirring with a wooden spoon until it thickens lightly, 2 to 3 minutes—if you draw your finger over the back of the spoon, it will leave a clear trail. Strain the custard into a bowl and leave it to cool—the vanilla bean can be rinsed, dried, and used again. Cover and set the custard aside to cool.

Purée the figs and marc in a food processor or blender and stir the purée into the cool custard. Freeze the ice cream until firm in a churn freezer, then transfer to a chilled container and store in the freezer. If the ice cream has been made more than a day ahead, let it soften for an hour or so in the refrigerator before serving.

Tranquility reigns in this whimsical garden of vegetables on the grounds of L'Espérance restaurant. Beds, bordered with lettuce and cabbage, are mounded in the center to make picking easier. In the kitchen (top) quiet moments are rare. ABOVE: *One of Marc Meneau's signature dishes.*

Promotion and the development of ancillary activities are an essential part of today's restaurant game. Chefs are celebrities, appearing on television talk shows much like rock stars. Indeed, chefs are often more successful media personalities than managers—a great meal, after all, is theater, a concert performance that has an overture, a theme, and a grand finale. The kitchen *brigade* forms a closely knit team with the same camaraderie and sense of drama as a theatrical troupe led by the stars. Says Alain Ducasse, another three-star mogul: "Chefs need to emerge from their kitchens to be visible to the world at large so that French cuisine maintains its international reputation." When a star chef has a competent substitute, often a family member, to take over at home, this suits everyone. With Jean-Michel Lorain up to speed at the Côte St. Jacques, he or his father can take engagements elsewhere.

Chefs also get tied in knots over merchandising. Constantly looking for ways to expand the limited income from meals, they sell branded jams and chocolates and put their name to frozen and vacuum-packed dinners. Bernard Loiseau declares that the shop where he sells monogrammed chef's jackets for kids beside the house Champagne makes more money than the restaurant itself (I hope he's joking). Spin-offs need careful handling, easily diluting the focused, essentially luxury image of a top name.

Sheer physical strength is another limitation in the kitchen. After forty the long hours and tough conditions start to take their toll. By mid-fifties a chef can no longer stand the pace of twenty years earlier, no matter how fit he may be. Stars rise, but they also fall and the question of succession becomes key. The smooth transfer that has taken place within the Lorain family is rare. For example, in the 1960s on our local food scene the Frères Godard were renowned, two brothers of a restaurant family, one in Sens, the other in Joigny, each with a Michelin star. Today the stars are gone but the brothers are still there, and so are their sons who are now in their mid-thirties and yearning for independence. In Sens, young Philippe Godard has found a steady tourist market for the poached fish and roasts that once formed the glory of the house, but each year his face is a little plumper and a little sadder as he follows his father around the dining room. In Joigny his cousin Claude has catered with success, but his father obstinately keeps a brigade of cooks for a half-abandoned dining room. This summer, Claude decided enough was enough and packed up his knives for a bistro in Manhattan.

The struggle to the top for one chef, in this case Bernard Loiseau, has been recounted in epic style by William Echikson in *Burgundy Stars.* For Echikson, "To aspire to three Michelin stars takes a special character: creative, durable, and, *mais oui,* a bit crazy." To find a chef who can inspire young, ambitious cooks and transfer great food to the plate reliably, year after year, is rare. At L'Espérance, Marc Meneau is inclined to philosophize, at least to judge by his dotty aphorisms ("In choosing a dish which allows us to run faster, higher, and stronger, we must activate our entire mind"), but when he puts knife to chopping board he becomes more practical. "We must take today's new products and show others how we make the most of them, following our classic traditions. We must pursue the *terroir,* which adds so much character and impact." How right he is! All too often, menus with their lobster, truffles, and chic allusions to the latest dining fad could play equally well in Los Angeles, New York, or Hong Kong. It was Escoffier who said, "*Faites simple* [keep it simple]," a lesson all cooks should take to heart.

The village church of St. Père sous Vézelay, near the luxurious L'Espérance restaurant, is no stranger to gourmandise, judging from this 12th-century gargoyle of a manikin stuffing himself with food.

Frogs' Legs on a Red and Green Field

The consistency of the tomato coulis is intended to be chunky and just stiff enough to hold a shape, as should the parsley purée. The recipe serves four and is good for scallops, too

> *20 pairs of frogs' legs (about 1 lb/500 g)*
> *3 to 4 tablespoons flour*
> *salt and pepper*
> *3 tablespoons/45 g butter*
> *1 to 2 garlic cloves, finely chopped*
> *1 shallot, finely chopped*
>
> **FOR THE TOMATO COULIS**
> *1 tablespoon butter*
> *1 shallot, chopped*
> *1 garlic clove, chopped*
> *1 ½ lb/ 750 g tomatoes, peeled, seeded, and chopped*
> *a bouquet garni*
>
> **FOR THE PARSLEY PURÉE**
> *a large bunch (about 4 oz/125 g) of flat-leaf parsley*
> *1 cup/250 ml crème fraîche or heavy cream*

For the tomato coulis, melt the butter in a sauté pan, add the shallot and garlic, and fry until soft but not brown, 1 to 2 minutes. Stir in the tomatoes with salt and pepper and add the bouquet garni. Simmer, stirring occasionally, until the tomatoes are very soft and thick, 15 to 20 minutes. Taste and adjust the seasoning, discarding the bouquet garni. Set aside.

For the parsley purée, bring a pan of salted water to a boil. Discard the thicker parsley stems, add the sprigs to the boiling water, and simmer for 1 minute. Drain, rinse the parsley with cold water, and drain it again thoroughly. Purée the parsley in a food processor with half the cream and season it to taste. Stir in the remaining cream and set aside.

To finish, put the tomato coulis and parsley purée over low heat to warm while you cook the frogs' legs. Wash the frogs' legs and dry them on paper towels. Toss them with the flour, salt, and pepper until coated. Heat half

the butter in a large frying pan until it stops foaming. Add half the frogs' legs and sauté them over medium heat until brown, turning them once, about 2 minutes on each side. Transfer them to a plate, cook the remaining frogs' legs in the same way, and remove them. Add the garlic and shallot to the pan and sauté until just starting to brown, 1 to 2 minutes. Replace the frogs' legs and stir so they are seasoned with the garlic and shallot.

Spoon the tomato coulis on one side of 4 warmed individual plates, then add the parsley on the other, or be imaginative and create your own design. Pile the frogs' legs on top and serve at once.

ABOVE: *How simple fine cooking can be: the Lorains' snails on a red and green ground (this version of mine substitutes frogs' legs).* OPPOSITE: *Truck stops offer simpler fare, though a three-course lunch is still the rule.*

So far we've looked at the top three chefs in our region, the success stories. It goes without saying that these restaurants are expensive. If I'm at each of them once a year, I consider myself lucky. It must be admitted that the overwhelming proportion of their customers are from Paris, or from overseas; the number of diners these restaurants attract locally is tiny. So where do our Burgundian neighbors go most of the time? For that matter, where do Mark and I like to eat out? My preference is always for establishments with a strong sense of place, which serve regional dishes, the best of them made with local ingredients in simple, comfortable surroundings that don't intrude. (You'd be surprised how much neon lighting has reached rural France.) When dining out, we test the terrain, assessing the number of cars parked outside and eyeballing the menu, which under French law must be displayed at the restaurant door. Our son Simon has a nose for good eating places. I've known him to grind to a halt outside a log cabin in the wilds of Russia. "The *gai* traffic police park here," he says, "that's a good sign." Sure enough, there was no electricity but the soup was delicious.

Take the Pavillon Bleu just down the hill in Villevallier, which was our first outing when we came to live at Le Feÿ. Madame extended a warm welcome (she recognized the car) and Monsieur stuck his head out of the kitchen to say hello. The cooking was respectable—a homemade pâté de campagne, ripe melon with country ham, and a remarkable coq au vin falling from the bone and clearly reheated several times so the sauce had mellowed to a rich nose-tingling bouquet. Monsieur's poached eggs in meurette red wine sauce, a featured specialty, were equally successful.

Poached Eggs in Red Wine Sauce
Oeufs en Meurette

Out comes our local fruity red Irancy wine for sauce
meurette, a grand Burgundian classic served with
poached eggs or fish. The quirky combination appeals
to modern tastes, so you'll find it popping up on contemporary menus. For extra flavor, I like to poach the
eggs in the wine, which is then used for the sauce—
they emerge an odd purple hue, but this is later concealed by the glossy brown veil of sauce. In France, this
recipe would serve four as two eggs are always allowed
per person, but we often stretch it to eight. For poaching, it's well worth looking for farm-fresh eggs as they
hold their shape better than store-bought eggs.

> *8 fresh eggs*
> *1 bottle (750 ml) red Burgundy wine*
> *2 cups/500 ml brown veal or chicken stock*
> *1 onion, thinly sliced*
> *1 carrot, thinly sliced*
> *1 celery stalk, thinly sliced*
> *1 garlic clove, crushed*
> *a bouquet garni*
> *½ teaspoon peppercorns*
> *salt and pepper*
>
> FOR THE GARNISH
> *2 tablespoons butter*
> *¼ lb/125 g mushrooms, sliced*
> *a ¼-lb/125-g piece of bacon, diced*
> *16 to 20 baby onions, peeled*
>
> FOR THE CROÛTES
> *8 slices of white bread, ¼ in/6 mm thick*
> *oil for frying (optional)*
>
> FOR THE BEURRE MANIÉ
> *2 tablespoons butter*
> *2 tablespoons flour*

To poach the eggs, bring the wine and stock to a vigorous boil in a large shallow pan. Break 4 eggs, one by one,
into the places where the liquid is bubbling so the bubbles spin the eggs. Lower the heat and poach the eggs
for 3 to 4 minutes, until the yolk is fairly firm but still
soft to the touch. Gently lift out the eggs with a slotted
spoon and drain them on paper towels. Poach the
remaining eggs in the same way. Trim off the stringy
edges of the eggs with scissors. Set the eggs aside.

Add the onion, carrot, celery, garlic, bouquet garni,
and peppercorns to the poaching liquid and simmer
until it is concentrated and reduced by half, 20 to
25 minutes.

Meanwhile, cook the garnish: Melt half of the butter
in a medium saucepan, add the mushrooms, and sauté
until tender, 2 to 3 minutes. Remove the mushrooms,
add the remaining butter and bacon, and fry until
brown. Lift out the bacon and drain it on paper towels.
Add the onions and sauté them gently until brown and
tender, shaking the pan often so they color evenly, 10 to
15 minutes. Drain off all the fat, replace the mushrooms
and bacon, and set the pan aside.

Make the croûtes. Using a round or oval cutter, cut
the bread into 8 shapes just larger than a poached egg.
For fried croûtes, heat ¼ inch/6 mm of oil in a frying
pan over medium heat. Working in batches, fry the
croûtes until browned on both sides, 1 to 2 minutes per
side. Drain them on paper towels. Alternatively, if you
prefer toasted croûtes, brush the rounds on both sides
with oil and bake them in an oven heated to
350°F/175°C for 10 to 15 minutes, turning them
halfway through so they brown evenly on both sides. Set
the croûtes aside.

To thicken the sauce, crush the butter on a plate
with a fork and work in the flour to form a soft paste
(called *beurre manié*). Whisk the *beurre manié*, a piece at a
time, into the simmering wine mixture until it becomes
thick enough to lightly coat a spoon. Strain the sauce
over the mushrooms, onions, and bacon, pressing the
vegetables in the strainer to extract all the liquid and
flavor. Bring the sauce to a boil, taste, and adjust the
seasoning.

To finish the dish, reheat the eggs by immersing them
in hot water for 1 minute. Set the croûtes on warm serving plates. Drain the eggs on paper towels, set one on
each croûte, and spoon over the sauce and garnish.

Another Burgundian dish that survives on contemporary tables is fish in sauce meurette with the traditional mix of red wine, bacon, mushrooms, and baby onions. In the old days, the fish (probably trout or perch) would have come from the Yonne River, only 100 meters from the back door of the Pavillon Bleu. Now salmon is a favorite, its pink flesh a stunning contrast to the highly reduced, almost black, wine sauce.

Salmon in Red Wine Sauce
Saumon en Meurette

Follow the recipe for Poached Eggs in Red Wine Sauce (opposite), omitting the eggs, using 2 lb/1 kg salmon fillet (with skin) and cutting it into 6 serving portions. Poach the salmon pieces in the red wine and stock over low heat on top of the stove until they just flake easily —they will take 7 to 10 minutes depending on their thickness. The sauce, garnish, and croûtes are made exactly as for the poached eggs.

The red wine sauce meurette is a Burgundian classic, whether served with poached eggs (as here, recipe opposite) or with fish (recipe above).

Le Pavillon Bleu, by the way, is next to a Relais Routier, part of the truckers' café network throughout France. Truckers everywhere are good trenchermen and French ones have their own guide, which lists such amenities as free showers and superior food, denoted by a little casserole. Our local Relais features "home cooking" with a three-course menu of such unbeatable classics as egg and tomato mayonnaise, pâté de campagne, or composed salad as appetizer, a choice of ten main courses including roast leg of lamb, beef with carrots, roast chicken, skate in cream sauce, or oven-roasted blood sausage, all followed by a cheese platter (help yourself) or dessert. It's an astonishing value for under $10. To my amusement, in between visits to carriage museums and underground grottoes, the guide urges truckers to seek out Ecole de Cuisine La Varenne at Château du Feÿ. So far we've had no takers!

The next direction our restaurant exploration took us was to Sens. La Madeleine was a disappointment at first: the chef, Patrick Gautier, seemed to try too hard; Madame Gautier was hesitant and shy. After a year or two the decor, installed on a shoestring budget (Chef Gautier was only twenty-six when the restaurant opened), began to wilt and I could see his face lengthening in defeat. Then Patrick struck gold. He opened a wine bar in the space next door, decorating at minimum expense and servicing it out of the main kitchen. The choice of a second Patrick as server (waiter is too polished a description) was brilliant. Gray-haired, slim as an eel, Patrick keeps thirty diners happy with a jocular word here, a free glass of wine there, turning tables two or three times, a feat almost unheard of in France where a table is yours for the night.

At first, Patrick Gautier had feared that the wine bar's success would undermine his main restaurant, but now he finds the contrary. Customers start out at the wine bar, then become regulars, graduating to the restaurant for more special meals and celebrations. La Madeleine is doing better each year, enough to finance a renovation of decor. For the chef, the pressure is relentless and Patrick has been known to fall asleep at the lunch table when he comes to give a class on his day off. But he looks five years younger than in quieter, less successful times and has no complaints: "Cooking is *la folie*—the restaurant business even worse. No leisure, no time for family, nothing. But we're not in it for that."

I asked Patrick if he wanted to enter the star circuit. "A Michelin star is a minimum," he says and then hesitates. "For me it is a personal thing, a recognition by my peers that I've arrived." When I mention the prospect of doing better financially with a star, he laughs. "Oh, that's double-edged. Yes, you get more customers, but they are the butterflies, the tourists that may never come again. By contrast, many chefs feel that when they gain a star, they lose their old clients who fear prices will go through the roof. If ever I am awarded a star, I won't make that mistake."

Now is his chance! Recently Patrick Gautier won that coveted first star. He can expect visitors from all over the world and a 20 percent increase in business during the first year; such is the power of the *Guide Michelin.* Both nationally and internationally, eyes are on him as one of the emerging young talents. By contrast, Marc Meneau, longtime leader in the region, has lost one of his three stars. He has been demoted from one of twenty master chefs at the top to relative obscurity among seventy-five others, a devastating blow.

Dominique Unsch, chef-owner of Le Pavillon Bleu, displays a dish of steamed mussels.

Sugar-Crusted Sponge Cakes
Biscuits de Savoie

Chef Gautier uses little bucket-shaped molds inherited from his grandmother for these individual sponge cakes, but I've found that small cans, for example portion-sized soup cans, do fine. They should be about 3¼ in/8 cm in diameter and at least 1½ cups/375 ml in volume. The cakes are coated with a crunchy sugar crust and are astonishingly light, thanks to the use of potato starch instead of flour and to the classic *biscuit* method in which the egg whites are whisked to a light meringue and then folded into the egg yolk batter. The recipe makes six individual cakes, and I like to serve them with a fruit coulis or with berries and Wine Sauce for Fruit (page 94).

> 3 to 4 tablespoons melted butter (for the molds)
> 1 cup/200 g sugar, more for the molds
> ⅔ cup/80 g potato starch
> large pinch of salt
> 5 eggs, separated
>
> six 1½-cup/375-ml cans

Heat the oven to 350°F/175°C. Next line the cans. (This takes longer than making the cake itself!) Thoroughly wash and dry the cans. Cut rounds of wax or parchment paper to fit their bases and strips to line the sides. Brush the rounds and then the strips on both sides with melted butter and press them into the cans so they adhere. Chill the cans for 2 minutes in the freezer and butter the paper again. Sprinkle very generously with sugar, tipping to coat the sides and shaking out the excess. Chill the cans in the refrigerator while you make the cakes. The aim here is a thick sugar crust on the finished cakes.

Sift the potato starch with the salt. Set aside 2 to 3 tablespoons of the sugar for the egg whites. Put the egg yolks with the remaining sugar in the bowl of an electric mixer. Sift the potato starch with the salt into the yolks. First stir until mixed, then beat with the mixer until the batter is light and forms a thick ribbon trail when the

whisk is lifted, 3 to 5 minutes. Stiffly whisk the egg whites, add the reserved sugar, and continue beating until the whites form a very long peak when the whisk is lifted, in effect a light meringue. Fold about one third of this meringue into the egg yolk mixture, with about one third of the sifted potato starch. Add the remaining meringue and potato starch in two batches, folding together as lightly as possible.

Spoon the batter into the prepared cans, filling them about one half full. Bake them until risen, lightly browned, and just beginning to pull away from the sides of the cans, 20 to 25 minutes. Let them cool in the cans before unmolding them. They keep surprisingly well but are still best the day of baking.

One of Patrick Gautier's specialties is a multiple dessert plate centered on a single flavor—caramel, lemon, or vanilla. A little warm chocolate cake very like this one forms part of his quartet of chocolate sorbet, chocolate ice cream, and a tiny chocolate tartlet.

Soft-Centered Warm Chocolate Cake

The chocolate dessert of the nineties, these little cakes are baked to a crisp outside and a warm, melting center that acts as sauce. The recipe makes eight servings, and one key to success is leaving the batter to stand overnight. Then the cakes must be baked just long enough to hold a shape while the center remains soft. Don't worry if they overbake and set firm; they are still the very best of chocolate puddings.

> *5 oz/150 g bittersweet chocolate, chopped*
> *¾ cup/175 g butter, cut in pieces*
> *4 eggs, separated*
> *½ cup/100 g sugar*
> *3 tablespoons/22 g flour*
> *vanilla ice cream, crème fraîche, or whipped cream,*
> * for serving*
>
> *eight 1-cup/250-ml ramekins*

Butter the ramekins, freeze them for 5 minutes, and then butter them again. Finally sprinkle them with flour, discarding the excess. Put the chopped chocolate and butter in a bowl set over a pan of simmering water and stir until melted and smooth, 5 to 8 minutes. Set the bowl aside to cool.

In another bowl, beat the egg yolks with half the sugar until thick and light, 3 to 5 minutes. Stir in the cooled chocolate mixture, followed by the flour. Using an electric mixer, whisk the egg whites with the remaining sugar to form a light, stiff meringue, about 2 minutes. Fold the meringue into the chocolate mixture. Fill the ramekins to the rim, smooth the top with a spatula, and run your thumb around the edge to detach the mixture from the sides. Cover and refrigerate the cakes for 8 hours or overnight.

To bake the cakes, heat the oven to 400°F/200°C. Set the cakes on a baking sheet and bake until puffed and set on the surface but still liquid in the center, 8 to 9 minutes. Take them out and let them cool for about 10 minutes so they shrink back into the molds. Run a knife around the edge and turn the cakes onto warmed individual plates. Top with a spoonful of ice cream, crème fraîche, or whipped cream, and serve at once.

Chocolate Sorbet

For an ultra-rapid sorbet, heat 5 oz/150 g chopped dark chocolate with 1 cup/250 ml water, stirring until the chocolate is melted. Add 1½ cups/300 g sugar with 2 cups/500 ml more water and a tablespoon of instant coffee powder. Heat, stirring, until the sugar has dissolved. Bring to a boil and simmer until the mixture thickens very slightly, 8 to 10 minutes. Let it cool, then freeze it in a churn freezer. This makes 1 quart/1 liter of sorbet to serve 6 to 8.

OPPOSITE: *Light-as-a-feather* Biscuits de Savoie *are baked in antique molds coated generously with sugar for a crisp crust.*

In the restaurant world, so much depends on location. The Auberge de Villeroi just outside Sens flanks a fast stretch of road so that cars speed by without even seeing the sign, simply creating noise and pollution. They miss the best foie gras around, superbly served on a salad of haricots verts dressed with Walnut Vinaigrette (page 64). The chef bakes the fattened livers in a terrine to intensify their flavor rather than simmering them in a cloth. (Simmering stifles taste, in my opinion, but it retains 10 percent more weight, so you can imagine which method is more common.) As with most restaurants, it helps to know your way around the menu at the Auberge as the chef can be distracted by a passing fad. Plump and sweet, his roast scallops are superb.

Roast Scallops with Sesame, Parsley Salad

I've added a little, but very little, Asian spice to traditional roasted scallops. Serve them with a lively fresh parsley salad as lunch or light dinner for four. Try the same idea with shrimps, too.

> *12 to 16 large scallops (1½ lb/750 g)*
> *2 tablespoons sesame seeds*
> *2 to 3 tablespoons flour*
> *salt and pepper*
> *¼ cup/60 g butter*
> *2 to 3 garlic cloves, finely chopped*
> *1 teaspoon dark sesame oil*
>
> FOR THE PARSLEY SALAD
> *a medium bunch (about 4 oz/125 g) flat-leaf parsley*
> *1 lime*
> *3 tablespoons vegetable oil*

Heat the oven to 450°F/230°C. Heat the sesame seeds in a small nonstick frying pan over moderate heat, stirring them until brown and fragrant, 4 to 5 minutes. Set them aside.

Prepare the salad. Wash the parsley and dry it on paper towels. Detach the sprigs, discarding the stems. Pare wide strips of zest from the lime with a vegetable peeler and cut them in julienne strips. Blanch the julienne by putting them in cold water, bringing to a boil, and draining them. Squeeze the lime juice and reserve it.

For the scallops, wash and trim the white muscle off the scallops, leaving the coral if there is any—often it has been removed. Dry the scallops very thoroughly on paper towels. Put the flour in a shallow dish and season it with salt and pepper. Roll the scallops in flour, patting to coat them evenly and shake off the excess.

Melt the butter in a large frying pan with a heatproof handle, heating until the butter stops sputtering. Add the scallops and sauté over high heat until just brown, 1 to 2 minutes. Turn and quickly brown the other side. Sprinkle the scallops with the chopped garlic and flip them so the garlic is underneath, shielded from the direct heat of the oven. Roast the scallops in the oven until firm around the edges but still soft in the center when you press them with a finger, 5 to 7 minutes; they should still be slightly translucent in the center.

Meanwhile, finish the salad. Whisk all but 2 tablespoons of the lime juice with the oil, salt, and pepper in a small bowl. Add the parsley leaves and lime julienne, toss, and taste for seasoning. Pile the salad on 4 serving plates.

To finish, set the scallops on top of the salad, sprinkle them with sesame oil, followed by the sesame seeds and remaining lime juice. Serve at once.

The Vaudeurinoise is another case of bad location. Chef André Delory had everything going for him—an attractive property installed with charm and impeccable training as sous chef to Marc Meneau in Vézelay. But no one came to Vaudeurs, a lost backwater just east of Sens, on the way to nowhere. Now the touch of Slav melancholy in his pale face seems justified. The restaurant is still open but he makes ends meet by vacuum packing meals. He grins, "You wouldn't believe how many working couples order from me. And forget the myth that the French family shares supper around the table every evening. These people order individual meals and eat them at different times!"

A salad of flat-leaf parsley (it grows all year in our garden) forms a crisp background to plump, golden Roast Scallops with Sesame.

A recent appearance on French tables, even at unpretentious places like Villeroi, has been the pre-dessert consisting perhaps of a tiny crème brûlée, or a miniature cookie flavored with herbs, or a liqueur glass of fruit or chocolate sorbet. Best of all, for me, is seasonal fruit—a handful of wild strawberries, a freshly sliced juicy pear, a perfect ripe fig bursting on the plate. However, I seriously wonder how long this pleasant addition to the menu will last as even a sorbet discourages dessert orders, always a lucrative add-on to the tab.

Cherries Under a Hood
Cerises en Capuche

André Delory has always had the light hand with pastry needed for these cherries hidden under a crust of pastry. (Burgundy is dotted with former monasteries so the title *en capuche,* meaning "under a monk's cowl," seems appropriate.) Steam from the hot cherries raises the dough to a crisp dome. Let each guest crack the dome to catch the delicious aroma and add a scoop of vanilla ice cream. The recipe serves four and is best direct from the oven.

If, instead of baking the cherries under a crust, you spoon them over vanilla ice cream while still hot from flaming, you have cherries jubilee.

> *1 recipe puff pastry (page 298)*
> *1½ lb/750 g dark sweet cherries, pitted*
> *2 tablespoons butter*
> *3 tablespoons/45 g sugar*
> *1 tablespoon red currant jelly*
> *¼ cup/60 ml Cognac*
> *1 egg, beaten to mix with ½ teaspoon salt, for glaze*
> *2 cups/500 ml vanilla ice cream, for serving*
>
> *4 ovenproof soup bowls or large ramekins*

Make the puff pastry and chill at least 30 minutes. Melt the butter in a large frying pan, stir in the sugar, and heat gently, stirring occasionally, for about 1 minute. Add the cherries and sauté over high heat 1 minute. Add the red currant jelly and stir until dissolved. Simmer until the cherries are almost tender, 3 to 5 minutes.

Flambé the cherries. Warm the Cognac in a small saucepan, and then stand back and set it alight. Pour it, flaming, over the cherries and baste them until the flames die. Set them aside.

Heat the oven to 400°F/200°C. Put the serving bowls on a baking sheet and heat them in the oven. Roll the puff pastry dough to about ⅛-in/3-mm thickness and cut out 4 rounds, each 2 in/5 cm larger in diameter than the bowls. Chill the rounds on a baking sheet in the freezer until firm, 5 to 10 minutes.

Brush the chilled dough rounds with egg glaze. Remove the bowls from the oven. Heat the cherries just to a boil and spoon them into the hot serving bowls. Brush the outside rim of the bowls generously with egg glaze. Lay a round of dough over each bowl and shape it to the bowl, pressing to seal the edges with the glaze. Work quickly so the dough does not soften from the heat.

Bake the cherries until the pastry is puffed and golden brown, 25 to 30 minutes; the steam from the hot cherries will puff it to a tall dome. If necessary, trim any ragged bits of puff pastry with a knife to neaten the edges. Serve the cherries at once with scoops of vanilla ice cream in a separate bowl. A delicious steam will be released at the table when the pastry is broken.

OPPOSITE: *A crispy beret of puff pastry is a beguiling cover for a compote of fresh cherries.*

All these restaurants rely on the classic French management structure—the family. Many chefs can cook well, some can also run a kitchen efficiently, but to do both and manage a stylish restaurant is a quantum leap. A wife who is as dedicated to the job as her husband is well-nigh indispensable. Sometimes she's not his wife at all, but what the French law quaintly calls a *concubine notoire,* i.e., an established live-in companion enjoying the same rights as a spouse. Whatever the relationship, the man is invariably in the kitchen where the physical work is hottest and hardest, while Madame keeps a tight control out front on the staff, the customers, and the cash. She greets, takes the orders, chivvies the servers (mainly women), and, toward the end of the service, she retires to a desk where she issues the *additions.* Most important of all, she sells the menu, explaining the dishes, reassuring hesitant diners, chatting on equal terms with connoisseurs. When Madame is relaxed and smiling, stylish but not showy (she should never make the error of rivaling the customers), she puts everyone at ease.

Notice, however, that I've mentioned no woman chefs. I'm often asked why there are so few women in professional kitchens in France and one answer is simple. Cooking is hot, sweaty work involving long hours on your feet often with inadequate equipment. A chef must be not just dedicated, but also physically fit. Speaking personally, there's no way I could ever have stood the pace and I'm no weakling. Other factors are more complex: the French are more realistic—or ruthless—about a woman's lack of strength, and the distractions of family and children. And many chefs are categoric about the complications of both sexes in one kitchen, wanting none of it.

However, along the road from us in the historic walled town of Villeneuve-sur-Yonne there is an anomaly: a woman proprietor. Leslie Caron of *Gigi* fame fills the role of restaurateur with aplomb. "I'm looking for country food which is simple, not frightening, something Burgundian but lighter than traditional recipes." The food is pleasant, the service erratic, but atmosphere overrides all. In the summer season the restaurant is packed seven days a week.

OPPOSITE: *Grapes on a rusted fence—perhaps a sign of welcome, of wine sold within.* ABOVE: *Leslie Caron created La Lucarne aux Chouettes (The Owl's Loft) from four derelict warehouses on the banks of the Yonne, letting the ancient oak beams and tall flint-encrusted walls speak for themselves. In summer the sun-baked terrace overlooks a placid river scene worthy of Monet and in winter the open fire beckons.*

Croustades of Red Peppers with Goat Cheese

In a restaurant, speed is of the essence. Dishes must be quick to make, easy to prepare ahead, and just a little bit different, like this little sauté of red peppers piled on crusty bread and broiled with a topping of goat cheese. We serve it as an appetizer or a snack for four people.

4 red peppers
3 to 4 tablespoons olive oil
2 onions, sliced
2 to 3 thyme sprigs
salt and pepper
2 garlic cloves, crushed
2 tomatoes, peeled, seeded, and chopped
2 tablespoons capers, drained
4 thick slices of country bread
6 oz/175 g soft goat cheese

Heat the broiler and broil the peppers on a baking sheet until black and blistery, turning them to cook evenly. Once they are blackened on all sides, fasten them in a plastic bag so they steam and the skin is loosened. Leave the broiler alight. When the peppers are cool, slip off their charred skins with your fingers. Don't worry about leaving a few flecks of black—it adds flavor. Cut the peppers in half and then in wide strips, discarding the cores and seeds.

Heat the oil in a large frying pan and fry the onions with the thyme, salt, and pepper until soft and starting to brown, 5 to 7 minutes. Stir in the garlic and cook until golden. Add the tomatoes and capers and cook, stirring often, until the tomatoes are cooked and thickened, 3 to 5 minutes. Add the peppers and continue cooking until tender, 3 to 5 minutes. Taste and adjust the seasoning.

Oil a baking sheet and set it aside. Toast the bread and arrange the pepper mixture on top. Slice the cheese and put the slices on the peppers. Broil the croustades on the baking sheet until the cheese is lightly browned and the edges are melted, 2 to 3 minutes. Serve warm.

One way to calm restive customers is to offer them nibbles *"pour faire patienter,"* in the untranslatable phrase. At Leslie Caron's you are soothed with tiny niçoise olives. At La Madeleine it is marinated salmon, or at Vaudeurinoise a chilled demitasse of soup.

Mussel Salad

This refreshing summer salad of mussels can be nibbled with the help of a toothpick, or served as a more substantial appetizer on its own.

Wash 3 quarts/3 liters mussels under cold running water, scraping off any barnacles and pulling off the beard; discard any that do not close when tapped on the counter. Put the mussels in a large pan, cover, and cook them over high heat, stirring once, until they open, about 5 minutes. Let them cool and then remove them from the shells, discarding the tough dark ring surrounding the meat. Put the mussels in a bowl with 2 chopped shallots, 1 chopped celery stalk, 2 tablespoons chopped fresh cilantro, and the grated rind of 1 lemon. Add ¼ cup/60 ml vegetable oil, the juice of 2 lemons, salt, and pepper, and toss until well mixed. Taste and adjust the seasoning. Chill the salad before serving on lettuce leaves. It is enough for 4 to 6 as an appetizer.

Dates with Foie Gras

In winter, one of the most tempting openings to a festive meal I've come across are these dates stuffed with foie gras. The same filling is delicious in prunes, too.

Slit open and remove the pits from 20 to 24 dates—fresh if you can get them. Open a 3¼ oz/100 g can of pâté de foie gras and cut the pâté in about 20 cubes. Stuff a cube into each date. For a more formal effect, you can pipe the foie gras into the dates using a star tube. This makes enough for 8 to 12 guests.

Croustades of Red Peppers with Goat Cheese are baked at the last minute to come browned and bubbling to the table.

ABOVE LEFT: *The roguish grin of this wild boar hints at cunning—the creatures are notoriously ferocious. Cooking the dark meat to tenderness in a rich wine sauce is one of Chef Pierre Siri's specialties.* ABOVE RIGHT: *Chef Siri clutches a bouquet of flowers from a well-wisher, while his wife, Raymonde, displays a slice of chocolate tart, the house specialty.*

When I think of the perfectly run restaurant, I think of La Chamaille near Auxerre where the stage is set by Raymonde Siri. Madame Siri is always at hand when needed, but she never intrudes; her memory for faces is amazing and at each visit she has a personal word for guests. She remembers what you enjoyed last time and proposes just the right bottle of wine. As we sip, time slows, a family of ducks parades on the pond outside the windows—rural bliss. Meanwhile Chef Siri, busy in the kitchen, never appears but the trainees from our cooking school who have worked with him report a mastery of technique and a discipline that extends to the whole team. Chef Siri has a lively sense of humor. Last winter, he hung a whole wild boar, hide and all, in the cold store for a young apprentice to find. The resulting scream will be long remembered.

Braised Wild Boar with Juniper

The woodsy flavor of juniper—and of gin—is one of my favorites. It is excellent with any game, so don't hesitate to try this recipe with venison, too. The thickening of rye bread and vinegar gives a nice bite to the sauce. I like to serve this recipe for four to six people with a butter-laced potato purée and possibly, for a touch of sweetness, with a side dish of quince compote from the Roast Pigeon with Quince Compote on page 155.

> a 3-lb/1.4-kg boned roast of wild boar, preferably
>   with the bones
> 3 tablespoons vegetable oil
> 2 onions, sliced
> 2 carrots, sliced
> 2 celery stalks, sliced
> 1 tablespoon juniper berries, crushed
> 1 teaspoon black peppercorns
> 4 to 5 tablespoons gin
> 1 tablespoon flour
> 1 bottle (750 ml) red Pinot Noir wine
> 3 garlic cloves
> a bouquet garni
> salt and pepper
> 2 cups/500 ml veal stock or water, more if needed
> 2 slices of rye bread, crusts removed
> 2 tablespoons red wine vinegar

Heat the oven to 325°F/160°C. Tie the roast into a compact shape with string. Heat the oil in a flameproof casserole or Dutch oven over high heat and thoroughly brown the wild boar on all sides. Remove the roast, lower the heat, add the onions, carrots, and celery, and cook them gently until soft and starting to brown, 7 to 10 minutes. Put the juniper berries and peppercorns into a plastic bag and crush them with the base of a heavy pan.

When the vegetables are brown, add half the gin and flame it. When the flames die, stir the flour into the vegetables and cook, stirring, for 1 to 2 minutes. Then replace the meat, add the wine, crushed berries and peppercorns, garlic, bouquet garni, and a little salt, and bring it to a boil. If you have any bones, tuck them down along the sides of the meat. Add enough stock to half cover the meat, put the lid on the casserole, and braise in the oven for 2 hours, turning the roast after an hour. It should cook very slowly, scarcely at a simmer. Meanwhile, pour the vinegar over the bread in a shallow dish and leave to soak while the boar braises.

After 2 hours, pull the soaked bread into crumbs with 2 forks and stir it into the cooking liquid to thicken it lightly. If it seems thick or the meat is dry, add a little veal stock or water. Continue cooking until the meat is very tender when pierced with a two-pronged fork; it may take 1 to 2 more hours, depending on its age—mature meat takes more coaxing to become tender.

Transfer the meat to a carving board and cover it loosely with foil to keep warm. Skim any fat from the surface of the sauce and strain it, pressing hard on the vegetables to extract all the flavor. If the sauce is thin, boil to reduce and thicken it. Add the remaining gin to the sauce, taste, and adjust the seasoning. Meanwhile, discard the strings from the wild boar and cut it in generous slices. Arrange them overlapping on individual plates or a platter and spoon over a little sauce, serving the rest separately.

CHAPTER 5

La Vie de Château

When I look back over sixteen years of living at Château du Feÿ, the progression from historic but shabby ancient monument to the modernized home of La Varenne Cooking School seems inevitable, but it certainly was not so at the start. We bought Le Feÿ, crazy though it sounds, as a weekend and summer home, a *résidence secondaire,* for our small family of four. Only gradually did we realize that we had acquired so much more—a living property with an active past and a future that was ours to create. We were betting that we could do something to bring Le Feÿ back to life—to animate the property, as Mark has put it.

Château du Feÿ dates back to the 1640s. It was the center of extensive lands detailed on the vellum map now hanging in our entrance hall and drawn in 1751 when the property changed hands. Tiny stakes are drawn on the map to mark hundreds of acres of vineyard running down to the valley, while on the upland, curlicues indicate the oak trees of the neighboring Forêt d'Othe. This was wealth indeed. Historically, the economic basis not only for the château but the entire region was wine and timber; both floated northward on the river Yonne, which joins the Seine downstream. It was the waterway of these combined rivers that provided this area's lifeline to Paris.

We are the seventh owners in the château's 360-year history and now scarcely 100 acres remain, just enough to protect our magnificent front view, with some woodland at the rear. We have a postcard showing vines planted up to our front door, but this conceals a sad story. By the end of the last century, wine making here had already been made redundant by the railroads, which assured the transport to Paris of cheap, high-alcohol wines from the south. Much of the wine that was made in this area in the 1850s was of low alcoholic strength—about 7.5 degrees—and had to be stabilized with stronger wines, so no wonder it could not compete. Then came the final blow from the phylloxera louse that wiped out vines throughout France. It arrived in Villecien in the late 1800s; wine, as a local industry, was finished.

A young British observer, John Cobbett, visited our area in 1824 and remarked "the whole country, indeed, except the meadows by the river's side, is vineyard, but now and then planted at the same time in standard fruit trees, such as peaches, apricots, apples, pears and mostly in plums." Looking at the landscape today, it is hard to credit such a description. But some fruit trees do remain and in our orchard, the three kinds of plum (purple, green, and golden) do particularly well.

Tricorne Puffs with Plums
Corniottes aux Prunes

These *corniottes* are triangles of puff pastry with the sides turned up like a tricorne hat. They may be stuffed with fruits or with cheese and I like to combine the two, stuffing a single plum with cream cheese. Apricots and figs make good *corniottes,* too. This recipe makes eight pastries—great with coffee.

> *1 recipe puff pastry (page 298)*
> *½ cup/125 g cream cheese*
> *2 to 3 tablespoons milk (optional)*
> *1 to 2 tablespoons sugar, more if needed*
> *8 large plums (about 1½ lb/750 g)*
> *1 egg beaten to mix with ½ teaspoon salt, for glaze*
> *confectioners' sugar, for sprinkling*
>
> *a 6-inch/15-cm cookie cutter*

Make the puff pastry dough and chill at least 30 minutes. In a small bowl, beat the cream cheese until smooth, adding a little milk if necessary to soften it. Beat in the sugar, adding more if the plums are very tart. Slit the plums along the indentation, leaving the halves joined. Force the halves apart slightly and scoop out the

pit. Fill each plum with a tablespoon of the filling.

To shape the tricornes, roll out the pastry dough to a 20x24-in/50x60-cm rectangle about ⅛ inch/3 mm thick and stamp out eight 6-in/15-cm rounds with the cookie cutter. Sprinkle a baking sheet with water. Brush the rounds with egg glaze and set a stuffed plum in the center of each. Fold up the sides from 3 directions to form a triangle that almost but does not quite cover the plum, pinching the folds firmly to set sharp neat angles and prevent the plum juice from leaking during baking. Set the tricornes on the baking sheet and brush the dough sides with glaze. Chill until firm, at least 15 minutes. Heat the oven to 400°F/200°C.

Bake the tricornes until puffed, golden brown, and the dough is thoroughly cooked, 25 to 30 minutes. Five minutes before the end of cooking, sprinkle the tricornes generously with confectioners' sugar and continue baking until the sugar forms a shiny glaze. Transfer them to a rack to cool. Serve them warm or at room temperature.

PREVIOUS PAGES: *The view from the terrace at Château du Feÿ is as serene today as it was a hundred years ago, despite the proximity of Paris and small industries burgeoning along the valley. Until the late 1800s, vines grew up to the front door (bottom left). The property has always been carefully documented in archives that date to the late 1500s, even before the château was built.* OPPOSITE: *The top of the pigeonnier.*

The map of 1751 outlines a property of 4,700 acres, confirmed by the grandeur

of our pigeon house (above). Its construction has that rational quality of the best farm buildings. Inside, ranks of boxes (hence the name pigeonhole) give shelter for well over 5,000 birds; in effect this is an early broiler house. Pigeon and pigeon eggs must have been standard fare at Le Feÿ.

Roast Pigeon with Quince Compote

The robust taste of pigeon takes well to fruit, and one year we had a bumper crop of quinces, an invitation to a happy marriage. Quinces are a curious fruit; looking like a craggy pear, they are inedible raw, but if cooked slowly for hours with plenty of sugar, they turn a deep rose pink. The flavor is mellow, almost musky, and well worth the wait. I've used ratafia to flavor the sauce, but port is an excellent alternative. Allow a whole pigeon per person; this recipe makes enough compote and sauce for four.

> *4 to 6 quinces (about 3 lb/1.4 kg)*
> *1 cup/200 g sugar, more to taste*
> *1 quart/1 liter water*
> *pared zest and juice of 1 lemon*
> *1 vanilla bean, split*
> *4 young pigeons or squab (about ¾ lb/ 375 g each)*
> *salt and pepper*
> *1 tablespoon oil*
> *1 tablespoon butter*
> *1 tablespoon flour*
> *1 cup/250 ml chicken stock, veal stock, or water*
> *2 tablespoons ratafia or port*

To cook the quinces, put the sugar and water in a medium saucepan and heat until the sugar dissolves, stirring occasionally. Meanwhile, rub the fuzz off the quinces with a towel. Peel, quarter, and core them, then cut each quarter into 2 or 3 chunks, dropping them at once into the syrup so they do not discolor. Add the lemon zest and juice, cover the pan, and poach the fruit over very low heat until tender and deep pink, 2 to 3 hours. It takes time for the color to develop, so be patient; add more water if the syrup evaporates too much. At the end of cooking the syrup should be slightly thickened but still cover the fruit.

To roast the pigeons, heat the oven to 400°F/200°C. Sprinkle the birds inside and out with salt and pepper and truss them with string (see the glossary). Melt the oil and butter in a roasting pan over high heat and brown the birds on all sides. Set them on their backs and spoon over 2 or 3 tablespoons syrup from the quince.

Roast the pigeons in the oven, basting often and adding more quince syrup if the pan juices are lacking. After 20 minutes, test by lifting a bird on a two-pronged fork and pouring out the juices from inside—if pink, the birds will be rare. If you prefer them well done, continue roasting for 5 to 10 minutes until the juice runs clear.

Transfer the birds to a serving dish or individual plates, discard the trussing strings, and keep them warm. Reheat the quince in the syrup. For the sauce, pour any fat from the roasting pan, then heat it to cook the pan juices until they darken and caramelize. Stir in the flour and cook for 1 minute. Add the stock and bring the sauce to a boil, stirring constantly. Strain it into a small saucepan and bring just back to a boil. Add the ratafia, a tablespoonful of syrup from the quince, salt, and pepper. Taste the sauce and adjust the seasoning.

Lift out the warm quince pieces with a draining spoon and set them around the pigeons. Spoon over a little sauce and pass the rest of the sauce separately. Use the leftover pink quince syrup for poaching other fruit—it is deliciously concentrated.

The Château du Feÿ was built in the 1640s by Nicholas de Baugy, counselor and officer of the household to King Louis XIII. Handsome paneling was added to the main rooms early in the eighteenth century, but little was done after 1756, when the then owner Baron Philibert de Chamousset died, leaving a young widow. After the Revolution, a local merchant bought Le Feÿ from Madame de Chamousset under an arrangement called a *viager.* This gave her the right to occupy the property until her death in return for a lump sum plus an annuity. You'd think that Madame de Chamousset, at eighty-six, would have been a good bet for the purchaser, but she survived to ninety-nine, outliving the merchant, whose son-in-law, Admiral Meynard de La Farge, eventually inherited Le Feÿ in 1819. A *viager* is nothing less than a wager (indeed, the words are identical): one party bets on a short life, the other on a long one. A very French gamble, which is still widespread today.

That first summer we lived like gypsies. Only half of the upper rooms were habitable and the rest had peeling walls and the occasional disquieting hole in the floorboards. In one courtyard, we pushed open the door of the farmhouse—no plumbing at all there. The last tenants had quit in a temper and taken the bathroom with them! This was our current neighbor Monsieur Pinta, by common consent *une tête dure* (bullheaded) but a good farmer. At harvest time we hear his machines working far into the night, snatching fine dry weather until the dew starts to fall. When we first arrived, we too had a lesson from Monsieur Pinta in the rural way of doing business. We thought to do him a good turn by offering him the use of a barn at very modest rent. A year and five legal letters later he was still pushing for an even smaller sum, to be linked to the price of a bushel of wheat. We declined.

The gardener's cottage was hidden in another corner, perfect rental property if only it were renovated. The roof was sound, no worries there, but when it rained the ramshackle gutters gushed in a ragged jet like the bathroom shower. *"Ah, ça pisse partout!"* was Milbert's lapidary comment. Then, providentially, an impecunious artist called Jean-Claude stepped in and volunteered to repair it himself. That left the gamekeeper's house, a tall pavilion forming part of the architectural ensemble of the main courtyard. We renamed it the *garçonnière* (the bachelor's pad) and set it aside for Simon in a few years' time.

Friends began to drop by to judge the extent of our folly in buying a French *monument historique,* then stayed for a week, beguiled as we were by the ambiance. Good, simple food quickly became a priority and the children tried their hand. Hot Goat Cheese Salad rapidly became one of Emma's specialties. She would take great care in the market to choose small round goat cheeses that were fresh, aged perhaps a week, just right for melting on toast in the oven.

Hot Goat Cheese Salad

So many small farms make goat cheeses around us that most are anonymous, though the archetypal *crottin de chavignol* is internationally known. If the name were translated—goat's droppings—it might be less popular! Four little cheeses, cut in two, make enough for eight appetizers.

> *a medium head of salad, such as Boston lettuce or*
>   *frisée (about 1 lb/500 g)*
> *a bunch of watercress or arugula*
> *8 slices of white bread*
> *4 round fresh goat cheeses, or 1 log (about 6 oz/175g*
>   *total)*
>
> **FOR THE VINAIGRETTE DRESSING**
> *3 tablespoons red wine vinegar*
> *2 teaspoons Dijon-style mustard*
> *salt and pepper*
> *½ cup/125 ml olive oil*

Heat the oven to 400°F/200°C. Wash and dry the lettuce, tearing the leaves into pieces. Discard the stems from the watercress or arugula, wash and dry the leaves, and mix them in a salad bowl with the lettuce. Chill the greens to crisp the leaves.

Lightly toast the bread, and using a pastry cutter or glass, cut out 8 rounds the same size as the cheeses. If you cut the rounds of bread larger than the cheese, their edges will scorch. Put the rounds on a baking sheet. Cut each cheese in half crosswise to make 2 disks and set them on the rounds of toast. (If using a log of goat cheese, cut it into 8 individual rounds.) Bake until the cheese is bubbling and starting to brown, 8 to 12 minutes.

Meanwhile, make the dressing. In a small bowl, whisk the vinegar and mustard with salt and pepper until mixed. Gradually whisk in the oil, adding it slowly at first so that the dressing emulsifies and thickens slightly, then more quickly in a steady stream. Taste and adjust the seasoning; it should be rather piquant. Add the dressing to the salad and toss well. Taste a leaf of greens and adjust the seasoning again. Pile the salad greens on 8 individual plates, set a warm cheese toast on top, and serve at once.

OPPOSITE: *The* garçonnière *catches the afternoon sun.* ABOVE: *Goat cheeses come in many shapes and sizes, some fresh and others aged to crumbling piquancy.*

Meanwhile the children frolicked in the pool and slept until noon despite

Simon's loud complaints of a cockerel crowing in the dry moat at 4 A.M. We basked in the sun reflected with Mediterranean intensity from the front of the house. "*Temps bourguignon* (Burgundian weather)," said Albert, a decorator who from time to time helped me choose the curtains. Albert was small and neat, beautifully dressed, with a lock of hair that fell becomingly over his forehead. He had a keen sense of period, indispensable in an old house, and an eye for color. It was Albert who bought us the vine-strewn plates that we still use for salad, an early pattern from the Gien potteries over on the Loire. But Albert was unreliable, disappearing without warning for months at a time until Mark finally lost his temper and said something very rude.

Good meals proliferated now that our stove was working and everyone lent a hand. Just sometimes on a very hot day, Mark is persuaded to fire up the grill so we don't have to cook indoors. Chicken is usually the focus of the meal, with as many vegetables as we can muster. (As another idea for grilled chicken, try the coriander chicken on page 199.)

Salad of Honey Roast Chicken Wings and Bacon

The first time I read this recipe, I shuddered but I have to admit that the sweet-salt combination of honey and bacon with chicken is a winner. Use the same glaze for other chicken pieces, too, to make a fine first course or lunch for four.

> *½ lb/250 g mixed salad greens*
> *1 tablespoon vegetable oil*
> *3 to 4 slices of bacon, diced*
> *8 to 10 chicken wings (about 1 lb/500 g)*
> *¼ cup/60 ml red wine vinegar*
> *1 heaping tablespoon honey*
>
> **FOR THE VINAIGRETTE DRESSING**
> *2 tablespoons sherry vinegar*
> *½ teaspoon Dijon-style mustard*
> *salt and pepper*
> *1 tablespoon port (optional)*
> *½ cup/125 ml olive oil*

Heat the oven to 425°F/220°C. Wash and dry the salad greens and pile them in a bowl. For the dressing, whisk the vinegar, mustard, salt, and pepper in a small bowl until mixed. If you like a touch of sweetness to balance the salty bacon, add the port. Gradually whisk in the olive oil, starting drop by drop so the dressing emulsifies and thickens slightly, then adding it more steadily in a slow stream. Taste, adjust the seasoning, and set the dressing aside while you cook the chicken wings.

If it has not already been done, chop off the tips of the chicken wings (they make a fine addition to a stock-pot), leaving you with the 2 meatier portions of the wing still joined together. Heat the oil in a large skillet or frying pan with a heatproof handle and fry the bacon until crisp, stirring occasionally. Transfer the bacon with a slotted spoon to drain on paper towels. Add the chicken wings to the pan and brown them on all sides over medium heat, taking 5 to 7 minutes. Remove the wings and set them aside. Discard all the fat from the pan, return it to the heat, and add the vinegar. Stir in the honey until dissolved. Return the wings to the pan and toss them to coat well with the honey mixture.

Transfer the pan of wings to the oven and roast until they are very tender and caramelized by the honey to a rich brown, 25 to 30 minutes. You'll need to stir them often and watch closely toward the end of cooking as they scorch easily.

To serve, add the dressing to the salad greens, toss them, and taste to see if more seasoning is needed. Pile the greens on 4 plates and arrange the hot chicken wings around the edge of each. Sprinkle the crisp bacon on top and serve at once.

Grilled Summer Vegetable Salad

For variety I've included half a dozen vegetables here, but you can use a few or even just a single vegetable if you are so inclined. I'm particularly fond of eggplant and onions grilled this way. Serve the warm vegetables in the spiced sauce as a lively salad for six to eight people.

1 eggplant (about 1 lb/500 g)
2 zucchini (about ¾ lb/375 g)
1 green pepper
1 red pepper
1 yellow pepper
4 small onions
2 fennel bulbs
⅓ cup/75 ml vegetable oil, more if needed for basting
salt and pepper

FOR THE SPICED SAUCE

2 tablespoons sliced or slivered almonds
1 tablespoon cumin seeds
2 garlic cloves, peeled
1 jalapeño chile pepper, cored, seeded, and sliced
1 tablespoon red wine vinegar
½ cup/125 ml olive oil

Trim the eggplant and cut it across into ½-inch/1.25-cm rounds. Lay the slices in a single layer on a tray, sprinkle them with salt, and leave for 30 minutes to draw out the juices. Rinse the eggplant slices, drain them in a colander, and pat them dry with paper towels.

Meanwhile, fire up the grill and oil the grill rack. Trim the zucchini and cut them into ½-inch/1.25-cm diagonal slices. Core and quarter the peppers, discarding the seeds. Peel and quarter the onions through the root. Trim the fennel bulbs, cut them in half lengthwise, and then slice them through the root and stem into ⅜-inch/1-cm slices. Put all the vegetables in a large bowl, add the vegetable oil, salt, and pepper, and toss so they are thoroughly coated.

Make the spiced sauce. Heat a nonstick frying pan, add the almonds, and toast them over medium heat until brown, stirring often, 5 to 7 minutes. Remove them, add the cumin seeds, and toast them until fragrant, 2 to 3 minutes. Put the almonds, cumin seeds, garlic, jalapeño pepper, vinegar, and half the olive oil in a food processor and work to a fine purée, about 2 minutes. With the blade turning, add the remaining olive oil in a steady stream. Add salt and pepper, taste, and adjust the seasoning.

Set the grill rack about 3 inches/7.5 cm from the heat. When the grill is hot, transfer all the vegetables to the grill rack without overlapping them; you may need to work in batches depending on the size of your grill. Reserve any leftover oil for basting. Grill the vegetables until they are tender and well browned (I like them a bit charred), basting them often and turning them once. The cooking time will vary from 5 to 12 minutes on each side depending on the maturity of the vegetables and the heat of your grill. Transfer the vegetables to a bowl when they are done and keep them warm while any tougher vegetables continue to cook.

To finish, add the sauce to the warm vegetables and toss them well. Taste and adjust the seasoning before serving.

We often have summer lunch on the terrace by the kitchen door.

The weather broke one night in a storm of tropical intensity (the wine harvest farther south in the Côte d'Or was severely damaged) and a single thunderclap exploded frighteningly close. The lights failed and it emerged that the transformer, housed in a barn, had been struck. No transformer, no electricity; no electricity, no water. *La vie de château* is not all that you might think. Everything is our responsibility. The transformer converting current from the main power network belongs to us and has burned out twice since that first occasion. The kilometer of avenue, so scenic with its great lime trees framing the entrance like a secret, fairy castle, must be maintained as a public right of way. As for the water—ever since the house was built, this has been a problem.

The château stands on the edge of a dry chalky plateau and was originally constructed, we think, on the foundations of a fort that relied for water on an immense medieval well. The well is still there in the farmyard, dug down for a dizzying 90 meters/300 feet, as deep as a twenty-five-story skyscraper. The flints of the medieval masonry still hold and the water is pure, though the flow cannot keep up with a twentieth-century lifestyle. A couple of local spelunkers visited one day and we watched entranced as they rappelled their way down in what seemed to us could have been free fall, climbing

ABOVE: *Nestling among the farm buildings at Le Feÿ is an ancient key to prosperity: a vast stone-lined well 300 feet deep, which still runs with clear, drinkable water. Two marble lions flank our long driveway, to Château du Feÿ, one standing guard while the other takes a quick nap.* OVERLEAF: *The main rooms of the château are blessed with 17-foot/4-meter ceilings and tall windows, so the sun streams in from both east and west. In the days before central heating, the alcove at right sheltered a large tiled stove.*

back with a carafe of chilly well water to toast their descent. When I wondered out loud how many laborers might have died in its making, Monsieur Milbert laughed gruffly. "And how many Germans did not fall down there at the end of the war!"

The eighteenth-century owners tackled the water problem by channeling the rain runoff from the immense roofs (we once calculated their area as over an acre) into three great stone cisterns under the main buildings. They kept the château supplied until after the Second World War, though there were thirsty times. A friend who lived here as a boy said that in summer he turned his undershirt inside out for lack of water for laundry. German troops occupied the house for three months in 1940, but fortunately moved on when the taps ran dry.

We inherited a water system cobbled together in the reconstruction days of 1947—two kilometers of private line and an antiquated pumping house in the valley that would fail at the smallest glitch. The pipeline route was uncharted and to find a leak meant casting outward from each end to find a wet spot. The village supply wasn't up to much either, so after a year or two we all got together and built a modern installation that delivered unlimited water for all: "low nitrate and not a drop of chlorine," boasts Claude, the village water man and weekend hunter. Even now, we sometimes have to call him hastily when the red alarm light blinks on, signaling a water shutdown.

At Le Feÿ the new installation came just in time to supply the bathrooms that our increasing flow of visitors required. We now have a dozen, three times the original number. Lighting, too, has been renewed and gradually the whole château has been redecorated—floors stripped and stained, *boiserie* painted, bedroom walls papered and curtains hung (my particular province—I must have made thirty pairs). Much was done in a single six weeks by an extraordinary couple, Lorraine and Dale Perkinson, known irreverently in the family as The Perks.

No sooner, it seemed, had we moved into Le Feÿ, than two years later we returned to the United States. Tenants, we decided, would be the answer to leaving the house empty. An unnerving collection of shady characters presented themselves. There was the smooth-spoken couple with Libyan connections. There was the fine art dealer who dreamed of bringing clients to France to view his antique statues of dubious provenance, a currency broker whose only reference was a numbered Swiss bank account. We despaired until Dale and Lorraine arrived, fresh from developing American shopping malls in the 1970s, decade of the consumer. "Well, Mark, this château sure makes a statement," observed Dale, gazing at the moon rising over the pigeon house, its roof adorned with a leaded lantern topped with a sculpted bird. "Would you mind if we made some renovations?"

Albert the decorator took charge; the plumber competed for space with the electrician and painters swarmed over the three main reception rooms, which emerged shimmering in a color kindly described by a friend as vanilla (it has mercifully mellowed since). Upstairs, disused doors were reopened to reveal the original configuration of suites, each with bedroom, bathroom, and salon, a lesson to us in French interior planning. Great houses like these were designed for extended families, grandparents, maiden aunts, and broods of children. Each group would have its own *appartement,* meeting in the central reception rooms for entertainment and meals. Over the years, needs would change and with them the disposition of the surrounding rooms. We have done the same, opening and closing off doors to find space for bathrooms, a study, and a laundry.

Pumpkin Soup with Wild Chestnuts

All four of the main ingredients for this eighteenth-century soup grow at Château du Feÿ: pumpkin, onions, and potatoes in the garden, and wild chestnuts in the avenue outside the gate. Wild chestnuts are lighter, more floury, than the familiar cultivated *marrons* and either can be used here. I prefer the sugar variety of pumpkin, with deep orange flesh and plenty of flavor. For a spectacular presentation, I use a second pumpkin as a soup tureen, hollowing it out and then warming it in a low oven before adding the finished soup. As this is a holiday recipe, quantities here are generous, enough for a large family gathering of ten to twelve.

> *6 to 8 lb/about 3 kg whole pumpkin or pumpkin pieces*
> *3 tablespoons/45 g butter*
> *a 4-oz/125-g piece of bacon, diced*
> *2 onions (about 1 lb/500 g), sliced*
> *2 potatoes (about 1 lb/500 g), diced*
> *2 garlic cloves, chopped*
> *½ teaspoon grated nutmeg, more to taste*
> *pinch of cayenne*
> *salt and pepper*
> *1½ quarts/1½ liters chicken stock, more if needed*
> *1 lb/500 g wild or cultivated fresh chestnuts*
> *1 quart/1 liter milk, more if needed*
> *crème fraîche or heavy cream for garnish (optional)*

For a whole pumpkin, cut a slice from the top and base using a sturdy knife. Set the pumpkin firmly on a board and cut away the peel, working from top to base in a curving motion. Cut the peeled flesh into 1-in/2.5-cm chunks, discarding the seeds. If using pumpkin pieces, cut away the peel, discard any seeds, and cut the flesh into chunks.

Melt the butter in a large soup pot, add the bacon, and fry it until crisp, 5 to 7 minutes. Lift it out with a slotted spoon and drain it on paper towels; reserve it for the garnish. Add the onions to the fat and fry until starting to brown, 5 to 7 minutes. Stir in the potatoes and garlic, and cook just until fragrant. Add the pumpkin pieces, nutmeg, cayenne, salt, pepper, and enough stock to just cover the pumpkin. Cover with a lid, bring to a boil, and simmer until the potato and pumpkin are very tender, 30 to 40 minutes.

Meanwhile, light the broiler to cook the chestnuts. Poke each chestnut with a knife so they do not burst, then broil them, turning often, until they are tender, 8 to 12 minutes. Let them cool enough to handle, then peel them—don't worry if some of the chestnuts crumble.

When the pumpkin is tender, let the soup cool to tepid, and then purée it in the pan with a hand-held immersion blender, or use a food processor. Stir in the milk and bring the soup just to a boil, adding more milk if necessary so the consistency is rich and thick but not sticky. Stir in the diced bacon and most of the peeled chestnuts (set aside a few chestnut pieces for garnish). Reheat the soup for 1 or 2 minutes, taste, and adjust the seasoning.

Serve the soup in a whole pumpkin, cleaned of seeds, and warmed in the oven for 10 to 15 minutes. Alternatively, use individual warm soup bowls, swirling a spoonful of cream into each bowl and topping it with the reserved chestnuts.

OPPOSITE: *Pumpkins abound in our garden and form a natural container for Pumpkin Soup with Wild Chestnuts, served here on the table in the main dining room.*

Outside the château, geography has changed less than in the main house. The walled *potager* (vegetable garden) has survived intact, partly because no one would want it nowadays; it requires far too much manual work for modern tastes. In the old days it was key, expected to nourish not just the château residents but a large labor force as well. In the contemporary *potager du roi* at Versailles twenty gardeners were employed per hectare and the number at Le Feÿ in its eighteenth-century heyday was probably a dozen. Our garden measures exactly one hectare, set out in four squares with a central watering pond, a classic plan that dates back well before the Christian cross. The squares were probably subdivided with hedges, some flowering and some of box, then planted with vegetables and herbs, both culinary and medicinal. Fruit trees were espaliered against the sunny south- and west-facing walls, a practice still followed by Monsieur Milbert, who has some vines and a remarkable bay tree at least 10 feet high and as much around. Twice I've seen it frosted to the ground, then regenerate from the roots.

With its high walls and sheltering trees, the *potager* is several degrees warmer than outside. The topsoil, Milbert tells me, is 15 in/40 cm deep, double that just outside, thanks to centuries of care and manure that not only enriches the soil but also warms it by fermentation. At Versailles, Louis XIV was able to eat figs in March, at least two months early, thanks to manure that was banked around the tree roots every other day. Monsieur Milbert, beaming with delight, has this minute delivered a bucket of tiny, purple-black potatoes and a handful of yellow pear-shaped tomatoes, both brought from the United States and novelties to him. Yesterday it was a basket of purslane, an ancient salad green with a slightly crunchy leaf: "volunteers from last year," he says. By far and away our favorite dessert at Le Feÿ is *tarte Tatin,* often made with pockmarked windfall apples from the garden. We look for varieties with little juice, which hold their shape during long cooking; Golden Delicious is a good candidate.

Apple Tarte Tatin

Starting with the basic *tarte Tatin* for caramelized apples baked with a pastry topping and turned upside down, over the years we have evolved such refinements as caramelizing the butter and sugar before adding the apples to ensure a deep color, and turning the apples so the halves are evenly browned. In early fall when apples are fresh and full of juice, I've resolved problems by peeling and then drying them in the oven to keep them firm. They will look shriveled and brown, but don't worry, this disappears during cooking. It is hard to beat the classic accompaniment to *tarte Tatin* of crème fraîche, but a scoop of vanilla ice cream is acceptable. One tart serves eight.

about 5 lb/2 to 2.5 kg firm apples
½ cup/125 g butter
1½ cups/300 g sugar

FOR THE PÂTE BRISÉE
1⅔ cups/200 g flour
7 tablespoons/100 g butter
1 egg yolk
½ teaspoon salt
3 tablespoons/45 ml water, more if needed

a 10- to 11-inch/26- to 28-cm Tatin mold, skillet, or deep heavy frying pan

Heat the oven to 350°F/175°C. Peel and halve the apples and scoop out the cores. Set the apples cut-side up on a baking sheet and bake for 12 to 15 minutes, until their surfaces are dry but they are still firm (if your apples are on the dry side, skip this step). Let them cool and turn up the oven temperature to 400°F/200°C. Meanwhile, make the pâte brisée using the ingredients listed and following the technique explained in the glossary (page 298). Then wrap and chill the dough until firm.

Melt the butter in the Tatin mold, skillet, or frying pan. Sprinkle in the sugar and cook over medium heat without stirring until it starts to brown and caramelize. Stir gently, then continue cooking until it is golden brown. Let it cool in the pan for 3 to 5 minutes—the butter will separate, but this does not matter.

Arrange the apples in the mold in concentric circles with the cut sides standing vertical—the caramel will help to anchor them. Pack them as tightly as possible as they will shrink during cooking. Cook the apples over medium heat until the juice starts to run, about 8 minutes, then raise the heat and cook them as fast as possible until the underside is caramelized to deep golden and most of the juice has evaporated, 15 to 20 minutes. With a two-pronged fork, turn the apples one by one so the upper sides are now down in the caramel, and continue cooking until this second side is brown also and almost all the juice has evaporated, 10 to 15 minutes. The time will vary very much with the apples. Let them cool to tepid.

Roll the pastry dough to a round just larger than the mold. Wrap the dough around the rolling pin and transfer it to cover the apples. Tuck the edges down around the apples, working quickly so their warmth does not melt the dough. Poke a hole in the center to allow steam to escape.

Bake the tart until the pastry is firm and lightly browned, 20 to 25 minutes. Take the tart from the oven and let it cool for at least 10 minutes, or until tepid. If you make *tarte Tatin* ahead, keep it in the mold, then warm it to tepid on the stove or in the oven before unmolding: this softens the caramel and loosens the apples.

Shortly before serving, unmold the tart onto a flat platter with a lip to catch any juice. To do this, set the platter on top of the tart pan and, in one swift motion, flip the tart onto the platter. Be careful because you can be splashed with hot juice.

Quinces make a spectacular deep pink tarte Tatin as you can see below.

The ingredient amounts remain the same as for the *tarte Tatin* (opposite), but quinces take much longer to cook than apples and so must be treated differently by cutting them into quarters and simmering them with water.

Quince Tarte Tatin

Begin by peeling, coring, and quartering the quinces (8 large ones weigh about 5 lb/2.25 kg). Melt the butter and add sugar to the pan, but do not cook it to a caramel. Arrange the fruit in concentric circles in the pan, packing it tightly. Cover the mold with foil or a lid and heat gently until the juice starts to run from the fruit. Add about ½ cup/125 ml water and continue simmering until the water is absorbed, 10 to 15 minutes. Continue adding water as needed (I find I need about ½ cup every 10 to 15 minutes). Keep the fruit covered and simmer it until tender and colored a deep pink. Turn the pieces halfway through cooking so they soften evenly and allow 1¼ to 1¾ hours for the fruit to fully soften —unlike apples, quinces almost never fall apart. At no stage should the liquid evaporate so much that the sugar starts to brown. When the fruit is fully cooked, take off the cover and then let the sugar caramelize by evaporating the liquid. Finish the quince tarte as for apple *tarte Tatin*; both versions serve 8.

Two versions of my favorite dessert, tarte Tatin, *made with apples (left) and quince (right).* ABOVE: *Pink-cheeked apples ripen in our orchard.*

In the old days, any agricultural property was expected to be self-supporting

and our outbuildings—called significantly the *communs* or common area—are extensive, arranged around two courtyards, one for the farm with its animals, the other for the poultry. The property is dotted with walnut trees, which yield small but succulent nuts encased in a green husk. The juices were used in ancient times as a dye, and even if you've the patience to let the husks wither to reveal the shells, your hands are still liable to be stained a deep brown.

Walnut Gâteau

I found this recipe in an old cookbook and at once adopted it. It uses bread crumbs instead of flour to make a moist cake, made crunchy by a crisp topping of caramel. It serves six to eight.

> 2 slices of white bread (1½ oz/45 g)
> 1¼ cups/150 g walnut pieces
> ⅔ cup/150 g butter
> 10 tablespoons/125 g sugar
> 4 eggs, separated
> grated zest of 1 lemon
>
> FOR THE CARAMEL TOPPING
> ⅓ cup/60 g sugar
> ⅓ cup/75 ml water
> 6 to 8 walnut halves
>
> a 9-inch/23-cm springform pan

Heat the oven to 325°F/160°C. Toast the bread in the oven until very dry and lightly colored, 8 to 12 minutes. Let the bread cool, then grind it to fine crumbs in a food processor or blender. Set these aside. Finely grind the walnut pieces in the food processor or blender, taking care not to overwork them or they will be heavy. Butter the cake pan, line it with a round of wax or parchment paper, and butter the paper.

Cream the butter, add two thirds of the sugar, and beat until soft and light, 2 to 3 minutes. Add the egg

yolks, one at a time, beating well after each addition. Stir in the lemon zest followed by the bread crumbs and the ground walnuts. In a separate bowl, beat the egg whites until stiff, add the remaining sugar, and continue beating until the egg whites are glossy and hold a long peak when the whisk is lifted, 1 to 2 minutes more. Fold about a quarter of the egg whites into the walnut mixture, then fold this mixture into the remaining whites, working as lightly as possible so as not to deflate the whites.

Transfer the batter to the cake pan and bake it until the cake is firm to the touch, shrinks from the sides of the pan, and a skewer inserted in the center comes out clean, 55 to 65 minutes. (If it browns too quickly at any time during baking, cover it loosely with foil and continue baking.) Let the cake cool for 4 to 5 minutes, then remove the sides and leave it on a rack to cool completely. Shortly before serving, lift the cake off the cake pan base, discarding the paper, and set it back on the rack. Set the rack on a larger baking sheet or newspaper to catch any drippings from the caramel.

Make the caramel topping. Heat the sugar and water over low heat until the sugar has dissolved, stirring occasionally. Raise the heat and boil the syrup, without stirring, to a golden brown caramel. Remove the pan from the heat, let the bubbles subside, and at once trail the caramel over the cake with a metal spoon, making a thin lattice pattern. Work fast, as the caramel will set as soon as it cools. While the caramel is still warm, arrange the walnut halves around the cake so they stick to the topping. Cut the cake in wedges for serving, cracking the caramel with the knife.

For years after we opened La Varenne Cooking School at Le Feÿ I had found our supply of herbs inadequate. Then Amanda Hesser came into our lives. Amanda was one of our trainees, a disciplined, talented young woman who came to learn cooking and stayed on to write a book, *The Cook and the Gardener,* about Monsieur Milbert and his *potager.* "You need an herb garden," said Amanda, and she was right. Now, thanks to her industry we have a graceful loop of brick paths in the shape of an 8, centered by a sundial and watched over by an elder tree, traditional symbol of good fortune.

Just where to plant the garden was a dilemma. In an ideal world, herbs grow near the kitchen but in full sun, unshaded by the house. They need watering and ready water would be a concern in our dry Burgundian summer. Finally we hit on a prime location at the end of the terrace, overlooking the valley. It has proved ideal and now, only three years later, more than fifty herbs have taken hold. We have half a dozen varieties of thyme, several sages, and a plethora of mints that engulf their neighbors and ramp over the paths. One corner is dominated by bushy angelica (when candied its fibrous stems turn vivid green). Pots hold aloe plants to soothe burns. We've even managed to grow token bulbs of saffron—one flower yields only two to three threads of this, the world's most expensive spice. The herb garden already forms an integral part of the landscape, an extension of the house. This is the clue, I think, to caring for an old property. Repairs and improvements should be neither new nor old, they should not be slavish reproductions but must give the impression they have been there from the start.

How we cooked without the herb garden, I do not know. It has led to all sorts of herbal salads, made vivid with the edible orange, purple, and blue flowers of nasturtium, chive, and borage. Favorite herbs include chervil (an early bloomer), dill, tarragon, arugula (which the French call roquette), wild spinach (known as Good King Henry in England), and lovage, which is akin to leaf celery but with a flavor all its own.

Salad with Herbs and Flowers

We usually mix a few generous handfuls of stronger-tasting greens, herbs, and edible flowers with up to three quarters their volume of lettuce, preferably with small crispy leaves for contrast of texture. Vinaigrette dressing is made with our own red wine vinegar (page 47) or sometimes with lemon and orange juice and olive oil in the classic proportions of one of acid to three of oil. ("Be a miser on the vinegar, a prodigal on the oil, and whisk like the devil himself" goes an old adage.) You won't need much dressing—½ cup is enough to dress green salad for 4 to 6 people. Be sure to taste the salad after it has been dressed—you'll be surprised how often more salt and pepper is needed—and serve it at once before it starts to wilt.

OPPOSITE: *Herbal heaven on the terrace.* ABOVE: *A salad made with herbs and flowers from the garden awaits a gentle shower of vinaigrette.*

Strategically placed near the kitchen door, the herb garden is popular with chefs and students on cigarette break (no smoking in the kitchen). I cannot remember who found the lemongrass and added it to *beurre blanc,* but it was a neat idea. Now that we have an abundance of herbs, we use them so much that I cannot resist just one more short recipe idea—Rosemary Lemon Sorbet.

Lemongrass Butter Sauce
Beurre Blanc à la Citronelle

For 4 to 6 people, peel and thinly slice the tender stems of 3 lemongrass stalks. Melt a tablespoon of butter in a heavy-based pan, add the lemongrass, and sauté it for 1 to 2 minutes. Add ½ cup/125 ml dry white wine and boil until it is reduced to about a tablespoon. Whisk 1 cup/250 ml cold butter into the sauce, adding it gradually in small pieces. Work on and off the heat so the butter softens and thickens the sauce without melting to oil. Strain the sauce, pressing to extract flavor from the lemongrass. Season to taste with salt and white pepper, and serve the sauce just warm. It is best with fish.

OPPOSITE: *Lemon sorbet is flavored with rosemary and served in champagne flutes.* ABOVE: *A basket of lovage and other herbs awaits delivery to the kitchen.*

Rosemary Lemon Sorbet

So many herb sorbets—verbena, lavender, rose geranium—taste to me of soap, but this combination of rosemary sharpened with lemon is wonderfully refreshing on a hot day. Try it, too, over ice as lemonade.

Heat 1 quart/1 liter water with 1 cup/200 g sugar until the sugar dissolves, then simmer it steadily for 2 to 3 minutes. Divide the syrup into 2 equal portions. Pound 6 to 8 rosemary sprigs with a rolling pin to release their aroma and add them to half the syrup. Cover and let the syrup infuse over low heat for 10 to 15 minutes. Add the pared zest of 2 lemons to the other portion of syrup, cover, and leave it to infuse also. Let both syrups cool, then combine them and strain the mixture into a bowl. Stir in the juice from the lemons and taste the mixture, adding more sugar or lemon juice to your taste—remember that sorbet served during a meal should be less sweet than for dessert. Freeze the mixture in a churn freezer until firm and serve the sorbet in chilled stemmed glasses or bowls, topping each with a curl of lemon zest or a rosemary sprig. This makes enough for 6 to 8 people.

As you'll have realized, I am less at home in the garden of Le Feÿ than in the kitchen. My mother was the grower, I am the cook of the family. It has always been so; in temperament my mother and I were opposite sides of the same coin. Where I enjoy roaming the world, my mother was never quite comfortable away from her small corner of northern England where she and her ancestors had lived for centuries. Our house is always full of people—children, friends, cooking school students and staff—whereas my mother would cross the street to avoid an acquaintance (if she were outside the garden gate, which was rare). White-haired and vigorous, she was something of a grande dame, famous for her quips. On Tony Blair, British prime minister: "talks like a parson, can't trust 'em an inch." On Princess Diana: "Given another ten years of life, her angelic reputation would never have survived!"

My mother did not suffer fools gladly, myself included. When I proudly showed her a pretty plant with hanging red bells I optimistically believed to be hiding cape gooseberries, she snorted with amusement. "Chinese lanterns, nothing more," she said and of course she was right. I was forced to buy the real thing in the market. But I haven't given up yet....

Medallions of Pork with Cape Gooseberries

Cape gooseberries are related to the tomatillo, and the cape refers to their papery covering that can be peeled back to form a petal-like decoration for the golden berry inside. You can substitute cherries or figs if cape gooseberries are hard to find. Using two pork tenderloins tied together, delicious little nuggets of meat are created to serve four—ideal with this sweet-sour sauce.

> *1 quart/250 g cape gooseberries*
> *2 pork tenderloins (about 1½ pounds/750 g total)*
> *2 tablespoons flour*
> *½ teaspoon ground cinnamon*
> *salt and pepper*
> *1 tablespoon butter*
> *1 tablespoon oil*
> *½ cup/125 ml red port wine*
> *1 cup/250 ml veal or chicken stock*
> *1 tablespoon red currant jelly*
> *1 teaspoon arrowroot mixed to a paste with*
> * 1 tablespoon cold water*
> *squeeze of lemon juice*
> *salt and pepper*

Peel the husk from the cape gooseberries, reserving 4 for decoration, and set them aside. Trim any skin and fat from the tenderloins. Lay them head to tail, and using 8 strings, tie them in an even cylinder. Cut between each string to make 8 medallions, each about 1½ inches/4 cm thick. Mix the flour, cinnamon, salt, and pepper and roll medallions in the flour, patting to remove the excess.

Heat the butter and oil in a frying pan until foamy. Add the medallions and sauté them until brown on one side, 2 to 3 minutes. Turn them over, lower the heat, and continue cooking until they are brown on the outside and no longer pink in the center, 7 to 10 minutes more. A skewer inserted in the center should be warm to the touch when withdrawn after 30 seconds. Transfer them to a plate and keep them warm.

While the medallions are cooking, pour the port into a small pan and boil it until reduced by half. Add the stock and the husked cape gooseberries and simmer for 1 to 2 minutes so the fruit is very lightly cooked. Drain the gooseberries, reserving the reduced port and stock.

Reheat the frying pan used to cook the pork and add the port-stock liquid with the red currant jelly. Simmer for 1 to 2 minutes over medium heat, stirring to dissolve the pan juices. Replace the medallions to reheat for about a minute. Remove them and discard the strings. Arrange the medallions on 4 warmed plates and keep them warm while you quickly finish the sauce.

Strain the sauce into a small pan and bring it to a rolling boil. Whisk in the arrowroot paste to lightly thicken it; if necessary, boil to reduce and concentrate the sauce. Add the lemon juice, salt, and pepper to your taste. Add the cooked gooseberries, heat briefly, and spoon the sauce and gooseberries over the medallions. Decorate the plates with the reserved berries.

Even if I had my mother's gardening talent, it would have been impossible to approach Monsieur Milbert's lifetime of Burgundian knowledge, both practical and intuitive. He's better at forecasting the weather than those puppets on TV with their charts and every computer known to man. He is a great believer in the phases of the moon, planting when the moon waxes to encourage growth and gathering when it wanes and the plants have maximum vitality. "*Pas avant Rameau* (Not before Palm Sunday)," he rules when I beg him to sow the sugar peas and arugula we have brought from the United States. "*A la Sainte Catherine, toute arbre prend racine* (On Saint Catherine's day—November 25—all trees take root)" is another of his dictums. He has even told me to cut my hair after the full moon so it will grow less quickly.

A born gardener, Monsieur Milbert nurtures anything that shows signs of sprouting. He is constitutionally incapable of pruning excess growth from the peach and pear trees with the result that their straggling branches break regularly under the weight of fruit. He shakes his head over the plum tree that unfailingly blooms "white as a sheet" he says, "but never a plum. *Ah, les plantes, c'est quelque chose* (plants are something else)." Now we have kiwi, persimmon, and blueberries growing beside the traditional quince and he has agreed, reluctantly, to plant corn. But eat it, never. "It's animal food." Nor does Monsieur Milbert touch sorrel, though it sprouts all summer.

Watering cans of handy modern plastic flank the ancient stone trough. Monsieur Milbert insists that water should be sun-warmed so as not to shock plants in the heat of summer. At left, my "cape gooseberries," which turned out to be Chinese lanterns.

Sorrel Soup

I cannot imagine why sorrel is sold in the United States in costly little bunches like an herb, because in our garden it grows like a weed. Sorrel resembles spinach with a more pointed leaf, but its puckering lemon taste is very different. Both sorrel and spinach are wonderful in this classic soup finished with an egg yolk and cream liaison. The recipe makes enough for six to eight bowls.

> *½ lb/250 g sorrel*
> *2 tablespoons butter*
> *1 medium potato, thinly sliced*
> *salt and pepper*
> *1½ quarts/1½ liters chicken stock*
> *2 egg yolks*
> *1 cup/250 ml crème fraîche or heavy cream*

Tear the stems from the sorrel and wash the leaves thoroughly. Melt the butter in a soup pot, add the potato, sorrel, salt, and pepper, and press a piece of foil on top to hold in steam. Cover the pot and sweat the vegetables over low heat until very tender, 20 to 25 minutes. Do not let the potato brown. (Sorrel discolors, which is normal.)

Add the stock, cover the pan, and bring the soup to a boil. Lower the heat and simmer it for 10 to 15 minutes to blend the flavors. Let the soup cool somewhat, then purée it in a food processor or directly in the pan using a hand-held immersion blender. The slightly coarse texture given by the processor or blender can be pleasant, but if you prefer a smooth creamy soup you should work it through a sieve or food mill.

Shortly before serving, bring the soup back to a boil. Mix the egg yolks and half the cream in a small bowl, then stir in a ladleful of hot soup. Take the pot of soup from the heat and stir in this liaison of egg yolk, cream, and hot soup. Reheat the soup briefly so the liaison cooks and thickens slightly, but do not let it boil and do not keep it hot for many minutes or it will curdle. Taste it and adjust the seasoning.

To serve, spoon the soup into warm bowls, add a spoonful of the remaining cream and stir to marble it.

Light Tomato Tart is perfect as an appetizer or paired with green salad for a light supper.

Tomatoes are chancy at Le Feÿ.

Some years they ripen in July, some years not until late August so there is scarcely a crop at all. Madame Maria has given us some excellent little cherry tomato plants, and I'm hoping that the tiny currant tomatoes I came across in California will take hold. As for ordinary Roma plum tomatoes, we like to caramelize them like this:

Caramelized Tomatoes

Cut 1 lb/500 g plum tomatoes lengthwise in half and sprinkle them with salt and pepper. Sprinkle 2 tablespoons sugar in a frying pan with an ovenproof handle and just large enough to hold all the tomatoes in a single layer. Cook the sugar over medium heat, stirring occasionally, until it melts and toasts to a golden caramel, 3 to 5 minutes. Remove the pan from the heat and at once add 2 tablespoons red wine vinegar, standing back as it will sputter and fume. Return it to the heat, stir to dissolve the caramel and then stir in ¼ cup/ 60 ml olive oil. Add the tomatoes, cut-sides down, with 2 or 3 rosemary sprigs and 2 or 3 bay leaves. Roast, uncovered, in a low oven at 275°F/140°C until the tomatoes are wrinkled, shrunken, and all liquid has evaporated, 3 to 4 hours—the longer they cook, the better they are. If you like, 45 minutes before the tomatoes are done, add the unpeeled cloves of a whole head of garlic to roast with the tomatoes. Both the tomatoes and garlic are delicious with roast lamb and beef.

Light Tomato Tart

Light apple tart, with wafer-thin slices of apple topping almost equally thin puff pastry, was one of the few triumphs of nouvelle cuisine to have become a classic. I love tomatoes treated the same way and scattered with a suspicion of garlic, basil, and olive oil—they are, after all, a fruit. This recipe makes six crisp, savory tarts.

> *1 recipe puff pastry (page 298)*
> *a small bunch of basil*
> *8 firm medium tomatoes (about 1½ lb/750 g)*
> *2 garlic cloves, finely chopped*
> *2 shallots, finely chopped*
> *2 to 3 tablespoons olive oil*
> *salt and pepper*

Make the puff pastry and chill it at least 30 minutes. Sprinkle 2 baking sheets sparingly with water. Roll the puff pastry dough to an 8 x 12-inch/20 x 30-cm rectangle and cut it into 6 squares. Roll each piece into very thin 7-inch/18-cm circles and transfer them to the baking sheets. Trim the rounds neatly with a knife, using a pan lid as a guide, and then chill them in the freezer until firm, 5 to 10 minutes.

Meanwhile, heat the oven to 400°F/200°C. Pull the basil leaves from the stems, and if you like, reserve 6 sprigs for decoration. Shred the leaves. With a serrated knife, cut the tomatoes into very thin crosswise slices across the "equator," discarding the ends—the slices should be so thin they almost dry when baked. Sprinkle the chilled pastry rounds with the chopped garlic, shallots, and basil. Arrange the tomato slices on top, overlapping them slightly but not too much, and taking care to cover the dough right to the edge so it does not scorch. Drizzle the top with olive oil, and season with salt and pepper.

Bake the tarts until puffed and the dough is crisp, 14 to 18 minutes. Serve them warm, topping each with a basil sprig if you wish.

The Milberts welcome the little yellow postal van that brings the mail to the gate and they filter all arrivals, acquiring a coterie of regulars like electrician Christian Moulinet, who stops for a quick Calva (Calvados apple brandy) on his way home. Bearded, intense, Monsieur Moulinet appears more folk singer or philosopher than electrician. He works late, weekends too, and to save time brews up lunch in his truck at noon rather than taking the customary two-hour break at home like everyone else. To him the tangle of cabling wound around 3-foot-thick walls is simple as a spider's web. In his way he's an artist, concealing the modern deftly within the old. Radio signals, hidden antennae—Monsieur Moulinet loves a complication, so much so that he can be too clever. Our ghost, George, was born thanks to his installing remote control on a bedroom light that took to switching on mysteriously in the middle of the night. Guests would leap to attention, convinced the end of the world, or at least the fire brigade, had come. Now any inexplicable happening (and there are many) is attributed to George.

We also have a more serious ghost, that of Ninon de Lenclos, seventeenth-century courtesan and intellectual (she must have had an eye for talent as in her will she left money to the eleven-year-old Voltaire to buy books). She is said to have slept in the downstairs bedroom and to have designed it with two separate entrances so that her departing lover did not run into the next one waiting outside. My father, who until then had little time for the paranormal, always swore he saw the latch lift and felt a cold presence when he overnighted in the same room. The other, more holy name associated with Le Feÿ is the missionary Vincent de Paul, who sent notes up the hill from Villecien entreating the "Mademoiselle du Feÿ" to join his charitable order. A saint and a courtesan; some châteaux have one, few have both as their yin and yang.

Monsieur Moulinet is a loner, but Monsieur Vergnaud the carpenter is always attended by a team of mates. He works in the best artisan tradition, building solidly to last like the château itself, peering over his half-moon spectacles to get the plans, and the estimated cost, just right. From bare walls, he and his right-hand man, another Claude, have installed our library, a whole wall 16 feet high of shelves in two overlapping tiers to pack in the maximum number of books. Of all our renovation projects, we are proudest of this. The stone fireplace once belonged in a farmhouse; the wallpaper was hand-blocked in England; the floor tiles we found in a loft. The final result looks as though it had been there from the start, or so we are assured.

ABOVE: *A manuscript cookbook dating to the 1600s, part of our collection.* OPPOSITE: *Zigzag, the Dalmatian, regards any chair by the fire as his. Here he waits hopefully in the library.*

We desperately needed the library to house our 4,000-plus collection of cookbooks, so many that Mark had started measuring them by the yard/meter of bookshelf. When I first started to cook, I'm ashamed to say that I possessed only a dozen cookbooks, partly a reflection of my nomadic lifestyle, but also of my hands-on approach to cooking. Mark the intellectual was appalled. I was working for *Gourmet* magazine at the time, so we cased their library, wrote down the 200 most useful books, and sought them out in secondhand bookstores. From this has grown a working library I consult constantly. Our most precious book, *Opera* by Bartolomeo Scappi, dates from 1570. With its jet-black italic print and vivid woodcut illustrations of kitchen scenes, pots, knives, and serving dishes, it is a work of art in itself. The following contemporary salmon recipe harks back to the medieval habit of spicing all meats and fish.

Crisp and Spicy Salmon with a Vegetable Julienne

This salmon is coated generously with powdered spices, then fried skin-side down so it emerges crisp as well as brown. By contrast, the vegetables are sweated in their own juices until tender, making a colorful dinner for four.

> *1 or 2 salmon fillets, scaled, with skin (about 1½ lb/750 g total)*
> *1 tablespoon Chinese five-spice powder*
> *1 tablespoon whole fennel seed*
> *pinch of cayenne*
> *1 tablespoon olive oil*
>
> **FOR THE VEGETABLE JULIENNE**
>
> *3 medium carrots (about ½ lb/250 g)*
> *2 medium zucchini (about ¾ lb/375 g)*
> *2 medium leeks (about ¾ lb/375g)*
> *2 tablespoons butter*
> *salt and pepper*
> *1 lemon*

For the vegetable julienne, peel the carrots and cut them into julienne strips. Trim the zucchini and cut them into julienne strips, including the skin for added color. Trim the leeks, leaving some of the more tender green tops, and halve them lengthwise. Cut them into julienne strips, wash them well, and drain them.

Melt the butter in a heavy frying pan or saucepan, add all the vegetables with salt and pepper, and stir well. Press a piece of foil on top and sweat the vegetables over low heat until tender, stirring them occasionally, 8 to 10 minutes. Do not let them brown. Cut 4 slices from the lemon for decoration, reserving the rest.

Heat the oven to 425°F/220°C. To prepare the salmon, run your fingers over the flesh and if you feel any bones (especially the tiny "pin" bones), pull them out with tweezers. Cut the salmon into 4 portions, sprinkle both sides lightly with salt, and leave them skin-side up. Mix the five-spice powder, fennel seed, and cayenne in a small bowl and sprinkle the spices over the salmon skin.

Heat the oil in a large frying pan with an ovenproof handle and add the salmon, skin-side down. Fry over quite high heat without moving the pieces for 2 to 3 minutes, until the skin is crisp—when done it will shrink and loosen from the surface of the pan. Turn the salmon pieces skin-side up, transfer the pan to the oven, and bake until done to your taste: 2 to 4 minutes for rare salmon, 5 to 8 minutes for well done. The cooking time depends on the thickness of the fillets.

Squeeze the reserved lemon over the vegetables, taste, and adjust the seasoning. Spread the vegetables on warmed dinner plates, set a piece of fish on top, skin-side up, and serve at once so the skin remains crisp.

A few books in our library date back to the 1500s—fortunately, cookbooks were not kept in the kitchen; otherwise, these treasures would not have survived.

Not all French craftsmen are as endearing as Messieurs Vergnaud and Moulinet. Every August we are hit by *les grandes vacances,* the three-, four-, even five-week vacations mandated by law. Kiss good-bye to any repairs. At the end of one July, the filter on our pool failed. *"Impossible, Madame,* vacation begins tomorrow," declared a triumphant voice at the end of the phone. "No hope before September," by which time the pool had quietly turned a virulent green. Same story when the refrigerator died, victim of one of Monsieur Moulinet's less happy techno-fixes. The manufacturer removed it at the end of July, delivering it back in mid-September, just in time for cooler weather.

You'll notice I have not yet mentioned the kitchen, the most important room in the house. Conventions of the seventeenth century when Le Feÿ was built dictated that, to minimize the attendant noise and smells, not to mention the constant danger of fire, the kitchen be far removed from any living quarters. Therefore the château's first kitchen was in the cellar, the door giving onto the walled dry moat and *basse cour* where the chickens and rabbits were conveniently housed. (The fattening of poultry for the table was always the cook's domain.)

Rabbit with Mustard

Now that the children are gone, rabbit has returned to our table, though there's still a lingering ghost of bunny when I see a whole carcass in the kitchen. This is the simplest way to cook rabbit—the mustard can be mild or hot as you prefer and you can use almost any herbs available. One rabbit makes a meal for four.

> *1 rabbit (about 3 lb/1.4 kg), cut into pieces*
> *3 tablespoons olive oil*
> *6 to 8 tablespoons Dijon-style mustard*
> *3 to 4 tablespoons chopped basil*
> *1 tablespoon chopped thyme*
> *1 tablespoon chopped rosemary*
> *a bouquet garni of 2 bay leaves and 3 or 4 sage leaves*
> *2 onions, finely chopped*
> *1 cup/250 ml dry white wine*
> *salt and pepper*

Heat the oven to 350°F/175°C. Generously oil a roasting pan. Brush the rabbit pieces all over with a few tablespoonfuls of mustard and set them in the pan. Sprinkle them with half the basil, thyme, rosemary, and some of the olive oil; add the bouquet garni. Roast the rabbit in the oven until tender and golden brown, ¾ to 1 hour.

During roasting, turn the pieces often, brushing them with more mustard and sprinkling them with more olive oil.

Transfer the rabbit pieces to a serving dish and keep them warm. Set the roasting pan on top of the stove, add the onions, and fry them, stirring, until they are very brown, 6 to 8 minutes. Add the wine and stir well to dissolve the pan juices. Simmer this jus for 2 to 3 minutes so it concentrates and reduces well. Taste it and adjust the seasoning with salt and pepper. Spoon the jus over the rabbit, sprinkle it with the remaining basil, and serve.

OPPOSITE: *We like to brush rabbit in Burgundian style, with plenty of mustard before baking it with white wine and herbs such as the fresh bay and sage leaves, which double as a table decoration here.*

Originally, the cooking at Le Feÿ was done in a great open hearth and food had to be carried up three twists of a winding staircase to the butler's pantry. This pantry we immediately made into our own kitchen. Imagine our surprise to find that what appeared to be an old mirror backed by a closet actually swung open as a hatch to the dining room. Still useful after 350 years! Sometime in the nineteenth century a majestic cast-iron range had been installed at ground level in one wing. It was still there when we moved in, lonely beside a chipped enamel sink. By tradition in France, departing owners take everything not "stuck to the wall," including the stove and kitchen appliances, but we soon discovered why the range had been spared. "*Bon à rien! Fendu!* (cracked)," lamented Madame Milbert, shaking her head at the rusty monster. It had to be dismantled, piece by piece, to load on the dump truck whose springs sagged under the weight.

Our first kitchen was frankly little better. Flung together in a hurry, appliances pushed against the wall and pans stacked on open shelves, it survived twelve years and the onslaught of hundreds of guests. It was here that we tested more than a dozen cookbooks; here Emma, age sixteen, apprenticed as a cook, turning out remarkably polished meals for family and visitors while Simon, with much more reluctance, learned to wash up. When we finally modernized our kitchen, I knew just what was appropriate. Our work surfaces are wood and marble and one of them, veined in pink and white, dates back to the eighteenth-century pantry. The walls are hung with tiles fired in an ancient kiln and glazed in traditional soft Burgundian grays, greens, and blues (see opposite, top left).

The Perkinsons' departure as tenants was the signal to build a separate, large-scale kitchen for the professional students of La Varenne. Large-scale equipment was combined with the old stone fireplace and a terra-cotta floor of hexagonal tomette tiles at least 100 years old. I left them as an economy measure, but they have proved superior to any modern material, as they are nonslip, comfortable to stand on for hours at a time, easy to clean, and resistant to grease. The back door leads directly to the *potager* and in fine weather students prepare vegetables and clean fish outdoors under the lime trees. As time has passed we've discovered more and more—the wild strawberries that carpet the woods in late spring; the field mushrooms that grow in the front pasture; the truffles that hide under a few of our oak trees; the abandoned ice house that is dug deep into cool earth, shaded by trees.

The longer I live at Château du Feÿ, the more I echo the devotion of so many owners of old property. A few years ago I wrote a book about how people live and cook in their châteaux and it was a revelation to discover how many ways they found to bring them alive. One enterprising châtelaine had founded a craft cooperative in the surrounding village, another an art gallery; several opened their properties to the public; others made wine, and a few simply farmed the land and lived as a family in the main house. I'm the only one to have founded a cooking school, a feat our French neighbors are the first to applaud —no chauvinism here. When asked why they continued what was often a losing battle against the costs of upkeep, the reply would be "*on aime*"—we love it. I can say the same. The initial *coup de foudre* (thunderbolt) when we bought Château du Feÿ has become a lifelong love affair. So complete is the château's own small world that I must confess we rarely feel the urge to leave it. I call it never-never land.

I'm rather proud to have added to Le Feÿ's already distinguished collection of tiled floors, which ranges from black-and-white checks to black-, red-, and gold-patterned squares, to ageless earthenware tomettes.

CHAPTER 6

Family and Friends Around the Table

The first party we attended at Château du Feÿ was not ours at all, but a farewell lunch given by the owner, Baron Fernand de Drouas. With very French élan, his wife Clothilde introduces us to neighbors with unlikely names like Pissepot Chassy, people whose forebears were seen off by the British at Waterloo (there were a few jokes about that), a papal count, and even a prince of Byzantium. ("*C'est faux!* Don't you believe it!" hisses Clothilde. She should know as her family, the de Saint Phalles, have lived in nearby Cudot since 1275.) However, the credentials of Henri de Montesquieu, scion of the great philosopher, are impeccable and he doffs a Panama hat worn especially to salute the English new arrivals.

The mood is extraordinarily convivial. Everyone seems to know everyone else and Mark rapidly dubs this inner circle the "château Mafia." Far from excluding us, they congratulate us on acquiring the prettiest place in the neighborhood. The view is superb, and a *potager* where fruit and vegetables are actually grown is much envied. Most of the guests suffer, they soon explain, from tumbled-down barns and general dilapidation. Many know Le Feÿ from childhood and recount stories from World War II—"we kept weapons in a *regard* (pit) just over here," says Michel Wallaert, whose family owned the château until the 1970s.

Once launched, we were included in a regular summer round of entertainment, which peaks in August, ending abruptly with *la rentrée,* the annual migration back to Paris in early September. Country dining, however, is not what you might think. Informal, yes, untidy, no. The women are carefully coiffed, their artlessly simple dresses bear a designer imprint; for men the blazer is the attire of choice. The food is often deceptively simple, too. French women seem to know by instinct (or a lifetime of attention to the plate) what will survive the rigors of a large party—dishes like Traditional Beef Bourguignon (page 26) and Seven-Hour Leg of Lamb (below) that improve on keeping, or root vegetable salads rather than greens, which wilt too fast.

Seven-Hour Leg of Lamb
Gigot de Sept Heures

This recipe is a favorite for entertaining since most of the work is done early in the day. The finished dish easily serves eight guests.

> *a leg of mature lamb or mutton (about 6 lb/2.7 kg)*
> *2 garlic cloves, cut into slivers*
> *a large bouquet garni*
> *salt and pepper*
> *4 quarts/4 liters water, more if needed*
> *3 carrots*
> *3 small turnips*
> *3 medium leeks*
> *2 small celery roots*
> *3 onions*
> *10 to 12 garlic cloves, chopped*

Heat the oven to 275°/140°C. Trim the lamb of excess fat and stud the meat with the slivers of garlic by first poking small holes in the outside of the roast with the point of a knife. Tie the meat tightly with string (it will shrink during cooking) and put it in a large flameproof casserole or Dutch oven with the bouquet garni, a pinch of salt, and enough water to cover it by three quarters. Bring the water to a boil on top of the stove and skim it well.

Cover the casserole, transfer it to the oven, and cook it for 2 hours. It is important that the meat poach gently with the water scarcely at a simmer, so if necessary turn down the oven heat. After 2 hours, turn the meat over

and continue cooking another 2 hours. Meanwhile, trim, peel, and cut the carrots, turnips, leeks, celery roots, and onions into 3/8-inch/1-cm slices. Mix them with the chopped garlic, salt, and pepper.

Lift out the meat, add the vegetables, and replace the meat on top. If necessary, add more water so that the meat is half covered. Replace the lid and continue cooking until the meat is very tender indeed and would fall off the bone if not tied with string, 1 to 1½ more hours.

Remove the meat to a warm place and cover it loosely with foil. If the vegetables are not very tender, continue simmering them, uncovered, on top of the stove until they almost collapse into a fragrant mélange. Transfer them with a slotted spoon to a deep platter, discarding the bouquet garni. Increase the heat so the cooking liquid boils and reduces.

Remove the strings from the lamb, lift it carefully on the vegetables, cover, and keep the platter warm. Continue reducing the cooking liquid to a concentrated broth to serve as gravy. Taste it, adjust the seasoning, and serve it apart from the lamb and vegetables. You will not need to carve the lamb as it falls apart into chunks with the touch of a spoon.

PREVIOUS PAGES: *Clockwise from top: In anticipation of visitors, we set the fountain going in the château courtyard; artichokes from the garden, their hairy chokes discarded, are a favorite summer appetizer; a field of sunflowers; and a church carving of wine drinkers.* OPPOSITE: *This recipe, a version of pot au feu in which the cooking liquid is boiled down to form a light gravy, was originally intended for tough old mutton. Very slow cooking was essential to render the meat soft enough to cut with a spoon. At this low temperature, today's young lamb still takes five hours to be meltingly tender and bursting with flavor from the vegetables.*

On all French tables a cheese course is mandatory, often a single wheel of Brie (made less than fifty miles away from Le Feÿ), or a group of fermier goat cheeses, or some smelly, aged Epoisses (the Burgundian favorite) so soft it must be spooned from its chipboard box.

Table seating is often left open, but for our first year I was invited to the host's right hand, which turns out to be in the center of the table rather than at the head as in Anglo-Saxon style. I find the French custom much more civilized as conversation can include at least a half dozen people by talking across the table. (Did my mother once say this is not done? How very English.) The French are ideal guests, launching themselves into an occasion with such gusto that success seems guaranteed. Conversation sparkles from the start and even little children are taught that the worst sin at a party is silence.

Emmanuel de Sartiges, who lives in a château where the chimneys tend to collapse, tells how he saved the local private lycée from extinction by a communist city council by converting it into a widely respected hotel school. The famous Gaullist military figure, Jacques Massu (universally addressed as "*Mon général*"), relives not his own campaigns, but the AD 841 battle between Charlemagne's grandsons at nearby Fontenay-en-Puisaye, where he has paced out the ground. Dominique Frémy, publisher of an ingenious encyclopedia called *Quid,* meets us one evening as we park the car before dinner. "We have Madame de Broglie here," he warns. "She's the one whose husband was gunned down in Paris. *Pas de gaffe!*" Little surprise, then, that the family brought the word *imbroglio* into half a dozen languages.

All this is strong meat for two expatriates, and it was at least a year before we plucked up courage to ask the château Mafia back to what had become our home. When they finally came to Le Feÿ I served as dessert a surefire success, star of every family festival in the Parisian household where I first learned French thirty-five years ago. Madame Charpentier, with a skeptical gleam in her eye, gave me a verbal rundown of the recipe, but it took me half a dozen tries to get the basic mix of five ingredients just right. Only later did I learn that every self-respecting Frenchwoman has her personal chocolate recipe, inherited from *mamie* (grandma), and never disclosed to outsiders.

ABOVE: *Artisanal goat cheeses are often rolled in wood ash, both to protect the surface and to add flavor. Eating the coating is optional, though it does taste rather good.*

Chocolate Snowball

You can keep the molded chocolate "ball" in the refrigerator up to three days, and it freezes well. Cover it with Chantilly cream as "snow" shortly before serving. One snowball serves at least eight to ten—it could hardly be richer!

½ lb/250 g dark chocolate, chopped
¾ cup/175 ml strong black coffee
1 cup/250 g butter, cut into pieces
1 cup/200 g granulated sugar
4 eggs, beaten to mix
8 to 10 mint sprigs, for decoration

FOR THE CHANTILLY CREAM
2 cups/500 ml heavy cream
1 to 2 tablespoons confectioners' sugar
1 teaspoon vanilla extract

a 1-quart/1-liter charlotte mold or deep bowl
pastry bag and small star tube

Line the charlotte mold or bowl with a single piece of foil, pressing it to the sides as smoothly as possible but without tearing the foil. Heat the oven to 350°F/175°C. Heat the chocolate with the coffee in a small saucepan over medium heat, stirring until melted. Bring the chocolate to a boil and simmer until it thickens but still falls easily from the spoon. Add the butter and sugar and continue stirring over the heat until the mixture is melted and smooth. Bring it just to a boil and then remove it from the heat.

Whisk the eggs into the chocolate mixture, adding them a little at a time and whisking steadily—the heat will cook and thicken them. Strain the mixture through a sieve and into the lined mold. Set the mold in a bain-marie and bring it to a boil on top of the stove. Transfer it to the oven and bake it until the chocolate mixture has risen and a light crust forms on top, 35 to 45 minutes. Take the mold from the bain-marie and let it cool—the snowball will shrink but don't worry. Cover and chill the mold until firmly set, at least 12 hours.

To finish the snowball, run a knife around the edge of the mold and turn the snowball onto a large flat serving plate. Peel off the foil—the chocolate will stick and be messy but this is no matter since it will later be completely concealed in Chantilly cream. If some chocolate sticks in the mold, simply scoop it out and reshape it.

For the Chantilly cream, beat the cream until stiff (it's best if the cream is rather cold to start with). Whisk in the confectioners' sugar and vanilla and continue whisking until stiff again—take care not to overbeat as the cream will stiffen further when it is piped through the small tube. Fill the piping bag with the Chantilly cream and completely cover the snowball with tiny rosettes so no chocolate is visible. Top it with a single large rosette of cream and dot the sides here and there with mint sprigs. Chill it until serving, then cut it in wedges like a cake.

Eskimo Ice Cream

Dessert on the French country table is a high point, but it is always simple. On one occasion we were served this upmarket version of an Eskimo pie.

Make or buy vanilla ice cream and let it soften so it can be stirred. Stir in generous amounts of raisins, chopped dried apricots, and coarsely chopped nuts such as walnuts. If you use hazelnuts, almonds, or pine nuts, they should be toasted for the best flavor. Pack the ice cream mixture into individual ramekins or small bowls, smoothing the top. Freeze it until firm. Melt some dark chocolate, allowing about a tablespoon per person, trail it in a lattice over the ice cream, and freeze again. Serve directly in the molds from the freezer. Perfect on a hot day.

Like everywhere else, summer is wedding time in Burgundy and we were invited to *assister* at the marriage of the daughter of Baron Arnaud de Bontin and his Swedish wife, Mona. This was a high point for the neighborhood as the festivitites were held in the sixteenth-century Château de Bontin, an architectural masterpiece of the region. Arnaud is one of those privileged individuals who need only follow their own name on the road signs to find the way home. I'm always flattered to note that Bontin looks a bit like a sophisticated Le Feÿ, with the same tall terra-cotta tiled roofs and elegant facade picked out in brick. Arnaud is a traditionalist. When we ran across him in 1989 during the long-drawn-out bicentennial festivities for the Revolution, he was grumbling. "What is there to celebrate? Nothing's been right ever since."

For years Arnaud has been restoring the vast outbuildings of his ancestral pile and this is the inauguration. Guests are streaming through the château itself to the garden beyond and a great courtyard a good 60 yards/55 meters square. Tables are set up in the shade of the open barn and the bride's father and then her brothers offer congratulations and toasts over a crackling loudspeaker system. I catch sight of a familiar face from La Varenne—Claude Godard, one of our visiting chefs, is catering the affair. He looks harassed, as well he might, with 500 people to feed on one of the hottest nights of the year. Keeping shellfish in aspic cold outdoors is a nightmare, but the jellied oysters in their shells, the little shrimp molds, and squid salad arrive in pristine condition on the plate, wonderfully refreshing. The wedding cake, a monstrous edifice a yard long in genoise sponge and pastry cream that re-creates Château de Bontin, is less happy. We hear the inside story from one of our trainees who is helping in the kitchen. The pastry cream had been made three days ahead and in the torrid heat had turned very slightly sour. But by the end of dinner, as the wine flowed faster and candles picked out shadows on the cheerful faces, no one gave a damn.

OPPOSITE: *The château of St. Fargeau, once the royal home of Louis XIV's sister, La Grande Mademoiselle, is a favorite spot for local weddings.* ABOVE: *When Arnaud de Bontin's daughter was married, the family home of Château de Bontin was the more logical background.*

191

Phyllo Tower with Red Berries
Feuilletés aux Fruits Rouges

This is a favorite caterer's dessert in our area, easy to prepare in advance and only needing to be arranged at the last moment. As a rule I'm against architecture on the plate, but I have to admit that these phyllo wafers, flavored with honey and cut in geometric shapes, do invite a modernist Le Corbusier approach. A vanilla pastry cream lightened with whipped Chantilly cream acts as mortar. For berries, there's a choice of raspberries, strawberries (with the hull), blueberries, blackberries, red or black currants on the stem, even cape gooseberries—the greater the variety and the prettier the fruit, the better. This recipe makes eight towers.

12 sheets of phyllo pastry
½ cup/125 g butter
5 to 6 tablespoons honey
about 2 quarts/375 g mixed red berries

FOR THE PASTRY CREAM

2 cups/500 ml milk
1 vanilla bean, split
5 egg yolks
7 tablespoons/90 g granulated sugar
3 tablespoons/22 g flour

FOR THE CHANTILLY CREAM

1 cup/250 ml heavy cream
2 to 3 tablespoons confectioners' sugar
2 tablespoons Cognac

3- to 3½-inch/8- to 9-cm round cookie cutter

For the pastry cream, scald the milk in a medium saucepan with the vanilla bean, cover, and leave it to infuse off the heat for about 10 minutes. Beat the egg yolks with the granulated sugar until thick and light, about 2 minutes. Stir in the flour. Whisk the scalded milk into the egg mixture and return it to the saucepan. Cook over low heat, whisking constantly, until the pastry cream comes to a boil and thickens. Simmer it and continue to stir for 1 or 2 minutes, then strain it into a bowl—the vanilla bean can be rinsed and used again. Press a piece of plastic wrap on the cream to prevent a skin from forming and chill it.

Heat the oven to 450°F/230°C. Brush 2 baking sheets with butter. Heat the honey and remaining butter in a small saucepan until melted. Lay a sheet of phyllo on the work surface and brush it lightly with the honey butter. Lay a second sheet on top and brush again. Repeat with 2 more sheets, keeping the remaining sheets covered with a slightly damp towel. Using the cookie cutter, stamp out as many rounds as possible from the dough and set them on the buttered baking sheet. You'll have some dough trimmings, so if you like, cut some crescents, too. Bake the rounds until the phyllo is golden and the glaze on top begins to caramelize, 5 to 6 minutes. The layers will puff and separate slightly. Gently transfer them to a rack to cool.

Meanwhile, layer 4 more sheets of phyllo with the honey butter and stamp out more rounds for a total of 24. Set the rounds, with any crescents, on the second baking sheet, bake, and let them cool as before. Layer the remaining pastry sheets and cut them in triangles or other shapes that you can later use to decorate the tower in a fanciful design. Bake them also.

Pick over the berries, washing them only if they are sandy. Leave them with some of their decorative hulls and stems, and slice them only if very large.

For the light pastry cream, whip the heavy cream for Chantilly until it holds a soft peak (this is quick work if the cream is well chilled). Add the confectioners' sugar and Cognac and continue whipping until the cream again holds a soft peak. Whisk the cold pastry cream to smooth any lumps that may have formed as it cooled, and then fold in the whipped Chantilly cream.

To assemble the dessert, set a round of pastry on each of 8 large individual plates. Add a spoonful of light pastry cream and top with some berries, using the less attractive ones for this bottom layer. Top with a second pastry round. Spread another spoonful of cream on top, add more berries, and cover with a third round. Pile a bit of cream on top of the round and stick the pastry shapes into it, creating your own fantasy construction. Decorate the plates with the remaining berries and serve as soon as possible.

Layers of honey-glazed phyllo and pastry cream adapt happily to a variety of fruits and fanciful presentations.

No sooner had we moved into Château du Feÿ than my parents came to assess the extent of our folly. My father shook his head at the half mile of private road, wincing as we hit the potholes. My mother smiled bravely at the mess indoors—she was one of those who dust the house before the cleaning lady arrives. Our priorities are different, and the atmosphere brightened once we sat down to table. My Yorkshire father, a confirmed meat eater who regarded salad as a waste of good space, always enjoyed a hearty slice of ham.

Ham Steaks with Butternut Coulis

Monsieur Milbert cannot read the English titles on the seed packets we bring him, so he eyeballs the picture, makes a stab at the planting season, and hopes for the best. Butternut squash, a rarity in France, was a success the first time—except that Monsieur Milbert mistook it for a summer squash and brought it in triumph with the first zucchini. Only with difficulty could I persuade him to wait until October to harvest these cold weather treasures when the flesh had ripened to a deep golden orange. Other winter squash such as pumpkin or acorn are equally good in this coulis, which I pair with ham steaks for an autumnal dinner for four to six.

4 to 6 cooked ham steaks (about 1 ½ lb/750 g total)
1 small butternut squash (about 1 lb/500 g)
¼ cup/60 g butter
2 medium leeks, white and pale green only, thinly sliced
2 onions, finely chopped
1 garlic clove, finely chopped
1 ½ cups/375 ml chicken stock
1 tablespoon dark brown sugar
1 tablespoon vegetable oil
salt and white pepper

Peel the squash and cut it into 1-inch/2.5-cm chunks, discarding the seeds. Melt half the butter in a medium saucepan, add the leeks (avoid the darker green part, which would discolor the coulis) and onions, and cook over medium heat until soft but not brown, 5 to 7 minutes. Add the garlic and cook until fragrant, about 30 seconds. Add the squash, chicken stock, and brown sugar. Cover and simmer until the squash is very tender, 20 to 25 minutes.

When the squash is soft enough to mash with a spoon, transfer it with the onions and leeks to a food processor. Purée it with a little of the cooking liquid until very smooth. Work the purée through a sieve into a saucepan. Stir in enough of the remaining cooking liquid to make a coulis that is just thick enough to coat the back of a spoon. Bring it just to a boil, remove it from the heat, taste, and adjust the seasoning. Set the coulis aside. Save any remaining cooking liquid as it may be needed to thin the coulis if you've made it ahead—it also makes a fine addition to a pot of soup.

To finish, heat the oil in a large skillet over high heat. Add the ham steaks and fry until brown on both sides, 3 to 5 minutes per side. Meanwhile, bring the coulis just to a boil. Remove it from the heat and add the remaining butter, cut in pieces, swirling the pan so that the butter is incorporated smoothly without melting to oil. Set the ham steaks on warm plates, spoon over a little coulis, and serve at once, passing the remaining coulis separately.

A winter table for four in front of a roaring fire in the grand salon. *Ham steaks are served with butternut squash coulis and leaf spinach.*

Meals on the terrace at Le Feÿ have become an institution; we may
set the table for six or sixteen. The view over the Yonne River valley embraces a patchwork of fields that change color daily as crops ripen and the harvest comes. One year hot-air balloons belonging to a local enthusiast would drift by, near enough to exchange greetings, and we are often buzzed by light aircraft as we are so visible on the skyline. As dusk closes in, bats from the wine cave dug into the hillside below us zoom past, as do mosquitoes—nothing in life is idyllic. Those early summers, we started out by serving purely French food—pâtés and dried sausages from the market, vinaigrette salads, and simple vegetable recipes like this one.

Deep-Fried Zucchini Flowers

"Plants are something else *(les plantes, c'est quelque chose)*," once again Monsieur Milbert reiterates his favorite phrase, reporting on the lack of zucchini flowers (and therefore zucchini) one year. "I was warned that they could be all male plants, but this is the first time." (He may talk about the shortcomings of nature but he clearly feels it is us, and our seeds from the United States, that have let him down.) The contrast is all the more puzzling given the previous year's seemingly endless supply of zucchini flowers that we deep-fried in tempura batter to eat plain or with a herb dipping sauce. I've added a little stuffing for the flowers to make a more substantial appetizer for four people, but they are good without it, too. For an even simpler batter, stir a cup of dark beer into a cup of flour.

FOR THE GINGER DIPPING SAUCE

½ cup/125 ml vegetable oil
3 tablespoons dark sesame oil
a 2-inch/5-cm piece of fresh gingerroot, finely chopped
the white and green part of 2 scallions, thinly sliced
salt and pepper

FOR THE TEMPURA BATTER

1 egg
1 cup/250 ml water
1 cup/125 g flour

FOR THE FLOWERS

12 to 16 zucchini flowers
½ cup/125 g cream cheese
1 to 2 tablespoons milk
a large pinch of grated nutmeg
vegetable oil for deep-frying

piping bag and medium plain tube

For the dipping sauce, heat the vegetable oil until very hot. Mix the sesame oil, ginger, scallions, salt, and pepper in a bowl, and stir in the hot oil. Let cool, then taste and adjust the seasoning. Pour the sauce into 4 small bowls for dipping and set them on 4 large plates.

For the batter, whisk together the egg and water in a bowl. Add the flour and whisk very briefly—the batter may be slightly lumpy but don't worry; if overworked it will be heavy.

For the flowers, wash the flowers and dry them thoroughly on paper towels. (Our flowers sometimes have live bees inside, so we take care!) In a bowl, soften the cream cheese by mashing it with enough milk so it just falls from a spoon. Season the cheese filling to your taste with nutmeg, salt, and pepper. Fill the piping bag with the filling and use it to stuff the flowers; each flower gets 1 to 2 teaspoonfuls of filling depending on their size. Twist the tips of the petals to seal the filling inside.

Heat about 2 inches/5 cm of vegetable oil in a deep frying pan until a drop of batter sizzles when dropped in the oil. Dip a flower in batter, lift it out by the stem, and let the excess batter drip off for 1 to 2 seconds. Carefully lower the flower into the hot fat. Repeat with 1 to 2 more flowers and fry them briskly until very pale gold, turning them once, for 1 to 2 minutes on each side. Drain the flowers on paper towels and keep them warm in a low oven with the door open while frying the rest. Never overcrowd the frying pan or the flowers will not fry evenly. Arrange the fried zucchini flowers on the plates with the dipping sauce and serve at once.

Soon our visitors and trainees began to influence the cooking. There was Southern-raised Virginia who distracted us with her "Yes, sir" and "Yes, ma'am." She beguiled us even more with her cooking, a potent mix of contemporary and Grandma, to whom Virginia spoke every week. It was during Virginia's time that we had to test gumbo thickened with okra for a cookbook. Okra is not a French favorite; we were forced to order a whole case from the Rungis wholesale market in Paris only to use a half pound. The gumbo was a disappointment, but Virginia's okra popcorn proved the hit of the cocktail hour. Virginia's Grandma's creamed corn was pretty good, too.

Popcorn Fried Okra

Cut a pound/500 g of okra into ⅜-inch/1-cm slices, trimming the stems. Put a cup or so of coarsely ground white or yellow cornmeal in a bowl (we used polenta) with a cup of flour and some salt and pepper. Break an egg into a second bowl, add 1 cup/250 ml buttermilk and ½ teaspoon salt, and whisk them until mixed. Stir about half the okra into the buttermilk mixture. Heat a good 2 inches/5 cm of vegetable oil in a deep frying pan until it sputters when a piece of okra is added. Using a slotted spoon, transfer the okra from the buttermilk to the cornmeal mixture—it will be unpleasantly gluey— and toss until well coated. Lower the okra into the hot fat and fry them, stirring often, until brown and crisp, 3 to 5 minutes. Lift them out with the spoon and drain on paper towels. (Inevitably, some of the coating will have fallen off into the fat, but ignore it.) Keep the okra warm in a low oven while you coat and fry the rest. Serves 6 to 8 as a snack or hors d'oeuvre.

Skillet Creamed Corn

Corn is one of our American imports. At first Milbert planted it in two long rows, with disappointing results. Then he was persuaded to try a compact block so the corn could cross-pollinate, and now most summers we have a respectable crop of plump ears. One year they sprouted the fabled grayish corn fungus so prized in Mexico—or so we believed, though we dared not put it to the test.

Cut the kernels from 4 to 5 ears of corn. With the back of the knife, scrape the milk from the corncobs into a bowl. Stir in the kernels and season with pepper and a little salt. Dice a couple of thick slices of bacon and cook them in a skillet or deep frying pan until brown. Add the corn kernels and corn milk, cover, and simmer, stirring often, until the corn is tender, 15 to 25 minutes depending on the age of the corn. If you like, stir in a few tablespoons of cream, taste, and adjust the seasoning. This recipe serves 4 to 6.

ABOVE: *No matter how many zucchini flowers we pick to deep-fry, they seem to keep on blooming and blooming.*

Jams and jellies are another summer project. I have before me the late fall inventory of preserves, which includes half a dozen jellies and as many different fruit alcohols, rhubarb-ginger and green tomato jams as well as the common plum, and a tomato and apple chutney. Some rather odd concoctions turn up, such as medlar marmalade and crab apple and tarragon jelly, but this cherry and raspberry jam, which I invented almost by accident, is a winner. Dark cherries ripen at the same time as raspberries in the garden at Le Feÿ, so one day I mixed the fruits together to get a worthwhile batch of jam. Perfection! The flavor of raspberries permeates the jam and their extra pectin helps set the cherry juice, which is often syrupy. What's more, there are far fewer woody seeds than in pure raspberry jam.

Spiced Apple and Green Tomato Chutney

Core 4 lb/1.8 kg green tomatoes. Immerse them a few at a time in boiling water for 10 seconds to loosen the skins, transfer to cold water, then peel them. Thickly slice them and combine in a large bowl with 1½ lb/750 g sliced onions, 2 cups/400 g dark brown sugar, 1¼ quarts/1.24 liters dark beer, 2 tablespoons salt, 1 tablespoon ground ginger, and 1 teaspoon nutmeg. In a piece of cheesecloth tie 2 teaspoons peppercorns and 2 or 3 dried hot red chili peppers and add to the tomatoes. Stir to mix, cover tightly, and leave overnight at room temperature to macerate. The next day, peel, core, and slice 4 pounds/1.8 kg tart apples and mix with the tomatoes. Bring to a boil in a large preserving pan and simmer until the mixture is dark, rich, and very thick, 1½ to 2 hours. Stir often, especially toward the end of cooking. Discard the cheesecloth bag, pack the chutney into sterilized jars, and seal. This makes about 3 quarts/3 liters.

Spiced Apple and Green Tomato Chutney is but one of the many preserves that come out of the kitchen at Château du Feÿ.

Our children have always been closely involved in the kitchen. Starting by chopping and slicing, not to mention washing up, they graduated to carving the chicken and piping the frosting on birthday cake. Friends from school would come to stay, the boys roaring through the back woods on an underpowered motor bike and the girls sporting a different hairdo at every meal. Dave was a creator of rap ballads, nicknamed The Pontificator by Mark for his habit of addressing the dinner table like a public meeting. He now edits a lively and successful counterculture art magazine, written mainly by himself under a variety of pseudonyms. Tom had a penchant for zoology (he keeps snakes) and was born with a straight eye. He and Simon undertook to renovate the two-roomed cottage called the *garçonnièr* and Tom was invaluable in keeping Simon's haphazard approach in line. One afternoon I found them carefully, laboriously, hanging the Laura Ashley lemon-printed wallpaper—upside down.

For a while Emma ran the kitchen, cooking daily for twelve or more with great aplomb. This was one of her favorites, a mild variant of barbecued chicken that reassures the most finicky of her friends.

Grilled Coriander Chicken with Yogurt

Given its Mediterranean overtones, it's not surprising that this chicken dish—enough for four servings—is as good at room temperature as when it is served hot. Yogurt plays a double role as tenderizer for the meat and also as the main ingredient in thickening the sauce.

> 8 chicken thighs or small single chicken breasts
> 2 cups/500 ml plain yogurt
> 1 tablespoon olive oil
> 1 onion, chopped
> 2 garlic cloves, chopped
> 2 tablespoons ground coriander
> salt and pepper
> ½ cup/125 ml crème fraîche or sour cream
> 2 tablespoons chopped cilantro

Leave the skin on the chicken pieces or remove it, as you prefer. Put the pieces in a bowl, add half of the yogurt, and stir so the pieces are coated. Cover and leave them to marinate in the refrigerator for 3 to 4 hours.

When it comes time to cook the chicken, heat up the grill or broiler and oil the rack. Remove the chicken from the marinade and wipe off the yogurt, discarding it. Dry the chicken pieces on paper towels and set them on the rack. Grill or broil them about 3 in/7.5 cm from the heat until they are very brown, tender, and no pink juice runs out when they are pricked with a fork near the bone. This will take 20 to 25 minutes and you should turn them once or twice as they cook. If at any time the chicken begins to scorch, move the pieces farther from the heat and continue cooking.

Meanwhile, make the sauce. Heat the oil in a saucepan over medium heat and fry the onion until soft, 3 to 5 minutes. Reduce the heat to low, add the garlic and ground coriander, and cook, stirring often, until the mixture is very fragrant, 1 to 2 minutes. Stir in the remaining yogurt off the heat, add salt and pepper, and purée the sauce with a hand-held immersion blender or in a food processor. Return the sauce to the pan, stir in the cream and cilantro, taste, and adjust the seasoning. Keep the sauce warm, but do not boil it or it will separate. Serve the chicken hot or at room temperature, with the sauce spooned on top.

It was around this time that we acquired Zulu, a Rhodesian ridgeback and sun lover. He is much admired by visitors. *"Un profil très noble,"* remarked Emmanuel de Sartiges, whose father-in-law was a duke. Like any French family, we can deduct Zulu's cost from our taxes providing he can bark and bite, thus qualifying as a guard dog. No problem there! His handsome profile and good nature are marred only by a tendency to bite children (Mark's nephew Lexi bears a scar to this day). Zulu and our neighbor Madame Andrea's poodle are great friends, meeting often at the gate for a forbidden breakfast of Madame Milbert's store-bought ladyfingers. In winter they are entertained indoors, doggie heaven with its frowst and smells.

One fateful summer, the children suddenly grew up: Simon acquired his first girlfriend and Emma, two years younger but always in competition, was taken up by his friend Luis. I had to admit Luis's dark-eyed charm, though as a mother I found his Mediterranean manner of lounging around the stove while the women worked deeply suspect. Indeed now I come to think of it, Emma's affairs of the heart often revolve around food—she met an Older Man while cooking in a summer villa on the island of Elba and in Washington, D.C., became romantically involved with the man who turned out to be her future husband after he lugged her groceries home from the store.

I'm a bit unkind—Emma is an excellent cook, organized and quick, with a good palate. Some of our happiest times together have been spent in the kitchen basting the Christmas goose or churning a quick batch of ice cream for unexpected summer guests. It's a shame her career in global finance leaves little time for anything but salads like this one, just right with her Grilled Coriander Chicken with Yogurt (page 199).

ABOVE: *Rhodesian ridgeback Zulu accompanies me from garden to kitchen.* OPPOSITE: *Now that a simple domestic version of the mandoline slicer is available in so many shops, salads like this one are easy.*

Zucchini and Squash Salad

For this recipe you'll need a mandoline—the domestic models with a plastic frame do just fine.

For a salad for 6 people, trim the ends from 4 small zucchini and 4 small yellow squash (about 1 lb/500 g of each). Cut them into 2-inch/5-cm lengths and slice them lengthwise on the julienne blade of a mandoline. Rotate the lengths of zucchini and squash as you slice, so that you come up with a julienne of the colorful outer peel and some of the flesh, but discard the seeds and central core. Make a vinaigrette dressing by whisking the juice of 2 lemons or limes with 2 chopped shallots, salt, and pepper. Then whisk in ½ cup/125 ml vegetable oil. Chop and add a couple of table-spoons of dill (or your favorite fresh herb). Toss the vegetable julienne with the dressing, taste, and adjust the season-ing. You can serve the salad at once, or after an hour or so, when the vegetables will have wilted and softened slightly though remaining crisp.

Simon seemed to be less involved in the kitchen than Emma. Then, six months after college graduation and still unemployed, in early 1993 he was offered the job of managing The Moscow Catering Company in Russia. Given that his only qualification was fluent Russian, I was skeptical, but my mother knew better. "My dear, you may not have taught him to cook, but you talk about food all the time!" she remarked sharply. (To her mind, cooking was at best a manual occupation.)

She was proved right, Simon took to catering like a duck to orange sauce, doubling turnover in two years and ending with thirty Russian employees. Together they turned out box meals such as tomato salad, Asian chicken with rice, flanked by brownies and garlic bread. Food production in Russia was in its infancy and for an individual to assemble this simple meal could take all day. Our weekly phone calls were half technical discussion, half story for a movie script and then, six weeks after Simon had taken over, the movie became reality. Igor, one of the company drivers, rear-ended a posh sedan and two men jumped out brandishing guns. "Five thousand dollars in cash for the car by tonight," yelled one, with a throat-slitting gesture. Back at the kitchen, Simon had never seen anyone so terrified as Igor. Paying up was Simon's first major business decision, and any since have paled by comparison. Back then in Russia, lemons were unobtainable but caviar was cheap and Simon would bring us jam jars full, bought with greenbacks in the Moscow market.

Blini with Caviar

With the minimum serving of caviar a half ounce, even modest sevruga becomes expensive, and beluga is a minor investment (when Simon is not around to play Father Christmas). Luckily blini are delicious with smoked fish so, rather than skimping on caviar, I prefer to substitute the best smoked salmon or eel. You can make the blini ahead and reheat them, but like all pancakes, they are best when freshly cooked. This recipe yields 24 to 30 small or a dozen large blini, enough to indulge six to eight guests.

> *1 cup/250 ml milk, more if needed*
> *1 tablespoon/10 g active dry yeast*
> *¼ cup/60 ml warm water*
> *½ cup/60 g all-purpose flour*
> *¾ cup/90 g buckwheat flour*
> *½ teaspoon salt*
> *2 eggs*
> *3 to 4 tablespoons melted butter for frying*
>
> FOR SERVING
>
> *6 oz/175 g caviar or 1 lb/500 g smoked fish*
> *1 cup/250 ml sour cream*
> *halved lemons, chopped red onion, thinly sliced*
> *   radishes, drained capers, chopped hard-boiled egg*

Scald the milk and let cool to lukewarm. Sprinkle yeast over the warm water and leave until dissolved, about 5 minutes. Sift both flours and the salt into a bowl and make a well in the center. Add dissolved yeast and three quarters of the warm milk. Stir with a wooden spoon, gradually drawing in the flour to make a smooth batter. Beat by hand for about 2 minutes—the consistency will be slightly sticky because of the buckwheat. Cover the bowl with a damp dishtowel and leave the batter to rise in a warm place until light and full of bubbles, 2 to 3 hours.

To cook the blini, separate the eggs and stir yolks into the risen batter. Stir in remaining milk and, if the batter does not fall easily from the spoon, add a little more milk until it does. In a separate bowl, whip the whites until they hold a soft peak and fold them into the batter. Heat 1 to 2 tablespoons of butter in a frying pan until it stops foaming and add spoonfuls of batter—you can make the blini large or small as you prefer. Cook until the undersides are lightly browned and the tops are bubbling, 1 to 2 minutes. Turn and brown the other side. Pile the blini one on top of another to keep them warm and moist while frying the rest.

Arrange the blini on a platter or on individual plates, and serve them warm, with the caviar and condiments.

OPPOSITE: *I learned from Simon that in Russia* blini *refers to any pancake, light or dark, large or small, though the best are made with buckwheat flour. Here they are served with caviar and the traditional condiments.*

A handful of Simon's Russian friends have come to Le Feÿ since the breakup of
the Soviet Union. Anya repaid her airfare by cleaning the more than 800 château windowpanes, which we
reckoned was fair exchange. Mischa drove all the way in a decrepit Lada, then ran out of money for gas
and had to be rescued at the tollbooth an hour away. As part of his college language exchange program,
Simon had stayed one summer with Liena Motienko in St. Petersburg and both families have since
become good friends. Liena's mother is a notable cook now that she is freed from ingredient shortages,
and for our last visit she made *solianka*, a vegetable soup seasoned with pickles and bolstered with every
sort of meat.

Piquant Russian Winter Soup
Solianka

The name *solianka* probably derives from *sol*, the Russian
word for salt, hardly a surprise as it contains a variety
of pickled ingredients—olives, cucumbers, capers, and
cabbage. *Solianka* is clearly a hearty winter soup and I
leave you to make a choice of meats, adding fewer or
none at all as you wish. This recipe makes six bowls,
filling enough for a main course if you include all of the
meats.

> *½ small head of white cabbage (about 1 lb/500 g),*
>   *shredded*
> *salt and pepper*
> *3 tablespoons vegetable oil or butter*
> *2 onions, chopped*
> *2 qts/2 liters beef, veal, or vegetable stock*
> *1 to 2 cups (about ½ lb/250 g) diced cooked beef or*
>   *pork*
> *6 oz/175 g country ham or salami, cut in julienne*
> *6 oz/175 g cooked tongue, cut in julienne*
> *3 tomatoes, peeled, seeded, and chopped*
> *2 large pickled cucumbers, cut in julienne, with their*
>   *juice*
> *1 tablespoon capers, drained*
> *6 to 8 black olives, pitted and chopped*
> *2 bay leaves*
> *3 to 4 dill sprigs, chopped*
> *juice of ½ lemon, or to taste*
> *sour cream for serving (optional)*

Toss the cabbage in a large bowl with 1 tablespoon of
salt and leave it to marinate for up to 4 hours if
possible.

Meanwhile, prepare the soup. Heat the oil or butter in
a large pan and fry the onions until lightly browned, 5 to
7 minutes. Add the stock and bring the soup to a boil.
Stir in the beef or pork, ham or salami, tongue, tomatoes, cucumbers, capers, olives, and bay leaves. Simmer
the soup for 20 to 30 minutes.

Put the cabbage in a colander and rinse it with cold
water to remove the salt. Stir the cabbage into the soup,
taste, and adjust the seasoning with salt and pepper (be
careful as the soup may already be quite salty from the
pickled ingredients). Simmer until the cabbage is tender,
10 to 15 minutes.

Discard the bay leaves from the soup, stir in the dill
and lemon juice, and taste again. Serve the soup very
hot, with a bowl of sour cream if you like.

Traditional meaty solianka *is a meal in itself.*

Liena always seems to visit Le Feÿ during raspberry season, when she's pressed into service with picking. This recipe for raspberry liqueur, brewed simply from raspberries and sugar, comes from her mother. Until I tried it, I was nervous that the raspberries would explode the jar and they do indeed ferment with vigor, so cover them only loosely. Wait six months and an amazing cardinal red liquid results, sweet but pungent, too, a potent pick-me-up on a cold day.

Liena's Raspberry Liqueur

Pack 2 lb/1 kg raspberries (do not wash them) in a quart/liter canning jar, layering them with an equal weight of sugar. Close the jar loosely so that air can escape and keep it in a cool place. The sugar and fruit will ferment and bubble and you should stir it every week or two. After at least 6 months, or when the bubbling stops, the liqueur is ready to drink but it will mellow and improve on keeping. You can strain out the raspberries and serve the liquid as a liqueur, or spoon the liqueur and fruit over ice cream or other fresh fruits. This makes 1 quart/1 liter of liqueur.

ABOVE: *Liena's raspberry liqueur, a combination of fresh raspberries and sugar (left), progresses over the months to a cloudy liquid which ferments (right) to a concentrated brew, delicious alone or served over ice cream.*

A succession of other regular visitors has developed over the years. Some specialize

in risqué limericks (Mark has a memory for them), others make a fuss about their food. Every family has a Cousin Caroline who offers homeopathic cures and indulges in vegetarianism. Bert Sonnenfeld, a professor of French literature at the University of Southern California, accumulates jokes in a notebook and is always ready with a quip ("beware of the Gorgon Zola"). Then there's Margo, journalist and self-styled Compulsive Clipper, who keeps us up to date with regular bundles of foodie articles from Boston and beyond. For years I've been trying to make a really moist muffin. Simple, you would think, but it took a New Englander to find me the answer. At Le Feÿ we replace the original maple syrup with our own honey.

Honey Walnut Muffins

While still hot, the tops of these deliciously moist muffins are dipped in honey to form a glaze. This recipe makes 12 muffins.

> 2½ cups/300 g flour
> 1 teaspoon baking soda
> ½ teaspoon salt
> 1½ cups/175 g walnut pieces
> 2 eggs
> 1 cup/250 ml sour cream
> 1¼ cups/300 ml clear honey
>
> a medium 12-muffin pan

Heat the oven to 425°F/220°C. Butter the muffin pan. Sift about half the flour with the baking soda and salt into a bowl. In a food processor, finely chop the walnuts with the remaining flour, but do not overwork or the nuts will be oily. Stir them into the flour mixture and make a well in the center.

In a separate bowl, whisk the eggs just until mixed. Whisk in the sour cream and 1 cup/250 ml of the honey until thoroughly combined, and pour the mixture into the well in the flour. Stir until the batter is mixed but still slightly rough. One of the secrets of light muffins is to never overmix—it makes them heavy.

Spoon the batter into the muffin pan and bake until the muffins are peaked and start to pull away from the sides of the cups, 18 to 22 minutes. A skewer inserted in the center of a muffin should come out clean.

When the muffins are done, let them cool for 2 to 3 minutes in the pan. Unmold them and while still warm dip their peaks into the remaining honey (if the honey is stiff, melt it by warming). Set the muffins on a rack to cool for a few minutes, but be sure to eat them at their best—while still warm.

Guests drop umbrellas by the front door—or borrow one for a visit to the garden in the rain.

Françoise from Normandy

Françoise from Normandy was housekeeper for Mark's parents when they lived near Dieppe. Françoise is that legendary treasure, a born cook. Even my mother-in-law's British penchant for overcooked vegetables and thick gravy could not mask her talent. Her roast meats were always crispy on the outside, juicy within, her sautéed scallops a marvel of sweetness, and her sole meunière, a test for professional chefs, was to die for. (Chef Chambrette—you'll meet him soon—was sacked from Prunier's in Paris in the 1930s because of the specks of burned butter on his meunière.) Inspired by the Norman rice dessert *tergoule*, Françoise also transformed English rice pudding with a touch of caramel and cream.

Françoise's Caramel Rice Pudding

Françoise makes several versions of rice pudding, and the best has a topping of dark, slightly piquant caramel. Be sure to use short-grain rice as it absorbs more milk, softening to make a creamy pudding lightly thickened with its own starch. The pudding is excellent made ahead as it is served cold. I've added a simple orange sauce, ample for four.

> 1 quart/1 liter milk, more if needed
> ½ cup/75 g short-grain rice
> 1 vanilla bean, split
> pinch of salt
> 3 tablespoons sugar, or to taste
> 3 eggs
>
> FOR THE ORANGE SAUCE
> 2 large oranges
> 3 to 4 tablespoons orange marmalade
> ½ cup/125 ml orange juice
> 2 tablespoons Grand Marnier (optional)
>
> FOR THE CARAMEL
> ½ cup/100 g sugar
> 5 tablespoons cold water
> squeeze of lemon juice
>
> ring mold or soufflé dish (1 quart/1 liter capacity)

Bring the milk to a boil in a heavy saucepan and stir in the rice, vanilla bean, and salt. Simmer the rice, uncovered, until it is very tender, 30 to 40 minutes. Stir it occasionally, particularly toward the end of cooking, and add more milk if it gets very thick. When ready, all the milk should be absorbed so the rice is creamy but still falls very easily from the spoon. Stir in the sugar, adding more to your taste.

While the rice is cooking, grate the zest from the oranges and stir it into the rice. With a serrated knife, cut out orange segments, setting them aside to garnish the finished pudding.

For the orange sauce, drain the juice from the segments into a small pan and add the measured orange juice and marmalade. Heat gently, stirring, until the marmalade is melted. Remove from the heat, stir in the Grand Marnier, if using, and leave the sauce to cool.

Make the caramel. Heat the sugar and water in a small heavy pan over high heat until the sugar dissolves. Add a squeeze of lemon juice (this helps prevent the syrup from crystallizing) and bring it to a boil. Boil it steadily without stirring until it starts to color. Lower the heat and continue cooking the syrup to a dark caramel—it will color quickly. Remove it from the heat, let the bubbles subside for 5 to 10 seconds, and then pour the caramel into the mold, turning so the bottom and sides are coated. (Beware, as it is very hot.) Leave the caramel to set.

Heat the oven to 350°F/175°C. Heat a roasting pan half full of water on the stove as a bain-marie. When the rice is cooked, take it from the heat and remove the vanilla bean (it can be washed to use again). Let the rice cool to tepid.

Whisk the eggs in a small bowl until mixed and stir them into the rice. Pour the rice into the caramel-lined mold and set it in the bain-marie. Bring the water back to a boil on top of the stove and transfer it to the oven. Bake the pudding until it is just set in the center, 30 to 35 minutes. Take it from the bain-marie and let it cool. Cover and chill it up to 2 days.

To finish, run a knife around the edge of the pudding and turn it out onto a deep plate. Arrange the plumpest orange segments in a flower pattern on top of the pudding. Add the remaining segments to the sauce and spoon it around the edge. Serve the pudding at room temperature.

Julia Child has been to Château du Feÿ several times. In this interna-

tional age, it always comes to me as a surprise that someone so legendary in her home country should be virtually unknown outside. In the United States, Julia has only to walk into the street to be saluted by smiling fans, but in Europe she is unrecognized. Such is the power of television. Julia first came to dinner when we were neighbors in Cambridge, Massachusetts, and I can remember the occasion exactly. Nine months pregnant with Emma, I was unable to beat the egg whites for a soufflé and felt overwhelmed. With her gift for being instantly at home, Julia walked in, remarked, "My, that looks good!" and cut herself a slice of pâté. Thus began a long and lively friendship founded on a passion for good food. I collect Julia quotes, like her tart comment when we were hurriedly autographing our cookbooks one day: "It's no good signing, dear, if no one can read your name!" Just last year at dinner at The Greenbrier in West Virginia, Julia surveyed the menu and to everyone's surprise chose the low-fat steamed fish. There was a pause . . . "and with it I will have some hollandaise," she said.

It turns out that Julia is two years and one day younger than my mother, so her birthday is always remembered in the family. Emma cooked for it one year when Julia was with us—roast duck, salad from the garden, and chocolate ice cream cake. Opposite is Julia's own recipe for chocolate gâteau.

Julia's Gâteau Victoire

This wonderfully rich cake is one of Julia's big-time hits and we've lost no time in adopting it—with her permission—here in Burgundy. In black currant season, I flavor the cake with Madame Milbert's Cassis Liqueur (page 68) instead of rum, serving it with whipped cream. Candied Rose Petals (page 236) form a romantic decoration, or the cake can be simply sprinkled with confectioners' sugar. This is a big cake, needing a 10-inch/25-cm or larger pan holding 2½ quarts/2.5 liters, and it must be watertight as the cake is baked in a bain-marie. You can still hear Julia talking in every line of the recipe, though some of the phraseology here is mine. In her words, the gâteau serves "ten or more."

> *1 tablespoon instant coffee*
> *¼ cup/60 ml hot water*
> *¼ cup/60 ml rum*
> *14 oz/440 g semisweet chocolate*
> *2 oz/60 g unsweetened chocolate*
> *6 eggs*
> *½ cup/100 g sugar*
> *1 cup/250 ml heavy cream*
> *1 tablespoon vanilla extract*
> *confectioners' sugar or whipped cream to finish*
>
> *a 10-inch/25-cm deep cake pan*

Heat the oven to 350°F/175°C and set the oven shelf near the bottom of the oven. Butter the cake pan, line the base with a round of wax or parchment paper, and butter the paper. Sprinkle the pan with flour, discarding the excess. Bring a roasting pan half full of water to a boil on top of the stove. In a medium saucepan, dissolve the coffee into the hot water, and then add the rum and both kinds of chocolate. Cover the pan tightly, set it in the roasting pan, and turn off the heat. Leave the chocolate to melt. (The cover prevents steam from contaminating the chocolate and making it "seize.")

Meanwhile, put the eggs and sugar in the bowl from your electric mixer, or any large bowl if you are beating by hand. Set the bowl over a pan of steaming water and stir the mixture by hand for several minutes until frothy and it feels warm to your fingers. Take it from the heat and beat vigorously, preferably with an electric mixer, until the mixture has tripled in volume and forms a thick ribbon trail when the whisk is lifted. Set it aside.

In another bowl, beat the cream until it stiffens enough to hold a soft peak (it is best if the cream is well chilled first), then stir in the vanilla. Take the saucepan of chocolate out of the bain-marie, and reheat the bath on the stove in preparation for the cake. The chocolate will have melted; stir it until smooth. Pour the melted chocolate into the whisked eggs, folding them together as lightly as possible. When partially mixed, add the whipped cream and fold that in gently, too. Pour the batter into the cake pan—it should be about two thirds full.

Set the cake pan in the bain-marie of hot water and transfer it to the oven. Bake the cake until firm in the center and a skewer inserted in the center comes out clean, 50 to 60 minutes. Turn off the oven, prop the door ajar, and leave the cake to cool in the bain-marie for 30 minutes so it sinks evenly. Take it carefully from the oven and leave it in the bain-marie for another 30 minutes so it cools to tepid. It will sink to about its original volume as it cools. Julia says the cake is at its most tender and delicious when eaten at this moment while still slightly warm. However, it can be cooked a day or two in advance and stored in the cake pan in the refrigerator. Simply warm it in a low oven at 200°F/95°C for 20 minutes before unmolding.

To serve the cake, run a knife around the edge and unmold it, discarding the paper. Sprinkle it with confectioners' sugar or add a decoration of whipped cream and candied rose petals just before serving.

OPPOSITE: *We candied some rose petals from the garden (recipe on page 236) to scatter over this rich chocolate Gâteau Victoire.*

CHAPTER 7

La Varenne: The School and Students

With the encouragement and expert advice of three food authorities—Julia Child, Simone Beck, and James Beard—I founded L'Ecole de Cuisine La Varenne in Paris in 1975. We opened our doors on November 10 in an old building with almost as much atmosphere as Le Feÿ. There were five students and one teaching chef, and I was terrified. I discovered it is a quantum leap from cooking professionally and writing about food, as I had done, to planning a school.

Choosing the name was the least of it and even that took several months. François Pierre de la Varenne was the first cookbook writer to define classical French cooking and, by coincidence, his *Le Cuisinier François* was published just a decade later than the building of Château du Feÿ. Then there was the focus of the school to decide. I had been trained at the London Cordon Bleu under Rosemary Hume not many years after England had ended postwar food rationing so that it was once more possible to think of food without counting coupons. The style of that school was robustly domestic, with an overlay of French technique. The Paris Cordon Bleu, where I went next, transcended time. The syllabus covered exclusively the grand classics, the *blanquettes* and braises, the sauces and soufflés of Escoffier. We cooked in a basement with a single oven without a thermostat, which heated top, bottom, or both together, take your choice. On a good day, the cantankerous old chef would pinch my knee, on a bad day he simply yelled. It was excellent experience as a soufflé that rose there would rise anywhere. My mother, arbiter of progress, remarked how much my cooking had improved.

Looking back, it was when I moved to France that I grew up, escaping from a cozy, predictable world as the much-loved only child of well-to-do parents. I was raised during the war in the depths of north Yorkshire, half a mile from the nearest farmhouse, a happy, solitary childhood full of books and folklore. Even then I was excited by food; for me baking day was the big event of the week when our old cook fired up the range and baked pastry and cakes for the seven days to come. Boarding school was another, less pleasant cocoon, but it led to the intoxication of Cambridge University where I was one of two women studying economics—I was quite unsuited to the academic life but loved it all the same.

On graduating, I was advised patronizingly to take a secretarial course, such were the prospects for a woman in the business world in 1959. I was damned if I would be a secretary and turned to teaching, first dressmaking, and then cooking at the Cordon Bleu School in London, causing my lawyer father to mutter, "Waste of a good education!" Good food led naturally to Paris, and when not studying at the Cordon Bleu (unconnected, in those days, to the London school), I filled in spare time with freelance teaching and catering. For a young Englishwoman to earn money while cooking in France was unheard of, but through a risky classified ad of the "young woman gives French lessons" variety, I lined up half a dozen clients. One was socialite Florence Van der Kemp, an American who had married the curator of the Château de Versailles (his taste, her money) and lived in a wing with a pack of Mexican servants. Soon I was installed there, too, a fourth national element, breezing my way through such classics as *vol au vent financière,* which we served to the Duke and Duchess of Windsor. This recipe for shortbread, with its English name and French method of mixing, dates from my stay in Versailles. It proved an early sign of the international direction my cooking would take.

PREVIOUS PAGES: *When La Varenne cooking school first opened in the late 1970s, our chef de cuisine, Fernand Chambrette, conferred often with Julia Child. An antique scale (top left) is still in regular use, while old menus provide inspiration for the students of today. Presentation at the end of class, when students display what they have cooked, is a La Varenne tradition. The chef and I make comments, while the students do their best not to look self-conscious.* PAGE 211: Boeuf à la Mode *(recipe on page 218).* ABOVE: *Chef Chambrette in the kitchen.*

Classic Shortbread

Whenever we can we have one of these shortbread cookies for breakfast, slightly overbaked and caramelized just the way I like them. Serve them also with ice cream made with ratafia (page 75) or with puréed seasonal fruits. The recipe makes sixteen shortbreads, but they disappear quickly.

> *2 cups/250 g flour*
> *½ teaspoon salt*
> *¼ teaspoon baking powder*
> *1 cup/250 g butter*
> *½ cup/75 g confectioners' sugar*
> *granulated sugar for sprinkling (optional)*
>
> *a 2½-in/7- to 8-cm cookie cutter*

Sift together the flour, salt, and baking powder. Cream the butter by hand with a wooden spoon or using an electric mixer. Add the confectioners' sugar to the creamed butter and beat until light and soft, 2 to 3 minutes. Sift in the flour mixture and stir to form loose crumbs. Lightly flour the work surface and knead the dough with the heel of your hand, pushing it out and gathering it up with your fingers, until it peels easily from the surface and becomes as smooth and pliable as putty, 1 to 2 minutes. Shape it into a cylinder, wrap it in plastic, and chill until firm, about an hour.

Heat the oven to 350°F/175°C. Line 2 baking sheets with wax or parchment paper. Cut the dough into 16 equal pieces by first cutting the cylinder in half, then in quarters, and finally into individual pieces. Shape each piece into a ball and roll them with a rolling pin into 2½-in/7.5-cm rounds that are about ¼ in/6 mm thick. Trim the edges with the cookie cutter and set them on the baking sheet. Prick the shortbreads all over with a fork and chill them again until firm, about 15 minutes.

Bake the shortbreads for 20 to 25 minutes. They should be lightly browned around the edges and underneath but still pale in the center. It is important not to overbake them; they scorch easily. Transfer the shortbreads to a rack to cool and, if you like, sprinkle them while still warm with granulated sugar.

Fifteen years after that first immersion into French food, I moved back to Paris from the United States, now an American citizen with a husband and two little children. The 1970s were revolutionary times in the cooking world: nouvelle cuisine was just beginning to oust the stately Escoffier classics that had reigned since the start of the century. Young iconoclasts like Michel Guérard were opening their own places, launching a wave of chef-owned restaurants that added another dimension to the French restaurant scene. French cuisine was, and I stoutly maintain still is, the most complex and challenging in the western world, constantly changing and renewing itself by drawing on age-old roots.

When we opened La Varenne, I was determined to teach the full French range—the classics, the regional dishes, a little bit of history, and also those novelties such as fish pot-au-feu or warm salad of foie gras with raspberry vinegar that were taking Paris by storm. I knew what it was like to be a stranger in France, and La Varenne, we knew, would draw on foreign students. We needed to allow for national tastes, not to mention foodstuffs back home. For years I lugged American flour to Paris so that everyone could succeed in making butter puff pastry the French way. There would be a strong insistence on practical training, on putting "hand to dough," *la main à la pâte,* as the French say. We'd provide *stagiaires,* or bilingual teaching assistants, to give instant meaning to the chef's words. To my dying day I will hear a *stagiaire* obediently reiterate, "Chef says . . ."

Indeed, students came from all over—Brazil, Australia, Japan, Hong Kong, Denmark, and Britain and, of course, North America. Gregory Usher was La Varenne director at this time, an affable, discerning American who went on to found the Ritz-Escoffier School before he died quite young. Gregory dearly loved a gossip over a good meal—his knowledge of up-and-coming bistros was unrivaled—and he would scan the menu for grilled pigs' feet or head cheese, dishes that were then totally out of style. Sweetbreads were one of his favorites.

Sweetbreads with Celery Root, Olives, and Bacon

The key with sweetbreads is to cook them thoroughly, first simmering them in court bouillon to dissolve that horrid chewy membrane surrounding the meat. Garnished with celery root, olives, and bacon, these make a fine dinner for six.

1½ lb/750 g veal sweetbreads
a small celery root (about 1 lb/500 g)
juice of 1 lemon
3 tablespoons vegetable oil, more if needed
a 6-oz/175-g piece of smoked bacon, diced
1 onion, chopped
salt and pepper
1½ cups/375 ml veal or chicken stock
½ cup/100 g mild green olives, drained and pitted
2 tablespoons chopped parsley

FOR THE COURT BOUILLON
1 onion, sliced
1 carrot, sliced
a bouquet garni
1 teaspoon black peppercorns
1 cup/250 ml dry white wine
3 cups/750 ml water, more if needed

Put the sweetbreads to soak in cold water for 1 to 2 hours. Meanwhile, make the court bouillon. Combine the onion, carrot, bouquet garni, peppercorns, wine, and water in a medium saucepan, cover, and simmer for 15 to 20 minutes, skimming from time to time. Set aside.

Drain the sweetbreads from the soaking water and trim off and discard the tubes, loose membrane, and any discolored parts. Immerse the sweetbreads in the court bouillon and add more water to cover them if necessary. Cover the pan and simmer for 25 to 30 minutes, until the sweetbreads are firm and white on the outside.

Trim and peel the celery root, then cut it into ¾-inch/2-cm cubes. Toss the cubes in the lemon juice right away so they do not discolor. Heat the oil in a large frying pan and fry the bacon until the fat runs. Remove the bacon with a slotted spoon and set it aside. Pour off all but about 2 tablespoons of fat from the pan, reserving the excess for frying the sweetbreads later. Add the diced celery and onion to the pan, sprinkle with pepper, and sauté, stirring often, until the vegetables are brown, 3 to 5 minutes. Put back the bacon, add the stock, cover, and simmer until the celery is tender, 20 to 25 minutes. Remove the lid and add the olives. Continue cooking over high heat until any liquid is reduced to a shiny glaze.

When the sweetbreads are done, let them cool for 5 to 10 minutes in the court bouillon, then drain and rinse with cold water. Peel them, pulling away the skin and membrane with your fingers. I often peel so thoroughly that the sweetbreads fall apart into small pieces—not very classic, but deliciously brown when fried. Drain the sweetbreads on paper towels and cut the larger pieces into ¾-in/2-cm slices.

To finish, heat the reserved bacon fat in a large frying pan, adding more oil if needed to make about 3 tablespoons. Add the sweetbreads with a little salt and pepper. Fry them briskly, turning and stirring often, until well browned and no transparent patches remain where they were sliced, 8 to 10 minutes. If necessary, reheat the celery and bacon mixture. Add it to the sweetbreads with the parsley and mix well. Taste and adjust the seasoning before serving.

Training is literally hands-on, starting with the most basic of tasks like pitting olives and juicing citrus, then moving on to straining sauces and roasting duck (with Chef Claude Vauguet as instructor).

Ten years later, the scene had changed again. American students no longer needed to come to France to learn basic knife skills and how to make stock. Sound basic training was available back home. The graduate experience was what was needed, an immersion in the cultural aspects of food in France as well as advanced practical expertise in the kitchen. I would like to think that I had already sensed the return to tradition that has become so characteristic of the 1990s, with its bistros and emphasis on *cuisine de grand-mère*. We made courses shorter, more diverse, more demanding. A new breed of student also appeared: the culinary tourist who comes for a week or two to learn a few amusing dishes, to hobnob with the pros and enjoy some memorable meals. Many are serious cooks, technically adept in the kitchen, and a few have gone on to turn professional, the classic career changer. It was this group to which we appealed more and more.

Here's where Château du Feÿ comes in, an ideal haven for the in-depth study of French cooking, surrounded by fine restaurants and top chefs, the region a source of outstanding ingredients, all within cracking distance of Chablis, the Côte d'Or, Champagne, and the Loire, with their world-class wines.

We started La Varenne in Burgundy very small, with a few students for just a few weeks, then added more and more courses until finally in 1991 all our programs transferred to Château du Feÿ. With us came the mainstays from La Varenne in Paris, the chefs who were the core of the school. Chef Chambrette, then in his early seventies, was already an habitué of the château, padding out to the vegetable garden every morning in his tattered espadrilles to talk to Monsieur Milbert and running a racket with him on the rabbits (wine from the school cellar in exchange for rabbits and fresh eggs to take back to Paris). The bucolic (though rigorous) country routine suited the chef perfectly, with its lunches outdoors under the lime trees and a quick siesta in the tiny blue bedroom he made his own.

Chef Chambrette had always been an instinctive cook who shone when left to improvise. Countryman by birth and an avid gardener, he understood better than any of us just when the basil would be at its best or how to test a peach for ripeness. The results in the kitchen were spectacular. He would commune with the ingredients, poking the vegetables to test their freshness and looking a fish straight in the eye. When Madame Milbert delivered what, for her, was a generous bunch of thyme one morning, he pursued her, shouting, "More, I need more!" He hated to make the same dish twice, so there would always be some subtle difference of garnish or flavoring, no matter how classic the recipe.

For me his cooking was a revelation, a combination of instinct and the knowledge acquired during more than fifty years in the kitchen (like others of his generation, Chambrette apprenticed at age thirteen). His little snippets of learning brought the background of food to life. He knew, for instance, that peas should be planted near beans and carrots but never, never beside onion or garlic. A few marigolds among the vegetables discourage slugs and bugs. He proved again and again that intelligence and education are as important to cooking as to any other art. I wasn't surprised to find Chambrette is an expert on seventeenth-century Dutch painting, or that in his spare time he would frequent the Salle Drouot, the leading Paris auction house. In the early 1950s, Chef Chambrette's Paris restaurant, the Boule d'Or, earned two Michelin stars and a write-up in *Paris Cuisine* by James Beard for such dishes as *filets de sole au vermouth* and *babas au rhum,* still quintessentially French.

Chef Chambrette's skill with leftovers was legendary. On Fridays, he would fling

open the refrigerator door and drag out the anonymous little packages and bowls that had been accumulating for five days. *"Débarrassons-nous de tout ça* (let's get all that out of here)," he would cry and the resulting feast was invariably the best of the week. Himself the most inventive of cooks, he was modest about his own talent and would scoff when an aspiring student displayed some supposedly revolutionary creation. "Nothing's new," he would insist, giving hot pasta salad as a case in point. The craze for salads of pasta swept the United States a decade ago, but the idea dates back to at least the early 1800s in Alsace when a dish called *totelots* appeared in an Alsatian cookbook. Here is Chef Chambrette's version.

Hot Pasta Salad
Totelots

Chef Chambrette delighted in assigning fresh pasta to self-important students, giving him ample opportunity to take them down a peg or two. He would shout at them when, inevitably, they got in the way as they stretched long ribbons of dough across the room, then lugged cauldrons of water for boiling, and finally had to sweep the flour-strewn floor. He would never have countenanced the quick method that I use here, where the dough is both kneaded and rolled with the pasta machine. If you use fresh noodles from the store, you'll have supper for six on the table in even less time— under 20 minutes.

> *1 recipe pasta dough (page 297)*
> *4 eggs for garnish*
>
> **FOR THE DRESSING**
> *¼ cup/60 ml white wine vinegar*
> *3 shallots, finely chopped*
> *a medium bunch (1½ oz/45 g) of parsley, finely chopped*
> *2 garlic cloves, finely chopped*
> *salt and pepper*
> *⅔ cup/150 ml vegetable oil*
> *½ cup/125 ml sour cream, or more to taste*
>
> *pasta machine*

Make the pasta dough and roll it as thinly as possible. Spread the fresh sheets of pasta onto a lightly floured work surface, and using a sharp knife, cut the sheets into long, 1½-in/4-cm-wide strips. Spread the strips on floured trays to dry for ½ to 1 hour. Repeat with the remaining pasta dough.

Meanwhile, bring the eggs to a boil in water, simmer them for 10 minutes, and transfer them to cold water to cool. Once cool, peel them, and cut into slices or quarters.

For the dressing, whisk the vinegar in a small bowl with the shallots, parsley, garlic, salt, and pepper. Gradually whisk in the oil so that the dressing emulsifies and thickens slightly. Whisk in the sour cream, taste, and adjust the seasoning. Transfer the dressing to a large bowl.

Just before serving, bring a large pan of salted water to a boil. Add the pasta and simmer for 2 to 3 minutes, or until it is tender but still firm—al dente—when you taste a piece. Drain the pasta and rinse quickly with hot water. Add it to the dressing, toss until thoroughly mixed, and taste again, adding more sour cream, salt, or pepper as needed. Pile the salad in a serving bowl, arrange the eggs on top, and serve it while still warm.

Quarters of hard-boiled egg top a traditional Hot Pasta Salad from Alsace. In back is an antique rolling pin—heavy and cold, glass is an ideal material for rolling dough.

Braised Beef in Aspic
Boeuf à la Mode

This time-honored local dish is greeted with cries of acclaim by our Burgundian neighbors, who nowadays rarely see what is essentially a homemade specialty. *Boeuf à la mode* can be served hot simply as a stew, but when cold and layered with its vegetables as a colorful terrine, the beef is spectacular—an ideal party dish to prepare ahead and enough to serve fourteen to sixteen guests. At first sight, the recipe closely resembles Traditional Beef Bourguignon (page 26), a slow braise in red wine with vegetables, but the results are quite different. Here, a pig's foot and veal bones contribute gelatin to the cooking juices that then set to an unclarified aspic used to hold the beef and vegetables in place. A firm, muscular cut, such as eye of round or bottom round, is best. Serve it completely plain, or with bowls of gherkin pickles, pickled onions, and olives.

> *a 4½-lb/2-kg beef pot roast, tied*
> *1 pig's foot, split*
> *2 lb/1 kg veal bones, cracked*
> *2 tablespoons vegetable oil*
> *1½ qt/1.5 liters brown veal or beef stock, more if needed*
> *1 tablespoon tomato purée*
> *4 tablespoons/30 g gelatin*
> *salt and pepper*
> *⅔ cup/150 ml Madeira or port*
> *a bunch of watercress for decoration*
>
> **FOR THE MARINADE**
> *3 onions, quartered and stuck with 3 cloves*
> *3 carrots, quartered*
> *3 celery stalks, cut in sticks*
> *1 garlic clove, peeled*
> *a large bouquet garni*
> *½ teaspoon peppercorns*
> *1 bottle (750 ml) red wine*
> *1 tablespoon vegetable oil*
>
> **FOR THE VEGETABLES**
> *1½ lb/750 g medium carrots*
> *2 cups/500 ml brown veal or beef stock*
> *1½ lb/750 g baby turnips*
> *1 lb/500 g green beans, trimmed*
>
> *a large piece of cheesecloth*
> *two 2-qt/2-liter loaf pans*

To marinate the beef, put the beef in a deep nonreactive bowl and add the onions, carrots, celery, garlic, bouquet garni, and peppercorns around it. Pour in the wine and spoon the oil over the meat so it does not dry out. Cover the bowl and store in the refrigerator for 12 to 24 hours.

When you are ready to braise the meat, blanch the pig's foot and veal bones by putting them in a large pan of cold water and bringing them slowly to a boil, skimming occasionally. Simmer them for 5 minutes, drain, and rinse them. Tie the pig's foot in cheesecloth. Remove the beef from the marinade and dry it on paper towels. Strain the marinade, reserving the vegetables and liquid separately. Heat the oven to 325°F/160°C.

Heat the oil in a large flameproof casserole or Dutch oven and brown the beef on all sides, coloring it well. Remove the meat, add the vegetables from the marinade, and brown them thoroughly also. Add the marinade liquid and the bouquet garni, bring it to a boil, and simmer for 5 minutes. Stir in the stock and the tomato purée. Replace the beef and add the pig's foot and veal bones, pushing them well down into the liquid—the casserole should be nearly full so that the meat stays moist during cooking. Cover the casserole and transfer it to the oven to cook until the meat is very tender when pierced with a skewer, 3 to 3½ hours. Turn the meat occasionally as it braises and add more stock if the pan seems dry.

Let the meat cool to tepid in the pot, then remove it and strain the cooking liquid, reserving the pig's foot. There should be about 2 quarts/2 liters of liquid. Add more stock if necessary or, if there is too much liquid, boil to reduce it. Meanwhile, sprinkle the gelatin over the Madeira or port in a small saucepan and leave it about 5 minutes until spongy. Then melt it over low heat and stir it into the stock to make unclarified aspic. Chill the aspic for several hours so that the fat solidifies on the surface.

Meanwhile, remove the strings from the meat, trim any dry surfaces, and pull the meat into shreds. Pull the meat and skin from the pig's foot (save the bones as they will help in a stockpot), and coarsely chop both the meat and the skin. Mix the shredded beef with the chopped pig's foot and set them aside to cool.

To cook the vegetables, peel and cut the carrots lengthwise into long ⅛-inch-/3-mm-thick slices, preferably using a mandoline. Put them in a shallow pan with half the stock and a little salt and pepper. Press a piece of parchment paper on top of the carrots and simmer until very tender, 15 to 20 minutes. Drain them, reserving the stock, and let them cool. Peel the turnips, cut them into thin wedges, and cook them like the carrots—they will take about the same time. Drain and reserve the stock. Trim the green beans and cook them, uncovered, in a large pan of boiling salted water until just tender, 10 to 15 minutes (if the beans are left too crisp, they are hard to slice when molded with the beef). Drain them, refresh with cold water, and drain them thoroughly.

To mold the beef in aspic, if the meat has been chilled let it come to room temperature, as it will have set. Skim all the fat from the aspic—it will be firmly set. Reheat it and add the reserved stock from cooking the carrots and turnips. Taste the aspic and adjust the seasoning with salt and pepper, remembering that the flavor will be milder when served cold. Pour a ⅜-inch-/1-cm-thick layer of aspic into the 2 loaf pans, set the pans in a pan of ice water, and chill until set. Layer the carrot slices in the pans on top of the aspic, overlapping them lengthwise, and add just enough aspic to cover the carrots. Chill again in ice water until set. Add a layer of green beans, arranging them lengthwise, top them with aspic, and chill. Add the turnip wedges in a layer, top with more aspic, and chill again until set.

Spread the meat in an even layer on top of the turnips.

Cover it with aspic, making sure all air is expelled. (The meat forms a firm bottom layer for the molds when they are turned out.) The loaf pans should be almost full and the meat must be completely immersed in aspic so it sits level on the board when turned out. Cover the molds and chill until firmly set, at least 6 hours and up to 2 days.

To serve, dip the loaf pans in warm water for 5 to 10 seconds to loosen the aspic, run a knife around the edge, and turn the molds onto a chopping board. Holding a wide spatula upright to support the first slice, cut the molds in thick slices using a very sharp knife. (I have to admit a bit reluctantly that an electric knife does well here.) Arrange the slices on a platter or on individual plates and decorate with watercress sprigs. Be assured that the sight of this dish will reward all your hard work!

ABOVE: *At Le Feÿ, Chef Chambrette taught us the real* boeuf à la mode, *with its three-day cycle of marinating; simmering with red wine, vegetables, and flavorings; then final molding in its own aspic with colorful layers of meat and vegetables.*

The second La Varenne chef to join us at Château du Feÿ was Claude Vauguet,

who had been "formed," as the French say, by his apprenticeship under Chef Chambrette. Far from being a shadow of his mentor, Chef Claude brought a contemporary lightness to the kitchen with Asian flavorings and plenty of color on the plate. Our trainees have always loved sunny-tempered Claude, who took all in his stride, declaring, *"Ça brûle normalement (it's burning normally)."* His patience with dull and/or lazy students was exemplary, in contrast to Chef Chambrette, who never suffered fools gladly. Chambrette would sum up new recruits within the day and parcel out the interesting jobs accordingly; weaker souls were ignored. Chef Claude came from the Loire, home of pears, pike, goat cheese, and good cooks.

Roast Pike with Piquant Herb Butter

Eric, our Joigny computer geek, asked me the other day for a recipe for pike-perch (*sandre*), which, with its cousin pike, is indigenous to the Yonne. Eric is a fisherman—he had just caught a 4-lb/1.8-kg pike—but only an innocent would suppose that the fish we see now in the local market are Burgundian. Most, I am told, come from eastern Europe—as do a lot of good things including snails and foie gras. I was delighted to pass on this recipe of Chef Claude's, which serves four to six and can be made with almost any four- to five-pound (about two kilos) whole fish.

> *a whole pike (about 4 lb/1.8 kg) with head and fins,*
>   *scaled, and cleaned*
> *2 to 3 thyme sprigs*
> *2 to 3 oregano or marjoram sprigs*
> *2 tablespoons olive oil, more for basting*
> *salt and pepper*
> *2 lemons cut into wedges, for serving*
>
> **FOR THE PIQUANT HERB BUTTER**
>
> *a medium bunch (½ oz/15 g) of watercress*
> *a medium handful (½ oz/15 g) of spinach leaves*
> *a medium bunch (½ oz/15 g) of parsley*
> *a medium bunch (½ oz/15 g) of chervil or chives*
> *3 anchovy fillets, soaked in milk*
> *1 medium gherkin pickle*
> *1 tablespoon capers, drained*
> *1 garlic clove, peeled*
> *6 tablespoons/90 g butter, softened*
> *¼ cup/60 ml olive oil*
> *2 teaspoons Dijon-style mustard*
> *squeeze of lemon juice*

Heat the oven to 375°F/190°C. Wash the pike inside and out and dry it on paper towels. Cut 2 or 3 diagonal slashes in both sides of the fish so the oven heat can penetrate and cook the fish more evenly. Tuck an herb sprig into each slash. Trim the tail into a neat V shape. Set the fish in an oiled baking dish or roasting pan and sprinkle it with olive oil, salt, and pepper. (If your dish seems small, stand the fish on its belly and curve it to fit—it will look as though it's swimming.)

Roast the fish, brushing regularly with more olive oil, until the skin is brown and crisp, 30 to 40 minutes. The fish eye will have turned white and the flesh should no longer be transparent; check it by flaking a bit from the backbone with a fork.

Meanwhile, make the herb butter. Bring a large saucepan of water to a boil. Discard the stems from the watercress and spinach and the large stalks from the parsley and chervil. Add the herbs to the boiling water and blanch them by simmering for 2 minutes. Drain, rinse with cold water, and pat them dry on paper towels. Drain the anchovies and work them in a food processor with the pickle, capers, and garlic until finely chopped. Gradually add the butter, puréeing it until smooth. Add the herbs and work until they are also finely chopped. With the blades turning, slowly pour in the olive oil. The herb butter will be creamy and a lovely shade of green. Add the mustard and season the butter to taste with lemon juice, salt, and pepper.

To finish, transfer the whole fish to a warm platter and decorate it with lemon wedges. Serve the herb butter in a separate bowl.

OPPOSITE: *From the start, plants have burgeoned in our herb garden, offering plenty of choice for a piquant herb butter for roast pike-perch (below). Giving an S shape to roast fish not only adds an appealing twist, but makes it fit more easily in the pan.*

I rapidly discovered that in at least one area, Chef Claude outshone Chef Chambrette—styling for food photographs. Claude seemed to have an instinctive knowledge of how dishes would appear on camera, of just how far to brown the skin of the chicken or how best to arrange the background bunch of watercress so it had no black holes, the bane of food on film. By no means does every recipe make a good portrait. For impact, a recipe should rise tall to be shot at an angle like the soufflé on page 232 ("a mountain," one photographer calls it), or should spread out attractively like a landscape, to be taken from above. Chambrette's Braised Beef in Aspic (page 218) is a good example. Ideally a dish holds up to changes in temperature and the jostling involved in arranging the background just right. As you can imagine, gelatin molds (which collapse), mayonnaise (which discolors), and soufflés (which shrivel) are the food stylist's dread, but Claude would take them all cheerfully in his stride.

Twice-Baked Spinach Soufflés

I have a mental short list of recipes labeled "Best of the Best" and this is one of them. The soufflés are prepared well ahead so that the only last-minute action is to bake them in the oven, where they puff, infallibly, to flamboyant size. Lacking the necessary individual dishes, you can bake these soufflés in muffin cups and then brown them in sauce for serving in one large baking dish. This makes six appetizer-size soufflés.

> *1 lb/500 g spinach*
> *⅓ cup/75 g butter*
> *1 onion, finely chopped*
> *salt and pepper*
> *¼ cup/30 g flour*
> *1½ cups/375 ml milk*
> *pinch of grated nutmeg*
> *1½ cups/375 ml light cream*
> *5 egg yolks*
> *6 egg whites*
> *½ cup/50 g grated Gruyère cheese*
>
> *six 1-cup/250-ml ramekins*
> *six 6-in/15-cm gratin dishes*

Pull the stems from the spinach and wash the leaves in several changes of water. Pack the wet leaves in a large saucepan, cover it, and wilt the leaves over medium heat, stirring occasionally, 5 to 7 minutes. Drain the spinach and let it cool. Squeeze handfuls of spinach in your fists to extract the water, and then chop it. Melt 1 tablespoon of the butter in the saucepan, add the onion, and sauté over medium heat until it is soft but not brown, 3 to 5 minutes. Stir in the spinach with salt and pepper and

continue cooking, stirring, until it is quite dry, 2 to 3 minutes. Set it aside.

To make a white sauce, melt the remaining butter in a saucepan, whisk in the flour, and cook until foaming but not browned, about 1 minute. Whisk in the milk, nutmeg, salt, and pepper and bring to a boil, stirring constantly until the sauce thickens. Simmer it for 2 minutes and then take it off the heat. Transfer about a third of the white sauce into a small saucepan and pour the cream on top so it coats the sauce and prevents a skin from forming. Set it aside.

Generously butter the ramekins and chill them. Stir the spinach into the remaining sauce and heat until very hot. Remove the mixture from the heat, taste, and adjust the seasoning; it should be well seasoned to make up for the bland egg whites. Beat in the egg yolks a bit at a time so they cook in the heat of the sauce and thicken it slightly. Cover the saucepan with plastic wrap to prevent a skin from forming on the spinach mixture.

Heat the oven to 350°F/175°C. Bring a roasting pan of water to a boil on the stove for a bain-marie. Beat the egg whites until stiff, adding a pinch of salt to help stiffen them. Warm the spinach mixture gently until the pan is hot to the touch. Add about a quarter of the beaten egg whites and stir until well mixed. The heat of the sauce will cook the whites slightly. Add this mixture to the remaining whites and fold them together as lightly as possible.

Fill the ramekins with the mixture, smoothing the tops with a metal spatula. Run a thumb around the edge of each dish to detach the mixture so the soufflé rises straight. Set the ramekins in the bain-marie, bring it back to a boil on the stove, and transfer it to the oven. Bake until the soufflés are puffed, browned, and just set in the center, 20 to 25 minutes. They should rise well

When unmolded and rebaked, spinach soufflés, shown here in front of a seventeenth-century engraving, will puff a second time and proudly hold their shape.

above the rim of the dish. Take the ramekins from the bain-marie and leave them to cool—the soufflés will shrink back into the ramekins, pulling away slightly from the sides.

Turn each soufflé out into a gratin dish. Whisk the cream with the reserved sauce until smooth and bring it just to a boil. Season it to taste with salt, pepper, and nutmeg, and pour on top of the soufflés, letting it pool around the sides. Sprinkle them with the cheese. The soufflés can be kept, covered with plastic wrap, for up to 24 hours in the refrigerator.

To finish, heat the oven to 425°F/220°C. Bake the soufflés until browned, slightly puffed, and the sauce is bubbling, 7 to 10 minutes. Serve them at once.

Twice-baked savory spinach soufflé was such a success that I made several unsuccessful attempts to develop a sweet version, only to be foiled by the deflating effects of sugar. Then British food stylist Jane Suthering supplied the key. "Use cornstarch as a thickener instead of flour," she advises.

Twice-Baked Vanilla Soufflé with Espresso Sauce

For a tipsy soufflé, substitute two tablespoons Cognac for the coffee granules. This makes six soufflés.

> *²/₃ cup/150 ml milk*
> *a vanilla bean, split*
> *¹/₃ cup/60 g sugar, more for the ramekins*
> *4 eggs, separated*
> *3 tablespoons/22 g cornstarch*
> *pinch of salt*
>
> **FOR THE ESPRESSO SAUCE**
> *1 ¹/₂ cups/375 ml light cream*
> *1 ¹/₂ tablespoons espresso coffee granules*
>
> *six ³/₄-cup/175-ml ramekins*
> *six 6-in/15-cm gratin dishes*

Generously butter the ramekins and sprinkle them with sugar; turn and shake them until they are evenly coated and discard the excess sugar. Bring the milk almost to a boil with the vanilla bean, cover the pan, and leave to infuse off the heat for about 10 minutes.

Whisk half the sugar with the egg yolks in a bowl until thick and light, about 1 minute. Stir in the cornstarch and salt, then the hot milk. Return this pastry cream mixture to the pan and bring it to a boil, whisking constantly, until it boils and thickens. Take it off the heat and remove the vanilla bean (you can rinse and dry it to use again). Press a piece of plastic wrap on the pastry cream to prevent a skin from forming and set it aside.

Heat the oven to 350°F/175°C. Bring a roasting pan of water to a boil on the stove for a bain-marie. Beat the egg whites until stiff, add the remaining sugar, and continue beating until the whites are glossy and form a long peak when the whisk is lifted, about 1 minute. Stir about a quarter of the whites into the warm vanilla pastry cream to lighten it. Tip this mixture back into the remaining whites and fold together lightly.

Fill the ramekins with the mixture, smoothing the tops with a metal spatula. Run your thumb around the edge of each dish to detach the mixture so the soufflé rises straight. Set the ramekins in the bain-marie, bring it back to a boil on top of the stove, and transfer to the oven. Bake until the soufflés are puffed, browned, and just set in the center, 20 to 25 minutes. They should rise well above the rim of the dish. Take the ramekins from the bain-marie and leave them to cool—the soufflés will shrink back into the dishes.

Make the espresso sauce. Heat the cream with the coffee granules until dissolved, then bring just to a boil. Set aside. Turn the soufflés into the gratin dishes and pour over the sauce so they and the base of the dishes are completely coated. They can be kept, covered with plastic wrap, for up to 24 hours in the refrigerator.

To finish, heat the oven to 425°F/220°C. Bake the soufflés until slightly browned, puffed, and the sauce is bubbling, 7 to 10 minutes. Serve at once, with the dishes set on cold plates to make handling easy.

ABOVE: *Chef Bouvier demonstrates how to whisk egg whites to exemplary stiffness in a copper bowl.*

Many students have remained with us for a year or two, first as trainees, then as staff members. Chef Randall Price first turned up at La Varenne after winning a competition in *Chocolatier* magazine. Five weeks was not enough and he stayed on to test recipes and help me with a couple of cookbooks. Since then Randall has cooked for the American ambassador in Hungary (it was still under communist control and he was detained with his knives on suspicion at the border), and has hosted a series for the television travel channel, as well as being chef in an American-style café near the Eiffel Tower. Randall is accident-prone: it is invariably Randall whose computer eats up his recipes and Randall whose airplane is mysteriously diverted to Dakar. A few years ago his picturesque Paris walkup took fire and he escaped suffocation only by immersing himself in the bath. A gifted, ingenious pastry cook, Randall loves to experiment and was exploring biscotti long before the current craze.

Randall's Biscotti

Randall rings many changes on these biscotti, adding different spices and substituting toasted hazelnuts, even walnuts, for the almonds. Amounts are generous and one batch makes about 50 cookies, but by their nature (*biscotti* means "twice cooked") they are designed to keep well.

> *1 cup/175 g whole blanched almonds*
> *4 cups/500 g flour, more if needed*
> *2 teaspoons freshly ground black pepper*
> *1 teaspoon ground aniseed*
> *1 teaspoon baking powder*
> *½ teaspoon salt*
> *2 cups/400 g sugar*
> *3 eggs*
> *2 egg yolks*
> *grated zest of 1 orange*
> *1 teaspoon vanilla extract*
> *½ teaspoon almond extract*
> *¾ cup/175 g butter*
> *3 oz/90 g bittersweet chocolate, very coarsely chopped*

To brown the almonds, heat the oven to 350°F/175°C. Spread the almonds on a baking sheet and toast them in the oven, stirring occasionally, until lightly browned, 12 to 15 minutes. Let them cool.

Sift the flour with the black pepper, aniseed, baking powder, and salt onto a work surface and make a large well in the center. Put the sugar, eggs, egg yolks, orange zest, vanilla, and almond extract in the center. Set the butter between 2 sheets of wax or parchment paper and pound it with a rolling pin to soften it. Add it also to the well.

With the fingertips of one hand, work the ingredients in the well until evenly mixed and smooth. Using a pastry scraper, gradually draw in the flour, working with your whole hand to form a smooth, slightly sticky dough. If it is very soft and sticky, work in a little more flour. Knead the dough, pushing it away with the heel of your hand and gathering it up with your fingers, until it is very smooth and peels easily from the surface, 2 to 3 minutes.

Pat the dough to a rough, flat rectangle, sprinkle it with the toasted almonds and chocolate, roll it up, and knead lightly to distribute the nuts and chocolate evenly. Don't worry if some bits of chocolate and nuts remain on the surface of the dough; it should be rough looking. Divide the dough into 3 portions. Lightly flour the work surface and shape each piece of dough into a log about 1½ in/4 cm in diameter and 16 in/40 cm long. Work quickly as the dough is quite soft and sticky. Transfer the logs to a baking sheet, cover loosely with plastic wrap, and chill them overnight.

For the first baking, heat the oven to 350°F/175°C. Unwrap the logs and bake them until lightly browned and firm on the outside but still soft, almost cakelike, in the center, 35 to 45 minutes. Let them cool and lower the oven temperature to 325°F/160°C.

When cool, cut the logs on the diagonal into ½-inch/1.25-cm slices (the end trimmings are the cook's reward). Space the biscotti out on a baking sheet so they can dry, leaving them upright. Rebake them until they are dry and lightly browned on the cut surfaces, 20 to 25 minutes. Let the biscotti cool on a rack and store in an airtight container.

Soon after La Varenne opened, I started to write books centered on the school. Even when I've been cooking a dish for years, it can be surprisingly hard to get a recipe down accurately on paper for a novice to follow. To explain succinctly when a roast chicken is done, for instance, or how to shape a loaf of bread is tricky. Cooking is a practical skill, seen with the eyes and felt with the hands, which is one reason I have always insisted on the importance of hands-on teaching classes. One aspect of cooking where chefs falter is in testing recipes. Chefs take techniques for granted and follow their own notions, not what is written down. If I do the testing, that is no good either—I know what I want and tend to read between the lines actually written on the page. So what's needed is an eager amateur like Linda from Los Angeles who had been in the film business. Linda cooked tirelessly for two months through the heat of summer and then came one day to say, "I'm sorry, I've had a great time, I've learned so much, but cooking is not for me. I have to go home." We get many career changers at La Varenne and the heat and turmoil of the kitchen is not for everyone. Linda left a legacy of good dishes, and this Shrimp Pistou is one of them.

Shrimp Pistou

This shellfish version of the classic Provençal vegetable soup, pistou, is rich with basil pesto and substantial enough to be a main course for six people.

> ¾ lb/375 g medium shrimps in their shells
> 1½ quarts fish or shellfish stock
> 1 long thin baguette (ficelle), for croûtes
> 1 tablespoon olive oil, more for croûtes
> 2 medium carrots, cut in small dice
> 2 shallots, chopped
> 1 garlic clove, crushed
> salt and pepper
> 1 tablespoon tomato paste
> 2 oz/60 g angel hair pasta
> 2 medium zucchini, cut in small dice
> 1 tomato, peeled, seeded, and diced
> grated Parmesan cheese, for serving
>
> FOR THE PESTO
> 3 tablespoons pine nuts
> a large bunch of fresh basil
> 3 garlic cloves, peeled
> 1 cup/250 ml olive oil

Peel the shrimps, devein them, and set them aside, reserving the shells. Make the fish stock (page 299) using olive oil. If the stock is already made, simply simmer the shrimp shells in it for 8 to 10 minutes for flavor. Strain the stock and set it aside.

Meanwhile, make the pesto. Toast the pine nuts in a small frying pan over low heat, stirring often until they are brown, 2 to 3 minutes. Pull the leaves from the basil stems (add the stems to the fish stock during simmering) and put the leaves in a food processor with the pine nuts and garlic. Purée with 1 to 2 tablespoons of the olive oil until smooth. With the blades turning, gradually add the remaining oil, starting slowly at first so the sauce emulsifies and thickens. Season the pesto with salt and pepper to taste and set aside.

Make the croûtes. Heat the oven to 350°F/175°C. Cut the baguette into ½-in/1.25-cm slices and set them on a baking sheet. Brush both sides with olive oil, then bake them until dry and lightly browned, 12 to 15 minutes. Spread them with a little pesto and continue baking for 4 or 5 minutes.

Meanwhile, make the pistou. Heat the tablespoon of olive oil in a soup pot, add the carrots, and sauté gently for 2 to 3 minutes. Stir in the shallots and garlic with salt and pepper, and cook over very low heat until the vegetables are tender, 7 to 10 minutes. Stir in the tomato paste, then the fish stock, and bring the soup to a boil. Stir in the shrimps, angel hair pasta, zucchini, and tomato and simmer until the shrimps and pasta are just tender, 2 to 3 minutes. Stir in a tablespoon of pesto and a sprinkling of Parmesan cheese, taste, and adjust the seasoning. Serve the soup at once so the flavor is fresh and vivid, passing the remaining pesto, Parmesan cheese, and croûtes separately.

We used to wonder what careers our students would choose, but we soon found out. Only a few have followed the traditional restaurant route of sous-chef followed by chef and, finally perhaps, restaurant owner. Many have combined their cooking experience with writing, so that there is now scarcely a food magazine in the United States that does not have a La Varenne graduate on the masthead. I like to think they pursue my insistence on accuracy with a leavening of lighter comment. Cooking careers have blossomed in the past decade, particularly for women, with openings in food styling, recipe development, catering, culinary newsletters, promotion, and most recently, on the Internet, to name a few. The La Varenne culinary training, with its emphasis on history, cultural background, and the importance of writing skills, helps students to escape from behind the stove into a wider world.

A recent group of graduates, instructed by Chef Patrick Gautier, pauses to record their achievement on the château steps.

Alex Bird was another colorful character with a flowing mane of gray hair that was straight from the Asian steppes—his family was of Armenian origin. Chef Alex was a loner, prowling the property at dawn and exchanging gossip with Monsieur Milbert, the other early riser. Alex therefore had a head start on garden produce, unveiling little surprises like vegetable gratin in herb pesto long before I knew the components were ready.

Gratin of Summer Vegetables in Herb Pesto

We can make this recipe all summer long with vegetables from the market but then, in early September, arrives the magic moment when every ingredient comes from our own garden. Basil is the traditional choice for the pesto (from the Italian *pestare*, to pound, as it was traditionally made by crushing the ingredients in a mortar with a pestle), but other aromatic herbs such as flat-leaf parsley or cilantro are just as good; mint is my particular favorite—an underestimated herb, I think. The vegetables serve four to six as a first course or as an accompaniment to lamb, chicken, or fish.

> *2 medium zucchini (about ¾ lb/375 g)*
> *2 medium yellow or scallop squash (about ¾ lb/ 375 g)*
> *1 lb/500 g tomatoes*
> *3 onions, thinly sliced*
> *salt and pepper*
>
> FOR THE PESTO
> *a large bunch (about 1½ oz/45 g) of basil, flat-leaf parsley, cilantro, or mint*
> *3 garlic cloves, peeled*
> *⅓ cup/30 g grated Parmesan cheese*
> *2 tablespoons pine nuts*
> *¾ cup/175 ml olive oil*
>
> *an 8 x 11-in/20 x 28-cm gratin or baking dish*

Heat the oven to 350F°/175C°. Wipe the zucchini and squash with damp paper towels and cut them into uneven ¾-in/2-cm chunks. Toss them into a large bowl. Core the tomatoes, cut them into chunks, and add them to the zucchini and squash with the onions, salt, and pepper. Brush the gratin dish with olive oil.

Make the pesto. Tear the herb leaves from the stems, discarding the stems, and, if you like, reserve some

sprigs for decoration. Purée the herb leaves, garlic, cheese, and pine nuts in a food processor with 2 to 3 tablespoons of the olive oil. Gradually add the remaining oil with the blades turning so that the sauce emulsifies. It should be a rather loose consistency, thinner than mayonnaise but thicker than salad dressing. Season it to taste with salt and pepper.

Add the pesto to the vegetables and toss so they are well coated with sauce. Spread them in the baking dish and bake until they are very tender and brown, 40 to 50 minutes. Decorate the vegetables with herb sprigs if you like, and serve the gratin hot or at room temperature.

ABOVE: *This herb-pesto gratin lends itself to all manner of vegetables, including the roots and squash of autumn.* OPPOSITE: *With a quick flick of his fingers, Jean-Michel Bouvier, chef/owner of L'Essentiel restaurant, salts the mushrooms for his ravioli.*

Alex's Dressing for Cold Meats

As kitchen director, one of Alex's responsibilities was using up leftovers and he was expert at it. This little sauce of his has given new life to many a slice of roast meat or poultry.

In a small bowl, whisk together ⅓ cup/75 ml balsamic vinegar, 3 chopped garlic cloves, 3 chopped shallots, salt, and pepper. Gradually whisk in ¾ cup/175 ml olive oil so the dressing emulsifies and thickens slightly. Core, peel, seed, and chop 3 large tomatoes and stir them into the dressing with the shredded leaves of a small bunch of basil. This makes 2 cups/500 ml of sauce to serve 6 to 8 people.

We have also been lucky in our guest teachers. Whenever he comes to Le Feÿ, Jean-Michel Bouvier is a strong presence in the La Varenne kitchen. As a young chef not yet twenty-five, he brought a popular Paris restaurant, the Pavillon Montsouris, to prominence and then left to follow the dream of all chefs, to open his own restaurant back home, in this case in Chambéry in the foothills of the Alps. For Bouvier, as for most chefs, training starts early with apprenticeship as a cuisinier at age sixteen. Then an ambitious young chef begins the crucial pilgrimage of top restaurants as *commis,* next slot in the hierarchy. "It's tough," says Jean-Michel Bouvier. "A young cook can earn good money very young in a mediocre bistro, but the experience of working with a great chef is irreplaceable." Jean-Michel's early career took him to the kitchens of Michel Guérard, an early exponent of nouvelle cuisine, where he worked long hours on double shift, an average twelve to fourteen hours a day, five and a half days a week. Wages at this level are at the legal minimum, the only consolation being there's no time to spend any money. A nucleus of good *commis* ensures the smooth running of a kitchen. Ability is rapidly recognized, so that a young cook may become sous-chef by twenty, in charge of roasting, and a year or two later move up to the coveted fish or sauce stations.

Tall, bearded, his girth increasing inexorably, Jean-Michel is a Rabelaisian figure and a prime example of the importance of vitality and physical strength in the restaurant business. He thinks nothing of leaving the restaurant at midnight after service, driving (at high speed) the four hours to Château du Feÿ, then appearing bright-eyed in the kitchen by 8:00 A.M. Generations of La Varenne *stagiaires* have completed their training in his kitchen, a trial by fire as L'Essentiel operates at full stretch on double shift seven days a week. The cuisine is a happy mix of the contemporary influence (it's mangoes and sea salt this year) with local, mountain ingredients such as reblochon cheese and omble chevalier, the unique species of salmon trout from nearby Lake Annecy. *"Le goût du terroir* (the taste of the soil), that's what matters," says Jean-Michel. Gathering wild mushrooms is one of his favorite pastimes.

Snail and Mushroom Ravioli with Parsley Sauce

A complex recipe this, but it results in some of the best ravioli I've ever tasted. If you're faint-hearted, there's a quicker alternative below. Plump, meaty escargots de Bourgogne come canned (rinse and drain them) or frozen (needing to be thawed). Serve these large ravioli as a fancy first course or as dinner for six to eight people.

48 small canned snails, rinsed and drained
½ recipe pasta dough (page 297)
¼ cup/60 g butter
1 carrot, chopped
1 onion, chopped
1 small leek, white and pale green only, chopped
salt and pepper
¼ cup/60 ml port
a bouquet garni
1 lb/500 g mushrooms, trimmed and roughly sliced
2 shallots, chopped
1 garlic clove, chopped
a few parsley sprigs for garnish

FOR THE PARSLEY SAUCE

1 tablespoon butter
2 shallots, chopped
a medium bunch (1 ½ oz/45 g) of flat-leaf parsley, chopped
3 cups/750 ml chicken stock
1 cup/250 ml crème fraîche or heavy cream

pasta machine

To cook the snails, melt half the butter in a frying pan over medium heat, add the carrot, onion, leek, salt, and pepper, and sauté until soft but not brown, 3 to 5 minutes. Stir in the snails and add the port and the bouquet garni. Cover and simmer until the snails are tender and all the port has evaporated, 10 to 12 minutes.

Meanwhile, coarsely chop the mushrooms, either by hand or in a food processor. (If using a processor, chop them a few at a time and be careful not to purée them.) Melt the remaining butter in another large frying pan over medium heat. Add the mushrooms, season with salt and pepper, and fry them until their juice runs. Stir in the shallots and garlic and continue cooking, stirring often, until all the moisture has evaporated, 5 to 7 minutes. Stir half of the mushroom mixture into the snails, taste, and adjust the seasoning—this is the filling for the ravioli. Set aside both mushroom mixtures to cool.

Make the pasta dough and roll it as thinly as possible. Spread the fresh sheets of pasta on a lightly floured work surface and cut them into 2-in/5-cm squares—there should be about 24 squares.

To assemble the ravioli, set a spoonful of the snail-mushroom mixture in the center of each square (you should have 2 snails per ravioli) and brush the edges with water. Fold over the dough to form a triangle and pinch the edges firmly together. If you like, trim the edges with a fluted ravioli wheel. Transfer the ravioli to a floured tray to dry for 1 to 2 hours.

Meanwhile, make the sauce. Melt the butter in a saucepan over medium heat and sauté the shallots until soft. Add the reserved cooked mushrooms, the parsley, stock, cream, salt, and pepper. Bring to a boil and simmer, uncovered, until reduced by about half and the flavor is concentrated, 15 to 20 minutes. Purée the sauce in a food processor and return it to the saucepan, or use a hand-held immersion blender.

To cook the ravioli, bring a large shallow saucepan of salted water to a boil and add about half the ravioli. Reduce the heat and simmer them very gently until just tender—al dente—3 to 5 minutes. If boiled too rapidly, disaster strikes and the ravioli will burst. Lift them out with a slotted spoon, drain on paper towels, and keep them warm while cooking the rest.

To serve, arrange 3 or 4 ravioli per person on warm plates or in shallow bowls. Reheat the parsley sauce, taste it for seasoning, and spoon it over the ravioli. Decorate with parsley sprigs and serve at once.

Fettuccine with Snails and Mushrooms

Substitute ¾ lb/375 g store-bought fresh fettuccine pasta for the ravioli dough in Snail and Mushroom Ravioli with Parsley Sauce (above). Cook the snail stuffing and make the sauce as for the ravioli. Cook the fettuccine in a large pan of boiling water until just tender—the timing depends on the dryness and thickness of the noodles. Drain, rinse with hot water, and pile them in 4 to 6 warm pasta bowls. Make a well in the center of the pasta and spoon in the snails. Coat with the parsley sauce and serve at once.

The preparation of Snail and Mushroom Ravioli is a lengthy process: first the wild mushrooms must be cleaned and trimmed; then the dough is mixed, kneaded, and rolled; until finally the little packages are filled with the stuffing and sealed.

In a restaurant kitchen, desserts are often a no-man's-land, some supervised by the cuisine chef, others originating in the pastry section. Jean-Michel Bouvier is a good example of a cuisine chef who also trained in pastry, the equivalent of a double major and a very different discipline. A pastry chef must be patient, meticulous, capable of turning out dozens, even hundreds of identical pastries at high speed, hour after hour. By contrast, a cuisine chef is flamboyant, adapting his dishes to the ingredients of the day. The discipline of pastry training can be invaluable in cuisine, but it is rare to find a *chef cuisinier* who makes a successful transition to pastry. Both crafts are equally creative, pastry relying much upon the eye and cuisine upon the palate. (Need I mention that the precision of pastry is not for me?) Chef Bouvier remembers the restrictions of the pastry apprenticeship, which he did first: "Even a vinaigrette was weighed out. After that, cuisine was easy for me."

Whole Tangerine Soufflé

The whole tangerine, peel, pith, and all, is simmered in orange sugar syrup to flavor this masterly soufflé, which is raised simply with a light meringue. The short list of ingredients gives a clue to its simplicity. It makes six individual soufflés.

> *1 lb/500 g tangerines*
> *2 cups/500 ml orange juice*
> *1½ cups/300 g sugar*
> *3 tablespoons Grand Marnier*
> *6 egg whites*
>
> FOR THE ORANGE STRAWBERRY SAUCE
> *1 quart/375 g strawberries*
> *1 tablespoon Grand Marnier*
> *2 to 3 tablespoons sugar*
>
> *6 ramekins (1 cup/250 ml each)*

Quarter the tangerines and discard any seeds. In a medium saucepan, heat the orange juice and two thirds of the sugar until the sugar is dissolved. Add the tangerines, cover the pan, and simmer until the tangerines are very tender, 25 to 35 minutes. Strain them, pressing gently to extract most of the juice, and set them aside. Measure ½ cup/125 ml juice and reserve the rest. Put the tangerines with the measured juice in a food processor and work for 3 to 4 minutes to form a fairly rough purée—this forms the base of the soufflé. Work in the Grand Marnier. The purée should just hold a shape without being sticky; if necessary, work in a little more juice. Return the purée to the saucepan.

For the orange strawberry sauce, hull the strawberries, washing them only if they are sandy. Purée them in a food processor with the Grand Marnier, sugar, and 2 to 3 tablespoons of the reserved tangerine juice. Taste and add more sugar if needed. Chill for serving.

For the soufflé, heat the oven to 400°F/200°C. Generously butter the ramekins, chill them for 10 minutes in the freezer, and butter them again. Set them on a baking sheet. Whip the egg whites with a tablespoon of the remaining sugar until the whites hold a stiff peak, 1 to 2 minutes in an electric mixer. Add remaining sugar and stir with a spoon until the whites are glossy and form a long peak when the spoon is lifted, about 1 minute.

Heat the tangerine purée until the edges start to bubble. Take it from the heat and add about a quarter of the whites, stirring until well mixed—the heat cooks and slightly stiffens the whites. Add this mixture to the remaining whites and fold together as lightly as possible.

To finish, transfer the soufflé mixture to the ramekins, filling them to the rim and mounding the mixture generously in the center of the dishes. (If you overdo this, the soufflés will look like volcanoes, but that can be fun, too.) Run your thumb around the edge of the mixture to detach it from the ramekin so it rises in a "hat." Bake the soufflés until puffed and brown, 12 to 15 minutes. Set the ramekins on small plates, preferably lined with a napkin or paper doily so the ramekins do not slip, and rush the soufflés at once to the table. Leave your guests to poke a hole in the center of their soufflés and pour in some cold sauce.

At the very last minute, preferably at the table, chilled orange strawberry sauce is poured into this soufflé flavored with whole tangerines.

A more recent arrival at La Varenne has been Frédéric Gauvin, a young pâtissier who at twenty-two was in charge of pastry decoration at Fauchon, one of the leading caterers in Paris. The kitchen was then headed by Pierre Hermé, top pastry chef of the new generation and Frédéric's mentor and inspiration. "I'm the SAMU (the ambulance service)," Frédéric would joke as he bounced to a grand reception in the back of a truck carrying multi-tiered, intricately decorated cakes as well as his pastry tools. "I'm prepared for emergency surgery." In a very French arrangement, Frédéric fulfilled his military service on pâtisserie duty in the officers' mess at the Ecole Militaire, then walked across the Seine to work a second evening shift at Fauchon for a total of sixteen hours a day. Today he and Pierre Hermé works in separate establishments, but Frédéric disclaims all thought of rivalry: "Pierre is my master," he says.

In his command of ingredients and flair for invention, Frédéric comes closest to Chef Chambrette, though in personality he could not be more different. He creates soaring chocolate sculptures and tiny, painstaking sugar flowers to decorate a simple chocolate mousse. Just as a challenge on a quiet day, in one eighteen-hour session in the military kitchen he built a 5-foot croquembouche tower of thousands of choux puffs filled with pastry cream and mounted with sugar caramel. *"Pourquoi tu te donnes autant de mal? (Why give yourself so much bother?)"* his superior officer asked and Frédéric dropped his eyes, unable to articulate his quest for perfection.

Frédéric's Chocolate and Candied Orange Tartlets

Like all great craftsmen, Frédéric is a master of the simple. Dark chocolate ganache is poured while still warm into these tartlets, completely covering slivers of candied orange and setting to a smooth, mirrored surface —dead plain and stunning to both eye and palate. This recipe makes eight tartlets—a special treat with afternoon tea or an indulgent chocolate lover's dessert.

FOR THE PÂTE SUCRÉE
1 ½ cups/175 g flour
½ teaspoon salt
½ cup/100 g sugar
3 egg yolks
1 teaspoon vanilla extract
7 tablespoons/100 g butter

FOR THE FILLING
4 oranges
¾ cup/150 g sugar
½ lb/250 g bittersweet chocolate, chopped
½ cup/125 ml heavy cream
6 tablespoons/90 g butter
2 tablespoons Grand Marnier

eight 3 ½-in/8-cm tartlet molds
a 4-in/10-cm cookie cutter

Make the pâte sucrée using the amounts listed above and the method outlined in the glossary (page 299). Shape it into a ball, wrap, and chill it until firm, at least 30 minutes.

While the pastry chills, prepare the filling. Strip the zest from the oranges with a vegetable peeler and cut it into the finest possible julienne strips with a large knife. Blanch the julienne by putting them in a pan of cold water, bringing them to a boil, simmering them for 5 minutes, and then draining.

The perfectionism of a master pâtissier is displayed in these chocolate tartlets, each one identical.

Squeeze the orange juice from the oranges and put it in a medium shallow saucepan with the sugar. Heat gently until the sugar dissolves, then bring the syrup to a boil and simmer for 2 minutes. Add the julienne, lower the heat, and simmer very gently without stirring until the orange zests are translucent and very tender and almost all the liquid has evaporated, 30 to 40 minutes. If the pan gets dry before they are done, add a little water. Lift out the julienne with a slotted spoon, spread them on a sheet of wax or parchment paper, and leave them to cool and dry. Strain the syrup and put 2 tablespoons aside in a small pan. (Any leftover syrup makes a fragrant base for Champagne cocktail, with a tablespoon or two of Cognac.)

Heat the oven to 375°F/190°C and butter the tartlet molds. Divide the dough into 8 equal pieces and shape each one into a ball. Roll out the balls to 4-inch/10-cm rounds and trim the edges with the cookie cutter. Line the molds with dough, pressing it well into the base. Prick the bases with a fork and chill until firm, about 15 minutes. If you have more molds, set a second mold inside each pastry shell so that the tartlets keep their shape during baking; alternatively, line the shells with foil, using dried beans or rice to weight it down. Set the molds on a baking sheet and bake the shells until set and the rims start to brown, 6 to 8 minutes. Remove the lining molds or foil and continue baking until the shells are golden brown, 5 to 7 minutes. Let them cool before removing the tartlet shells from the molds.

To assemble the tartlets, reserve about 2 tablespoons of the orange julienne for decoration, chop the rest, and spread it flat in the tartlet shells. Make the ganache filling. Put the chopped chocolate in a small bowl. Stir the cream and butter into the reserved orange syrup and heat until the butter is melted. Bring the cream mixture just to a boil, pour it over the chopped chocolate, and let it stand for 1 minute to melt the chocolate. Stir the mixture until it becomes smooth, then stir in the Grand Marnier. Pour this ganache into the tartlet shells, covering the orange zest completely and filling the shells almost to the rim. Tap them gently on the counter to level the ganache. Leave the tartlets at room temperature until set, about 30 minutes. Top the tartlets just before serving with a large pinch of the reserved candied orange zest. The tartlets are best eaten within a few hours of making and should not be refrigerated so they keep their lusciously smooth and creamy texture.

One year we had an amazing Indian summer. The vintage in Chablis was
the finest of the decade (some said of the century) and the roses bloomed and bloomed. Frédéric crystallized the petals in egg white and sugar to scatter around his chocolate tartlets.

Candied Rose Petals

Lightly whisk an egg white in a small bowl just until broken up. Brush the top side of single rose petals (preferably pink ones) quickly with the egg white and set them on a baking sheet lined with wax or parchment paper. Sprinkle very lightly with a small pinch of sugar on each petal—coarse sugar, if you have it, will be prettiest, shining and crisp. Bake the petals in the lowest possible oven, around 140°F/60°C for 3 to 4 hours, until dry and crisp. Scatter them as decoration on cakes and dessert plates.

Pineapple Sputnik

Frédéric's roasted pineapple extravaganza, speared with vanilla beans so it looks like a sputnik, must be tasted to be believed.

Heat the oven to 325°F/160°C. Peel a whole fresh pineapple. If you like, use a small knife to outline and remove the eyes in a spiral pattern (see picture at right). Cut out the core with an apple corer. Cut 4 or 5 vanilla beans each into 2 or 3 shorter pieces and spear the fruit with these, pushing them as far as possible into the flesh —if necessary, use a skewer to help poke holes. Set the pineapple standing upright in a baking dish.

Make a syrup by heating ½ cup/100 g sugar with 1 cup/ 250 ml water, the grated zest and juice of 1 orange and 1 lemon, and about a tablespoon of grated fresh gingerroot until the sugar is dissolved, and then simmer it for 2 to 3 minutes. Pour the syrup over the pineapple and roast it, basting often, until the pineapple starts to brown and the syrup starts to caramelize, 1¼ to 1½ hours. It will be fragrant with vanilla. Toward the end of cooking, keep a close watch as the syrup will caramelize rapidly once it is reduced to a glaze. Slice the pineapple into thick rings for serving and serve it warm, basted with the cooking syrup. Leave the vanilla beans for decoration, though I'm afraid you cannot eat them. A medium pineapple serves 4.

Chef Frédéric Gauvin's roasted pineapple is worth every one of the vanilla beans used to perfume it.

One of the constant amusements of life at Château du Feÿ is the subplot that roils with almost Shakespearean intensity whenever school is in session. How is it that the consumption of wine has doubled from one week to the next? What happened to the cherry tree, laden with ripe fruit yesterday but today stripped bare? Madame Milbert swears the birds got them but this is surely impossible? Our stocks of firewood, in the charge of Monsieur Milbert, are also subject to something more than "seasonal variation." Which of the students are romancing together? (Housekeeper Maria is the expert here but she holds her tongue.) Some speculations are less pleasant: one year we had a kleptomaniac in residence who shredded favorite dresses and stole treasured personal belongings in a manner guaranteed to cause distress. I felt we had a real-life Agatha Christie novel on our hands, overlaid by the need to pretend that nothing was wrong. By the end of the season we had eliminated all suspects but two, and to this day I do not know which was the culprit.

I often mull over what makes a good cooking teacher. They may be cantankerous like Chef Chambrette, patient like Chef Claude, or an inspiration like Chef Frédéric. That technical expertise is needed goes without saying. It is the different personalities I find fascinating, and in the kitchen at Le Feÿ we reckon we've seen them all, from gray-haired, venerable Maurice Ferré, chef pâtissier at Maxim's, to the bombastic know-all who bullied the students and was not asked again. All the young chefs seem to be slim and athletic, constantly on the move, chopping, whisking, hefting hot stockpots, on their feet twelve hours a day and usually more. The double-shift American system does not extend to smaller restaurants in France as it's too expensive.

The kitchen can be cruel to the health. In older chefs, heredity takes over and the father's little *brioche* (paunch) begins to show in the son. Varicose veins are chronic, reactions are slowed, leading to more cuts and burns in the dangerous environment of the kitchen. Most insidious of all is alcohol, constantly available, constantly a temptation in the debilitating heat of most kitchens. Auguste Escoffier installed a vat of that most English of refreshments, lemon barley water, in his kitchens, a curious choice for a French chef.

I've come to the conclusion that passion is the key to a good teacher—the total commitment to cooking at every level, from choosing the potatoes to mastering the complexities of sugar and chocolate work. I'm often reminded that the French word *chef* has the double meaning of "head cook" and "leader." Tyrannical, irascible, it is nonetheless Chef Chambrette who is remembered with awe as a teacher, while mild-mannered, diligent Claude Vauguet, who was so much liked by his students, fades into the background. Life is not fair.

CHAPTER 8

The Heart of Burgundy

"Cherchez, cherchez," I hear as two fluffy little Pyrennean sheep dogs roam and snuffle around our oak trees under my skeptical eye. Suddenly one starts to scratch and, quick as a flash, their master, Michel Jalade, darts forward. Hollowing the ground with his hunting knife, he uncovers a dark, cindery ball the size of a large walnut. The unmistakable, pungent aroma of fresh truffle fills the air. Truffles! At Château du Feÿ! We could scarcely believe it. To be sure, not the intense, assertive *tuber melanosporum* of Provence and Périgord, but *tuber uncinatum,* a genuine truffle nonetheless. It turns out that Burgundian truffles were big business a century ago, with yearly production more than double today's output for the whole of France. Novelist Colette, who was raised not far from Le Feÿ, remarked of the Burgundian truffle: "it has a good smell, but no taste whatever . . . eat it on its own, scented and grainy-skinned, eat it like the vegetable it is, hot, and served in munificent quantities." How I long for the chance!

Marinated Salmon Checkerboard with Truffles

In the kitchen, I found that Colette is right: our Burgundian truffles smell wonderful but have little taste and are best eaten raw. Beware of that tempting cheap bottle of truffle oil. Chances are it will contain a bland Burgundian truffle or even one of the false truffles from China, a tasteless look-alike that bears no relation to the real thing.

Luckily truffles are valued as much for their jet-black color as for their flavor and this recipe makes the most of it. Very thinly sliced salmon is briefly marinated with truffle oil and lemon, then topped with sliced truffles —spectacular when carefully lined up as a checkerboard on the plate. If you can find, and afford, a fresh truffle, here's the ideal showcase for it, or you can use canned truffles, adding the truffle juice to the salmon marinade. I'm using a minimum of truffle (two large truffles for four servings), but double would not be amiss if you feel like a splurge.

> *a single salmon fillet, with the skin (about 1 ¼ lb/*
>   *600 g)*
> *2 large fresh or canned truffles (about 2 oz/60 g total)*
> *2 to 3 tablespoons truffle oil*
> *salt and white pepper, freshly ground if possible*
> *2 lemons, halved*
> *sea salt for serving*

Pull out any tiny "pin" bones from the center of the salmon fillet using tweezers. Trim away the soft flesh and any bones from each long edge of the fillet, leaving only the meat. With a very sharp knife, cut the thinnest possible diagonal slices of salmon, cutting away from the head end and toward the tail. As you cut the slices, lay them on plastic wrap to roughly form four 8-in/20-cm squares. Trim the edges of salmon and of the plastic wrap to leave you with 4 neat squares. Lay the squares,

plastic wrap upward, on 4 large serving plates; flat plates without a raised rim make the nicest presentation if you have them. Set another plate on top of the salmon and press down to flatten it evenly. It can be prepared to this point 3 to 4 hours ahead and stored in the refrigerator.

If using fresh truffles, trim off the crusty peel. (Stuff it into Brie cheese [opposite] or use it to flavor olive oil, making truffle oil for another time.) Drain canned truffles, reserving the juice. Very thinly slice the fresh or canned truffles, using a mandoline if possible.

Shortly before serving, peel the plastic wrap from the salmon squares and brush the surface with truffle oil. If using canned truffles, sprinkle the salmon with the reserved truffle juice as well. Season the salmon lightly with salt and white pepper. Brush or dip the truffle slices in more truffle oil and arrange them on the salmon squares in a checkerboard pattern. Just before serving, drizzle the lemon juice over the salmon. Serve it at once, as the lemon juice quickly "cooks" the fish—you will see the brightly colored salmon turn opaque within minutes. Pass a cellar of sea salt for sprinkling at the table.

Thanks to recent advances in propagation, *trufficulture* is on the up and up in Burgundy. Monsieur Jalade is our local crusader. His brisk bearing and neat moustache hint at his naval background—he was a submarine engineer—and he takes a disciplined approach with his dogs, initiating them with truffle oil on their mothers' nipples. It is thanks to Michel Jalade that we have ploughed part of our front pasture and planted it with baby oaks inoculated with the truffle mycelium, the white fibrous tubes that spawn the truffles. We won't have results for at least five years, he says, but we should have success with *uncinatum,* which is already indigenous. *Melanosporum* is a different matter, delicate, requiring specific soil conditions, and easily overwhelmed by other fungi. We've gambled on two dozen trees and we'll see.

In fact, the problem with truffles is not so much growing but gathering them. I cannot imagine our charming, witless Dalmatian, Zigzag, in the role of truffle hound even if I had the patience to train him. But so far Monsieur Jalade has the monopoly and nobody with truffle ambitions can do without him and his dogs. He now manages twenty acres of truffle trees and airfreights them, washed and vacuum-packed, to Tokyo. During the season, which lasts from September to January (in Périgord it begins and ends later), he is outdoors twelve hours a day. Last year he gathered about 700 pounds of saleable truffles, worth about $150 a pound wholesale, half the price of the superior *melanosporum* type. However, in a dry year—so much depends on the weather—the crop may drop below 200 pounds, hardly a commercial proposition. Until some hi-tech method is found to detect the elusive fungus underground (truffles are covered with 6 in/15 cm or more of earth), gathering them will remain an artisanal affair, at the mercy of the weather and of human ingenuity, and priced accordingly.

PREVIOUS PAGES: *To hunt for truffles, dogs must be trained from birth. At lower left, Michel Jalade directs operations, displaying the results of his digging to an admiring apprentice. On page 239, neat rows of baby lettuces sprout in the shelter of a greenhouse.* OPPOSITE: *Thinly sliced truffles are sliced to serve on a bed of marinated raw salmon.* ABOVE: *The Burgundian truffle is gray, with an intense perfume but a milder taste than the more famous and pungent Provençal variety.*

Truffled Brie

If you're ever lucky enough to have leftover truffle trimmings, you cannot do better than sandwich them inside a generous slice of ripe Brie. Slice the Brie in half horizontally and scatter truffle slices or pieces—the more the better—on the cut surface. Replace the top, wrap the Brie tightly in plastic wrap, and store in a cool place (around 60°F/13°C and preferably not the refrigerator) for a week so the flavor of truffle permeates the cheese. Serve with a baguette.

In this science-driven world, Michel Jalade is a rarity, but we've found other such idealists in our small corner of Burgundy, artisans who have made a deliberate commitment to traditional methods and to high quality. Take Jean-Marie and Véronique Cochon, makers of goat cheese, for example. "We are producers from start to finish, from raising the goats to making the cheese to meeting our customers, that's what I enjoy," says Monsieur Cochon. Their modest farm stands on a hill, open to the winds that breeze through the barn full of goats. As you enter, horned heads pop out—goats are insatiably curious—and within seconds they are amiably chewing your clothes. I turn from the goats to their master and Jean-Marie Cochon's neat beard, dark eyes, and receding hairline are an irresistible reminder that animals so often resemble their owner.

The Cochons live just west of Château du Feÿ in the Puisaye, a region of small holdings and poor soil where it is hard to scrape a living. Goats, however, can be raised almost anywhere. The flavor of their cheese varies with the cheesemaker, the time of year and, most importantly, with the feed. "In Provence, with its wild thyme and herbs, the cheese tastes very different," explains Jean-Marie. His 150 mature goats yield about 500 liters of milk a day in summer, enough for about 600 of the small round cheeses called *crottins*. Production is seasonal, dwindling to nothing in January and February until the kids are born. Goats are prolific and the Cochons' small herd produces about 400 kids each year, some of them quintuplets. The males are sold for meat—baby goat is an Easter delicacy—with the best females kept for milking.

Terrine of Artichokes with Goat Cheese

"Turning" a raw globe artichoke, or cutting away all the leaves and choke to leave only the edible meat, requires strong fingers and a sharp knife. I rarely get the chance, as the artichokes in our garden seem to wither with frost one winter out of two. Then I cheat and buy cans of cooked artichoke bottoms—expensive but worth it for making this sumptuous terrine layered with fresh goat cheese and a bit of tomato. Serve these individual terrines with good bread, preferably a baguette, as a first course for six.

> *12 large globe artichokes*
> *2 lemons*
> *2 tablespoons flour*
> *3 medium tomatoes*
> *salt and pepper*
>
> **FOR THE GOAT CHEESE MIXTURE**
> *a bunch of chives*
> *½ lb/250 g soft goat cheese*
> *2 garlic cloves, chopped*
> *3 to 4 tablespoons heavy cream, more if needed*
>
> **FOR THE LEMON VINAIGRETTE**
> *2 tablespoons lemon juice*
> *1 teaspoon Dijon-style mustard*
> *⅓ cup/75 ml olive oil*
>
> *six ¾-cup/175-ml ramekins*

To turn the artichokes, first break off the stem of the artichoke. With a sharp knife, shave off all the large bottom leaves, leaving only a cone of soft small leaves in the center on top. Trim the base of any remaining green parts, exposing all the lighter colored "meat" of the bottom. Cut off the soft cone of leaves on top, leaving only the choke behind. Rub the base of the artichoke well with a cut lemon to prevent discoloration and drop it into a bowl of cold water while trimming, or "turning," the rest. Reserve the squeezed lemons.

Prepare a *blanc* for cooking the artichokes: Bring a shallow pan of salted water to a boil. In a small bowl, make a soft paste by stirring 5 to 6 tablespoons of water into the flour. Whisk this into the boiling water and add the juice of a half lemon, again saving the squeezed lemon half. The flour and lemon will keep the artichokes white (or *blanc*) as they cook.

Add the artichokes to the *blanc* with the squeezed

lemon halves. (If you are using canned artichoke bottoms, they will not need cooking.) Put a heatproof plate on top to submerge the artichokes and simmer until they are tender when pierced with a knife, 15 to 20 minutes. Drain and let them cool. Line the ramekins with plastic wrap, leaving an overlapping border.

Core the tomatoes, immerse them in boiling water for 10 to 15 seconds to loosen the skins, then drain and peel them. Cut 2 perfect, thin round slices from the center of each tomato and set them aside (each ramekin will get one slice). Discard the seeds from the remaining tomato trimmings and coarsely chop them. Season the trimmings with salt and pepper and leave to drain in a sieve as a concassée.

For the cheese filling, chop the chives, reserving 12 stems for decoration. Soften the cheese in an electric mixer with the garlic, chopped chives, salt, pepper, and enough cream to make the filling easy to spread.

Scoop the hairy choke from the cooked artichokes with a teaspoon and cut the bottoms into 2 or 3 horizontal slices to make a total of 18 rounds. Trim the rounds if necessary to make them flat and even. Coarsely chop the artichoke trimmings and stir them into the cheese mixture. Taste and adjust the seasoning. Press an artichoke round into the base of each ramekin, if necessary trimming them to fit. Add a thin layer of cheese filling, spreading it with a spoon. Top with a tomato round, then with more cheese. Add the remaining artichokes and cheese in layers, ending with the artichoke. Cover with the overlapping plastic wrap and set a small can that fits just inside the edge of the ramekin on top of each to press together the layers. Chill for at least 6, and up to 24, hours.

Shortly before serving, make the vinaigrette dressing. Whisk the lemon juice in a small bowl with the mustard, salt, and pepper. Gradually whisk in the olive oil so the dressing emulsifies and thickens slightly. Taste and adjust the seasoning. Unmold the terrines onto individual plates, discarding the plastic wrap. Coat each one with vinaigrette, then top with a spoonful of tomato concassée and 2 crossed chives. Serve chilled.

OPPOSITE: *Market shoppers, above, inspect before they buy. Below, the countryside in Burgundy is dotted with homemade signs for farm cheeses. Goats are insatiably curious.*

East of the Cochon property, beyond Chablis and the historic town of St. Florentin, the land is richer: cow country. Here Philippe Gillot recently inherited the family farm with its 40 cows. It has been famous for cow cheese "forever," and last year Philippe earned two medals, one silver, one gold, at the Salon de l'Agriculture in Paris. Recently I arrived just as neighbors were dropping by with their enamel cans for the evening's fresh milk. Many buy crème fraîche and soft fresh cheese, but mature cheeses are also offered. They range from St. Florentin, only a few days old, to rich, ripe Soumaintrain, aged for six weeks and washed regularly with brine so it develops a yellow crust and deep, pungent flavor. Marketing is tough: small producers like the Gillots, who cannot guarantee the regular supplies demanded by supermarkets, must personalize their approach, selling directly at the farm and taking a stall at the local market. Philippe Gillot has a few restaurant chefs as customers, but demand tends to be seasonal, and he has yet to build up a regular clientele like Jean-Marie Cochon, who himself delivers his goat cheeses as far as Paris.

Even more restrictive are European Union regulations and the obsession with standardization. For his cheese to pass the hygiene rules, Philippe Gillot has had to invest in a good deal of equipment and each week the number of forms to fill in seems to grow—"it drives you crazy." I follow him from the dairy, with its racks of draining fresh cheese and fusty aroma of soured milk, through one refrigerated aging room to another where the odor is frankly ammoniac and the cheeses have shrunk to half their original volume.

Phyllo Purses with Soumaintrain Cheese
Feuilletés au Soumaintrain

An elegant first course for six, these giant cheese-filled phyllo cases are served with a vivid brick-colored cream sauce flavored with vodka and paprika. For the filling, a young, mild Soumaintrain cheese is best; firm Camembert, Brie, goat cheese, or even cream cheese can be substituted.

> *⅔ cup/100 g walnut pieces*
> *a small bunch of sage*
> *½ lb/250 g Soumaintrain or soft cheese*
> *3 celery stalks, sliced*
> *3 to 4 tablespoons heavy cream*
> *large pinch of grated nutmeg*
> *salt and pepper*
> *⅓ cup/90 g butter, more if needed*
> *a 1-lb/500-g package phyllo pastry*
>
> **FOR THE SAUCE**
> *1 tablespoon butter*
> *1 onion, very finely chopped*
> *1 tablespoon paprika*
> *2 tablespoons vodka*
> *1 cup/250 ml heavy cream*

Heat the oven to 425°F/220°C. Spread the walnuts on a baking sheet and toast them in the oven, stirring occasionally, until they are brown, 5 to 8 minutes. Let them cool, leaving the oven on. Strip the leaves from the sage stems and chop the leaves.

For the filling, discard any rind from the cheese and crush it in a bowl with a fork. Stir in the toasted nuts, chopped sage, celery, cream, nutmeg, and pepper. Taste and adjust the seasoning—salt may not be needed if the cheese is salty.

To shape the packages, melt the butter and butter a baking sheet. Lay a damp dishtowel on the work surface and unroll the phyllo dough sheets onto it. Cut the sheets crosswise to form 2 squares or wide rectangles; cover one pile of sheets with a damp towel so they do not dry out while you work with the rest. Brush the top exposed phyllo sheet very lightly with the melted butter and transfer it to the work surface. Brush a second sheet and lay it diagonally on the first. Repeat with 2 or 3 more sheets, setting them each time on the diagonal. Spoon about a sixth of the filling into the center of the buttered sheets. Bunch the sheets up and around the filling to make a purse with a frill of pastry corners at the

top. Tie the purse loosely with string, and then pull the corners apart and down to resemble flower petals. Transfer the purse to the baking sheet. Repeat with the remaining dough and filling to make 6 purses. Drizzle them with any remaining melted butter. You'll probably have phyllo dough left; it can be kept to use again if you wrap it tightly at once and freeze it.

Set the baking sheet low down in the oven so that the purses cook underneath before the tops scorch. Bake them 10 to 15 minutes, until browned and a skewer inserted in the center of a purse is hot to the touch when withdrawn after 30 seconds.

Meanwhile, make the sauce. Melt the butter in a small pan and sauté the onion until soft, 3 to 5 minutes. Stir in the paprika and sauté, stirring, for 1 minute. Add the vodka and flame it. When the flames die, stir in the cream and bring the sauce just to a boil. Season it to taste.

To serve, spoon the sauce onto 6 warm individual plates and set a purse on top; snip and discard the strings. Both the sauce and the purses may be served warm or at room temperature.

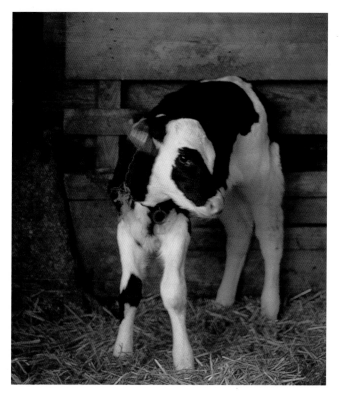

OPPOSITE: *Soumaintrain cheeses are left to drain in molds, left, before being transferred to mature in a climate-controlled room.* ABOVE: *A young calf must compete with the dairy for his mother's milk.*

This delicious recipe uses the delicate fresh cheese called *fromage blanc,* the very best only a few hours old. Mascarpone is the closest substitute. (Philadelphia-style cream cheese contains stabilizer and is not suitable.) Don't shudder at the thought of cheese in ice cream. After all, we freeze yogurt and many of the very first ice creams, made in the eighteenth century, were called *fromages,* or cheeses.

White Cheese Ice Cream

Mix 2 cups/500 ml milk in a saucepan with ½ cup/ 100 g sugar and ½ cup/125 ml light corn syrup. Heat gently, stirring until the sugar dissolves, then bring just to a boil. Take the pan from the heat and let the milk cool to tepid. Whisk 2 cups/500 g of *fromage blanc* in a large bowl until smooth and stir in the cooled milk with a teaspoon of vanilla extract. Chill the cheese mixture and then freeze it in a churn freezer. The recipe makes just over 1 quart/1 liter of ice cream and is outstanding with fresh berries.

Tomatoes Stuffed with Goat Cheese

Good promoter that he is, Monsieur Cochon hands out recipe leaflets for his goat cheese, and these baked tomatoes are one of them.

Core 4 large tomatoes, cut a shallow lid from the top of each one, and discard it. Using a sharp spoon, scoop out the seeds from the tomatoes and sprinkle the insides with salt and pepper. Turn them upside down and leave them to drain for 10 to 15 minutes—this keeps them from getting too soggy when baked. Toast 4 slices of white bread and stamp out the largest possible rounds from the center of each with a cookie cutter or thin-rimmed drinking glass. Brush the rounds lightly on both sides with olive oil and set them on a small oiled baking dish. Cut 2 small fresh goat cheeses (about 8 oz/250 g total) in half horizontally, or cut a log into 4 disks. Finely chop together 2 garlic cloves, 3 to 4 thyme sprigs, and 3 to 4 parsley sprigs, and sprinkle half the mixture in the tomatoes. Set a piece of the cheese in each one, crumbling it to fit, add the remaining herb mixture, and drizzle the top with 1 to 2 tablespoons olive oil. Set the tomatoes on the toast rounds and bake them in a 400°F/200°C oven until the cheese is hot and the tomato skins start to split, 15 to 20 minutes.

You'll often find walnuts paired with goat cheese, as in this Goat Cheese Quiche with a cabbage and walnut salad. Both walnut trees and goats do well on the same thin soil, so perhaps it's no coincidence that the flavors marry happily on the plate.

Like all farmers with animals, the Cochons and Gillots are on call seven days a week, with the additional burden of milking twice a day. Monsieur Gillot is one of only five remaining makers of Soumaintrain *fermier*. The rest is produced in industrial quantities from pasteurized milk, which yields a bland, sticky cheese, the rind an artificial yellow. Many young people opt out—of the two Cochon children, one has gone into wine and the other may become a vet. So Jean-Marie Cochon says he'll probably sell out when the time comes. Meanwhile, in an effort to diversify, he takes groups around the farm, over 7,000 people each year, talking with missionary fervor: "We artisans must maintain traditions and quality. Big producers—eighty percent of French goat cheese is made by only two manufacturers—would like to squeeze us out, but they need us. We offer them the promotional image of nature and the earth—just look at the ads on television."

Cabbage and Goat Cheese Quiche

The crisp little cabbage salad on the side of this creamy goat cheese quiche is just right as a lunch or supper for eight. Don't be distracted by the long list of ingredients—the recipe is really very simple.

> *1 small Savoy cabbage (about 1 ½ lb/750 g)*
> *½ lb/250 g soft goat cheese*
> *2 to 3 tablespoons chopped chives*
> *1 egg*
> *2 egg yolks*
>
> **FOR THE PÂTE BRISÉE DOUGH**
> *1 ⅔ cups/200 g flour*
> *1 egg yolk*
> *½ teaspoon salt*
> *3 tablespoons cold water, more if needed*
> *7 tablespoons/100 g butter*
>
> **FOR THE WHITE SAUCE**
> *3 tablespoons/45 g butter*
> *3 tablespoons/22 g flour*
> *1 ½ cups/375 ml milk*
> *pinch of grated nutmeg*
> *salt and pepper*
> *1 cup/250 ml crème fraîche or heavy cream*
>
> **FOR THE CABBAGE SALAD**
> *¼ cup/60 ml red wine vinegar*
> *1 teaspoon Dijon-style mustard*
> *½ cup/125 ml walnut oil*
> *3 to 4 tablespoons coarsely chopped walnuts*
>
> *an 11-inch/28-cm porcelain quiche pan*

Heat the oven to 375°F/190°C. Prepare and blind-bake the pâte brisée pie shell using the ingredients above and the technique as described in the glossary. Let the shell cool in the pan. Leave the oven on.

Discard the tough outer leaves of the cabbage and finely shred the inner leaves, discarding the core. Bring a large pan of salted water to a boil, add the cabbage, and bring it just back to a boil. Drain, rinse the cabbage with cold water, drain it again thoroughly, and set it aside.

For the white sauce, melt the butter in a saucepan, stir in the flour, and cook until it foams. Whisk in the milk, add the nutmeg, salt, and pepper, and bring the sauce to a boil, whisking constantly until it thickens—it will be very thick. Whisk in the cream and simmer the sauce for 2 minutes. Taste, adjust the seasoning (be generous), and let the sauce cool.

To assemble the quiche, squeeze about a third of the drained cabbage in your fists to extract any water. Spread it in the pie shell and crumble the goat cheese on top. Stir the chives, egg, and egg yolks into the cool sauce and pour the mixture evenly over the filling. Bake the quiche until it is firm and brown, 40 to 50 minutes.

While the quiche bakes, make the salad. Whisk the vinegar with the mustard, salt, and pepper in a small bowl until mixed. Gradually whisk in the oil so the dressing emulsifies and thickens slightly. Toss it with the reserved cabbage and the walnuts, taste, and adjust the seasoning. Serve the quiche warm, in the pan, with the salad on the side.

The small size of the Cochon and Gillot businesses (both farms are

under 200 acres/80 hectares) makes it hard to eke out a living. In contrast, just across the fields from Monsieur Cochon, the Ferme des Perriaux is four times as large and can support three families with a good balance of mixed farming. Madame Gillet senior is a *force de la nature*, scarcely slowing down though now approaching her sixties. Twenty years ago she decided the farm and four children were not enough. "Work is life for me," she says briskly. At the time, green tourism, as vacationing in the countryside is called in France (so much more enticing than blue tourism, which evokes the packed beaches of the ocean), was just beginning. Marie-France Gillet joined the Fermes Auberges, a loosely knit group of farms offering meals and hospitality. Here was an outlet both for her natural talents as a cook and for the farm produce, especially poultry. She made a good choice. Now three generations are involved and on busy summer days they may serve over 100 people. The Auberges pledge to employ only farm staff, and to grow 70 percent or more of the ingredients at home (though Marie-France admits that some members cheat a bit).

For the Gillets, one activity soon led to another. "Everyone asked for duck, not chicken," Madame smiles reminiscently, "so I thought I'd better go one further and learn to make foie gras." Foie gras is not a Burgundian tradition, so she consulted the experts in the Lot region of central France, learning how to fatten flocks of 100 birds at a time by feeding them a simmered mash of corn grown on the farm. Ducks are hardier and easier to fatten than geese, so now Marie-France raises over 1,000 ducks a year, fattening them fifteen to eighteen days on this special diet. In the kitchen, the precious liver is cleaned of membrane, marinated briefly in port wine, and then baked in a terrine with generous quantities of cracked pepper, the Gillet trademark. Very gentle cooking is vital to terrine of foie gras—if the liver gets too hot, the fat melts and separates.

At the time, Marie-France Gillet was a pioneer in our region of Burgundy, but now foie gras is produced here and there throughout France, always saleable though by no means always very good. Color is no indication of quality as the liver may be pink, yellowish, even tinged with gray but equally fine. "I judge more by the weight," explains Marie-France. "A pound is a good size as larger livers can dissolve to almost nothing in the pan." The rest of a foie gras bird is almost as valuable as the liver. "Nothing is lost," confides Madame Gillet. She serves the breast as magret, either grilled rare in the manner of a steak, or smoked and sliced for salad. Trimmings are baked as rillettes, a soft, rich pâté with a characteristic rough texture, and the legs are preserved as confit. "Only two legs per bird, I wish there were more!" Marie-France Gillet has no trouble selling everything she can produce. Her problem, and that of all artisanal producers, is how to increase production without compromising quality.

Warm Salad of Foie Gras with Asparagus

I prefer green asparagus to the plump stems of white and Escoffier agreed with me, though white is regarded as a greater delicacy. Either is good here, so the choice is yours. This recipe makes four individual salads.

> *a ½-lb/250-g piece of fresh foie gras*
> *salt and pepper*
> *1 to 1½ lb/500 to 750 g green or white asparagus*
> *1 shallot, finely chopped*
> *¼ cup/60 ml sherry vinegar*
> *¼ cup/60 ml walnut oil*
> *1 tablespoon chopped tarragon*
> *1 tablespoon chopped parsley*

Bring a large shallow pan of salted water to a boil. Peel the asparagus. Tie the spears with string in 4 bundles, lining up the tips, and then trim off the woody stems so all are the same length. Boil the asparagus, uncovered, until it is just tender when pierced with the point of a knife, 5 to 8 minutes for green asparagus and 10 to 15 minutes for white. Drain the asparagus and rinse quickly with cold water to set the color but not long enough to chill the spears. Leave the asparagus in the colander, cov-ered with the upturned boiling pan to keep them warm.

Meanwhile, with a small knife, cut out any membranes from the foie gras. Cut it on the diagonal in 4 slices about ⅜ inch/1 cm thick and sprinkle them with salt and pepper.

When the asparagus is cooked, heat a frying pan until very, very hot. Add the foie gras slices—fat from the surface will melt and oil the pan at once. Sauté the foie gras over high heat until brown but still pink in the center, maximum 1 minute on each side. Very short cooking is enough or the foie gras will dissolve to fat—what a catastrophe! Transfer the slices to a plate and keep them warm.

For the sauce, pour off all but a tablespoon of the foie gras fat. Add the shallot and cook for 30 seconds. Pour the vinegar into the pan and bring it to a boil, stirring to deglaze the pan juices. When it is reduced by half, add the walnut oil and heat for 1 minute. Remove from the heat, stir in the herbs, taste the sauce, and adjust the seasoning.

Arrange the asparagus tips in a fan on 4 warm individual plates and lay the foie gras on top. Spoon over the sauce and serve at once.

Duck breast—often called by the French term *magret*—is more and more often to be found

beside the chicken breasts in the supermarket. However, it is tricky to cook, turning rapidly to shoe leather if overdone. I've found I do well if I treat duck breast like steak, rapidly browning the outside and then cooking it only until rare. All the same tests for cooking steak apply to duck breast.

Sweet-Sour Duck Breast with Cherries

As a devotee of crispy skin, I particularly like the following method in which the skin is detached from the breast and cooked separately from the meat. We make this dinner for four with whatever fruit is in season—cherries, black currants, gooseberries, mirabelle plums, even prunes.

> *½ lb/250 g cherries or plums, or 6 oz/175 g black*
>   *currants, gooseberries, or pitted prunes*
> *3 tablespoons cassis liqueur*
> *4 small duck breasts* (magrets), *with the skin*
> *salt and pepper*
> *1 tablespoon vegetable oil*
> *1 tablespoon butter*
>
> FOR THE SAUCE
> *2 tablespoons sugar*
> *3 shallots, finely chopped*
> *½ cup/125 g red wine vinegar*
> *1 cup/250 ml red wine*
> *½ cup/125 ml veal or chicken stock*
> *1 teaspoon arrowroot mixed to a paste with 2 table-*
>   *spoons water*
> *2 tablespoons butter, cold and cut into pieces*

Wash the fruit and drain in a colander. Pit the cherries, discarding the stems, halve and pit the plums, pull the black currants from the stems using the tines of a fork, or snip off the blossom ends and stems of the gooseberries. Put the fruit in a saucepan with the cassis. Cover the pan and cook very gently until the juice of the fruit runs, 5 to 10 minutes depending on the fruit. Set it aside.

Strip the skin from the duck breasts and cut it into thin strips, discarding any membrane. Sprinkle the breasts with salt and pepper. Heat the oil and butter in a heavy pan until very hot, add the breasts, and brown them over quite high heat, 1 to 2 minutes on each side. Lower the heat, cover the pan, and continue cooking the breasts for 4 to 6 minutes for rare meat (still flabby if you press with a finger) or 2 to 3 minutes longer if you

prefer it well done (firm when pressed). Slit the center of a breast with the point of a knife to check the inside if you like. Transfer the breasts to a cutting board and cover them with foil to keep warm.

Pour the fat from the frying pan into another small pan and add the strips of skin to it. Fry them, stirring from time to time, until brown and crisp, 3 to 5 minutes. Lift them out with a slotted spoon and set aside to drain on paper towels.

Meanwhile, make the sauce: Discard any remaining fat from the frying pan. Sprinkle in the sugar and shallots and cook until caramelized, 1 to 2 minutes. Add the vinegar and boil until reduced by half, 3 to 5 minutes (stand back as it may sting your eyes). Add the wine and simmer for 2 minutes, stirring to dissolve the pan juices and caramel. Add the stock and bring the sauce to a boil. Whisk in the arrowroot paste and let it simmer for a moment to thicken. Remove the pan from the heat and add the butter in small pieces. Swirl the pan until the butter is incorporated—don't let it melt to oil—and then strain the sauce over the fruit.

Carve each duck breast into 4 or 5 slices, cutting on the diagonal, and arrange the slices in a fan on warm individual plates. Reheat the fruit and sauce, taste, and adjust the seasoning. Pile the fruit beside the duck breasts, spoon over the sauce, and top with the crispy skin.

PREVIOUS PAGES: *Left, ducks are never far from water. Right, Madame Gillet talks to her flock, which comes eagerly for a snack. The birds will soon be ready to move indoors and fatten for foie gras.* OPPOSITE: *Fresh foie gras, served here with asparagus and a warm vinaigrette, must be sautéed only briefly or it will dissolve in the pan.*

Confit was invented as a happy ending for the duck or goose legs, which are left when the breast is removed for *magret*. Unlike *magret*, which is cooked and served immediately, confit benefits from weeks, even months of mellowing.

Confit of Duck Legs with Hearty Greens

To balance its richness, confit is sometimes served with sorrel, which gave me the idea for this side dish of hearty greens that can be made with kale, turnip greens, broccoli rabe, radicchio, or familiar green Savoy cabbage. This recipe makes a full dinner for four with no need for any accompaniments other than good bread.

> *4 duck legs*
> *3 tablespoons kosher or coarse salt*
> *1 teaspoon black pepper*
> *2 to 3 thyme sprigs*
> *2 to 3 bay leaves, broken into pieces*
> *3 lb/1.4 kg lard, melted, more if needed*
>
> FOR THE HEARTY GREENS
> *3 cups/750 ml chicken stock*
> *2 bay leaves*
> *1 lb/500 g kale or other greens*
> *3 shallots, finely sliced*
> *2 to 3 garlic cloves, finely chopped*
> *2 tomatoes, peeled, seeded, and chopped*
> *salt and pepper*
> *splash of red wine vinegar*

Rub each piece of duck with some of the salt and put the pieces in a bowl. Sprinkle with the remaining salt and pepper and add the thyme and bay leaves. Cover and keep in the refrigerator, turning the pieces occasionally, for 6 to 12 hours depending on how strong a salt cure you want.

Rinse the salt from the duck and dry the pieces on paper towels. Heat the oven to 300°F/150°C. Lay the duck pieces, skin-side down, in a frying pan and fry gently over quite low heat for 15 to 20 minutes so that the fat runs and they brown evenly.

Transfer the duck pieces and fat to a small casserole and add enough melted lard to cover them. Cover with a lid and cook in the oven until the duck has rendered all its fat and is so tender that it is almost falling from the bone, 2 to 2½ hours. By tradition, it should be soft enough to pierce with a straw.

To preserve the duck, pour a layer of the rendered fat from the casserole into the base of a preserving jar or small terrine. Pack the pieces of duck on top and pour over enough fat to cover and seal them completely, adding more melted lard if necessary. Be sure all air bubbles are excluded. Cover and refrigerate for at least a week to allow the flavor to mellow. If you seal the jar or terrine with a cloth sprinkled with salt and then tightly cover it, confit will keep for several months. The longer it is left to mature, the better it will be.

To finish the confit and cook the greens, heat the oven to 400°F/200°C. For the greens, put the stock and bay leaves in a large skillet and boil rapidly until reduced by half, about 15 minutes. Discard the stalks from the greens, loosely roll the leaves, and shred them as fine as possible. Add them to the stock, cover, and simmer, stirring often, until they are wilted and almost tender, 10 to 20 minutes depending on their toughness.

Meanwhile, warm the jar of confit in a bain-marie to melt the fat. Lift out the pieces of duck, wiping off excess fat, and put them in a shallow baking dish. (Be sure to keep all of the remaining fat as it is wonderful for frying potatoes.) Bake the duck pieces in the oven for 5 minutes, then pour off 2 or 3 tablespoons of the melted fat into a small pan for cooking the greens; discard the remaining fat from the baking dish—once it's been reheated it's not worth saving. Continue baking until the legs are very hot and the skin is crisp, 10 to 15 minutes more.

When the greens are nearly done, remove the lid and cook them until almost all the stock has been absorbed and evaporated. Heat the 2 to 3 tablespoons of reserved duck fat over medium heat, add the shallots and garlic, and cook until soft but not brown, 2 to 3 minutes. Stir the shallots and garlic into the greens with the tomato. Sprinkle with salt, pepper, and a splash of red wine vinegar. Taste the greens, adjust the seasoning, and serve them with the crispy duck legs.

Crisp legs of duck confit are served on a bed of bitter greens to contrast with the richness. In back, a crock of confit is sealed under its protective layer of fat.

GROUPE D'EMPLOYES 1895

GEANTS

EXTRA GROS

TRES GROS

GROS

MOYENS

PETITS

BILLOT
Française de Gastronomie
118 Grande Rue
89400 BASSOU

Tél. : 03.86.73.37.00
Fax : 03.86.73.37.01

You must be wondering when I'd ever get around to Burgundy's famous snails. Just near us on the road south, a small village called Bassou depends on them for its livelihood and I'd like to say that they are locally grown—goodness knows there are plenty of them on the prowl in the woods at Le Feÿ after any shower of rain. But no, snail hunting takes time and almost all snails on the French table—30,000 tons were consumed last year—are imported from eastern Europe. The lengthy journey by truck is just enough to fast and purge them of any toxic herbs they may have ingested. Each truck carries 10 tons, and at 5 grams a shell, I'll leave you to calculate how many snails are crawling about in the interior. On arrival the snails must be washed, blanched, taken from their shells to remove the black stomach, then simmered in court bouillon before they are ready for the final treatment of butter and garlic, or an herb sauce.

I frankly haven't the patience (or is it the nerve?) to do this myself, though snail hunters are sufficiently persistent for our neighbors to post no-trespassing notices saying DÉFENSE DE RAMASSER LES ESCARGOTS when snails come out of hibernation in spring. One year Chef Claude, who was country-born, disappeared into the woods and returned in triumph with a bucket of our big beige gastropods (the excellence of *helix pomata*, the Burgundian variety of snail, was recognized by the Romans). He sprinkled a big circle of wood cinders in the barn and put the snails inside—they cannot cross the ash —with an inner circle of flour for them to eat. After the required week of purging, they were plump and ready for the pot, but Claude had long since gone back to Paris. . . .

Snails with Anise en Croûte

So proud are Burgundians of their snails that they call them *les ducs de Bourgogne*, the dukes of Burgundy. Here I suggest serving them as an appetizer in a hollowed crispy bread roll, or you may like to try them as a main dish over fresh fettuccine. A handy quickie, this recipe uses canned or frozen snails, takes 20 minutes at most, and makes enough for six to eight appetizers.

> *8 round crusty dinner rolls*
> *¼ cup/60 g butter*
> *4 dozen cooked canned or frozen snails*
> *2 garlic cloves, finely chopped*
> *2 shallots, finely chopped*
> *2 cups/500 ml crème fraîche or heavy cream*
> *1 teaspoon aniseed*
> *pinch of grated nutmeg*
> *salt and pepper*
> *1 tablespoon Pernod or other anise liqueur*
> *2 tablespoons chopped parsley*

Heat the oven to 350°F/175°C. Melt half the butter and set it aside. Cut the tops off the rolls and hollow out the crumb to make a bread shell. Brush the insides with the melted butter, set them on a baking sheet, and toast in the oven until the edges are crisp and starting to brown, 10 to 15 minutes.

Meanwhile, heat the remaining butter in a deep frying pan and sauté the garlic and shallots until soft and fragrant, about 1 minute. Add the cream, aniseed, nutmeg, salt, and pepper and simmer until the sauce is reduced by about half and tastes good, 10 to 15 minutes.

Add the snails to the sauce and simmer until very hot, 3 to 5 minutes. Add the Pernod and parsley, taste, and adjust the seasoning. Set the toasted bread shells on warm plates and spoon the snails and sauce into them, piling the snails up well. Serve at once, so that the bread is crisp and the snails piping hot.

OPPOSITE: *Packers at a local snail farm line up for the record in this century-old photograph, top. Below left, graded snail shells on show—only the French could classify them into six different sizes! A tempting dish of Snails with Anise en Croûte, right.*

Even though Madame Fontaine lives over an hour south of us in the
wild uplands of the Morvan, I'm sneaking her into this story because she exemplifies so much of what is
best in Burgundy. Quarré–les-Tombes is a bleak town, known for its hams, dried sausages, and eerie
tombstones fashioned by a prehistoric culture. The air must be bracing, however, for into the twentieth
century local wet nurses were in demand by the upper classes, such was the excellence of their milk.

For Roseline Fontaine, Quarré is a perfect home for the jams and jellies that are her passion. "I'm an
eccentric," she smiles. In her pastry shop on the central square, the walls are lined with vivid pots:
golden tomato jelly, purple wild peach jam, pink grenadine, green damson, red cherry jam with honey.
Strange names abound such as love-in-a-cage (cape gooseberry), scratch-your-backside (rose hip), par-
adise (wild plums and cranberry), and wedding night (apple, wild pear, and candied ginger). Over the
years she has collected old cookbooks in bric-a-brac stores, researching time-honored combinations.
"So much has disappeared," she laments. "In the old days much less was discarded. Did you know that
the stalk on lettuce was preserved as *gorge d'ange* (angel's throat)—it tastes a bit like rhubarb. Stringy
beans were candied in sugar as lollipops for the children."

Les fruits du vieux garçon (old bachelor's fruits) are yet another of Roseline's preserves, a homemade version
of the attractive jars of fruits preserved in alcohol you'll find all over France. Depending on the region, it
will be cherries in Cognac around Bordeaux, plums in white alcohol in Alsace, or figs in Armagnac from
Gascony. In Burgundy, marc is the liquor of choice and here I suggest a combination of fruits, starting
with cherries and then adding different colored layers throughout the season. Alternatively, you can use
just one fruit—Mark, for instance, likes to make a gin version with sloes from the autumn hedgerows.

Les Fruits du Vieux Garçon

Choose perfect fruits that are ripe but not soft. Firm
fruits such as cherries, apricots, and plums do better
than berries. Discard the stems and wipe the fruits with
a cloth (if you wash them, be sure to dry them thoroughly). Prick the skins with a needle so the alcohol
penetrates; large fruits such as peaches should be halved,
discarding the pit.

Measure the fruit approximately in a measuring jug—
this recipe is very free-form—and arrange them in a
large glass jar without packing them down. Add about a
third their volume of sugar. Pour alcohol over the fruits
to cover them, using vodka for a neutral taste or your
favorite Cognac or other alcohol, as you prefer. Store the
jar, loosely covered, in a cool dark place. As fruits come
into season, keep adding them with more sugar and alcohol, using different colors so the layers are distinct—
this is all part of the charm. When the jar is full, seal it
and, if any sugar remains undissolved, turn the jar
upside down. Store the fruits at least 3 months so the
flavor mellows. Serve them over ice cream or a slice of
cake, with their alcohol, or pour the alcohol into a sepa-
ate liqueur glass.

*After macerating for months in marc and sugar, these "old bachelor's
fruits" form a brisk pick-me-up with a couple of Randall's Biscotti (recipe
page 225). The glass globe in back is an old wasp trap: The bottom should
be filled with a lure of sticky jam or honey.*

To preserve the fresh flavor of fruit, Roseline Fontaine makes her jams in batches of nine pounds/about 4 kg, never more. For maximum taste, she recommends macerating fruits with sugar for 24 hours before cooking. What she makes depends very much on the season. Dandelion flower jam, for instance, is a spring favorite—"it takes 365 flowers to make three one-pound pots." Then comes the June glut of cherries, while September is the time for rose hips, elderberries, figs, and wild plums. Winter brings rhubarb, and it is thanks to my mother that I've always made rhubarb jam, simmering it with the English favorite, ginger. It was a surprise to find that Madame Fontaine is no stranger to the combination, including it as one of the more than 200 preserves she has on sale.

As is the case with most local jam makers, preserves are just a part of the Fontaine family business. Roseline's husband is a chocolatier, his pride being a yearly Christmas exhibition of chocolate sculptures and figurines, over 2,000 of them. Daughter Létitia is a pâtissier and married to the local butcher, Fabien Perrault, who is renowned for his home-cured *rosette* dried sausage and hams. These are salted Morvan-style for five months before smoking, then Fabien hangs them in a drafty loft above his shop to catch the dry mountain breezes. Nothing can be left to chance, not given all the industry rules about altitude and humidity. (You may have noticed that all the world's famous hams such as Parma and Serrano come from mountain areas.) In the old days in the Morvan, the pigs were left to run free in the

A serious jam-maker is wise to protect his arm, left, from the burns of bubbling jam. OPPOSITE: *Fresh baguette and homemade jam—the perfect snack.*

Rhubarb and Ginger Jam

Trim 3 lb/1.4 kg rhubarb stalks and if they are tough on the outside, peel them with a vegetable peeler. Cut the stalks into 1-in/2.5-cm sticks and layer them in a bowl with 6 cups/1.2 kg sugar. Cover and leave the rhubarb overnight to macerate. Transfer it to a preserving pan or large saucepan and stir in 2 to 3 tablespoons finely chopped fresh gingerroot and 5 tablespoons/90 g chopped candied ginger. Heat gently, stirring occasionally, until the rhubarb softens to pulp and the sugar dissolves, 7 to 10 minutes. Bring to a boil and cook the jam to the jell point, 20 to 30 minutes. The temperature should measure 220°/105°C on a candy thermometer, and the jam should set if you drop a little on a chilled plate. Let it cool for 5 to 10 minutes, then ladle it into sterilized jars and seal them. This makes 1 quart/1 liter of jam.

local oak forests, giving wild flavor to the meat, which is sliced thin to serve raw. So great is the demand that I must order our Christmas ham six months in advance.

Morvan ham is one of many artisanal products subject to various regulations. Not even snails escape in France: a national law passed in 1979 governs how and when they can be harvested. Food safety is of course an issue here, but French politicians are closer to my heart than most because they are equally passionate about the quality and authenticity of ingredients. It was, after all, the French who invented the concept of *appellation controlée* for the finer Bordeaux wines as long ago as 1855. To earn *appellation* status, a product must come from a specific place or area and have distinguishing characteristics that reflect "local, faithful and constant methods of production." Over the last seventy-five years many foods, including the chickens of Bresse in southern Burgundy, have been added to the system. Which reminds me that I have not formally introduced you to Epoisses, Burgundy's premier *appellation controlée* cheese, which is made not far from Quarré-les-Tombes. Epoisses is aged for six weeks, its rind washed with brine and finally with a brisk solution of marc. The cheese inside softens to be intense, tangy, and frankly reeking. Our Burgundian neighbors love it, but it's a bit much for me on its own and I prefer to temper the taste in a handy soufflé (overleaf).

Epoisses Soufflé

The ripest possible domestic Brick or French Munster can be substituted for Epoisses. This makes a fine supper for four when accompanied by a green salad.

> *½ Epoisses cheese (½ lb/250 g)*
> *6 eggs, separated*
> *2 tablespoons crème fraîche or heavy cream, more if needed*
> *salt and pepper*
>
> *a 1-quart/1-liter soufflé dish*

Heat the oven to 400°F/200°C. Brush the soufflé dish with melted butter, chill it in the freezer, and butter it again. Chop the cheese, including the rind, and put it in a food processor with the egg yolks, heavy cream, and a generous amount of fresh black pepper. Work it until smooth, adding more cream if necessary, until the mixture just falls easily from the spoon. Transfer it to a bowl.

Stiffly whisk the egg whites, adding a pinch of salt to help stiffen them. Stir about a quarter of the egg whites into the cheese mixture to lighten it. Add this mixture back to the remaining whites and fold them together as lightly as possible. Tip the soufflé mixture into the buttered dish—it should be almost full—and smooth the top with a metal spatula. The mixture is quite soft. Run your thumb around the edge of the dish to detach the mixture so the soufflé rises straight.

Set the soufflé on a baking sheet and bake it until puffed and brown, 20 to 25 minutes. When shaken, it should wobble slightly, showing it is still soft in the center. Transfer the dish to a cold plate for easy handling and serve it at once, cutting to the center with 2 spoons so each guest has some of the firm outside with the soft center as a sauce.

Over the hill from Quarré-les-Tombes, Gérard Maternaud also struggles with

the elements. After twenty years in business his biggest problem remains the same—the weather. His fourteen-acre truck farm is chilly at 1,600 feet and all but a tiny portion is outdoors. "It keeps us fit!" he says with a grin. Gérard supplies many top Burgundian chefs with fifty or more types of salad greens, squash, and baby roots, including such rarities as parsley root and Japanese artichoke. Tiny, finger-thin leeks are a specialty, deliberately planted so close together that they cannot expand—the opposite of Monsieur Milbert's philosophy. Like his vegetables, Monsieur Maternaud is small, a concentrated bundle of energy covered with a dusty glaze of good Burgundian earth.

Asian Stir-Fried Green Beans

This recipe will enliven all sorts of vegetables, not just green beans. Try it with broccoli or cauliflower florets, shredded cabbage, and of course, with yellow beans. It makes a tasty side dish for three to four people.

> 1 lb/500 g green beans
> 1 tablespoon sesame seeds
> a ½-in/1.25-cm piece of fresh gingerroot, finely
>   chopped
> 1 tablespoon fermented Chinese black beans, finely
>   chopped
> 3 garlic cloves, finely chopped
> 2 tablespoons peanut or vegetable oil
> 2 tablespoons dark soy sauce
> 1 tablespoon rice wine
> 1 teaspoon sugar
> 1 teaspoon dark sesame oil, more to taste

Toast the sesame seeds in a nonstick frying pan over medium heat, shaking the pan occasionally, until they are fragrant and brown, 8 to 10 minutes. Set them aside to cool. Trim the green beans. Mix the gingerroot, black beans, and garlic in a small bowl and set aside.

Heat a wok over high heat for about 1 minute. Drizzle in the oil to coat the bottom and sides of the wok. Add the ginger-black bean mixture and stir-fry just until aromatic, 5 to 10 seconds. Add the green beans and stir-fry them over high heat until they turn a darker green and start to pop, 5 to 7 minutes. Stir in the soy sauce, rice wine, and sugar and continue stir-frying until the beans look slightly blackened and withered, 3 to 4 minutes longer. If the beans are mature and still tough, cover the pan, lower the heat, and continue cooking them a few minutes until tender.

Remove the wok from the heat, add the sesame oil and toasted sesame seeds, and stir to coat the beans. Taste and adjust the seasoning with soy sauce and sesame oil.

OPPOSITE: *Pungent, runny Epoisses cheese, its rind washed with marc, is the base of a memorable soufflé.* ABOVE: *Fresh baby fava beans are a short-lived treat. When more mature, they are good stir-fried but must be peeled as well as shelled.*

Many of our regional foods are displayed at their best at the Christmas market, high point of the year in Bailly, a wine village on the Yonne River. Feeling like one of the seven dwarfs, you drive several hundred yards into the hillside into a huge cave, originally a quarry for the stone used to build the Panthéon in Paris. First comes a 50-yard/meter bar (throughout the year, tastings of the local sparkling *crémant* are offered). The air is warm, lights glint under the low ceilings, and the festive atmosphere is palpable as the crowd roams past small stands of artisanal producers. Where better to buy your home-smoked salmon trout, local foie gras, venison, or the free-range turkey of the *reveillon* feast, held by tradition in the early hours of Christmas morning on return from midnight mass. Boxes of hand-dipped chocolates and jams from the farm are here for the last-minute gift. Over there I recognize Gérard Maternaud with his baby vegetables and Madame Jalade with a miniature volcano of fresh truffles.

All of us who are here enjoy the carnival but we come for much, much more. This market epitomizes the French concept of *terroir*, the roots that pull Parisians back each year to that little bit of countryside they call their own. *Terroir* means much more than *terre* or "earth," it embraces culture and history, famous names, and of course, the food and wines. That's what is meant by the heart of Burgundy.

Artisan sausages, above left, are a natural marriage with crusty bread. Market day is prime time for conversation. RIGHT: *Chicken medium-brown or toasty, it's your choice.*

CHAPTER 9

Les Grandes Fêtes

When I first came to France I could not believe how much everyone enjoyed themselves on Sunday—bakers doubled their daily turnover, food shops stayed open, little girls dressed up, and restaurants did their best business of the week. I was living in a family to learn French and Marielle Charpentier, the mother, would cross Paris to buy her Sunday chickens from the finest poulterer. To her butter-roast chicken and butter-fried potatoes, each week she would add a surprise such as tiny Channel sole or baby gray shrimp, which had to be peeled laboriously by hand. The children were expert at it, much faster than I. In comparison to dank, Protestant Britain it was a festival. "Latin culture," scoffed my father, but my mother looked more wistful; in her teens she had wintered on the Riviera and been exposed to the blandishments of the Mediterranean lifestyle.

Today I still notice the same joie de vivre in our neighbors. Summer is the time to show off old properties, to display the new paint work and rattle on about retiling the château roof. The French government puts quite a bit of money into preserving *la patrimoine* (the national heritage), including houses that are privately owned. A caretaker is deductible from income and so are repairs to listed buildings like Château du Feÿ. There are even subsidies, but the historic buildings architect gets in on the act and takes a certain percentage to top up his salary. We've found it easier—and cheaper—to get on with it quietly ourselves.

Great houses had no place in post-Revolutionary France and it is only recently, with modern communications and business done worldwide, that properties like Château du Feÿ, even without the land that was once their livelihood, have once more come into their own. It is easy for us to run La Varenne cooking school from here, offering classes in the summer and responding electronically to inquiries year-round. To say that the satellite links have brought Australia to Europe's doorstep is already a cliché. Mark believes there is more activity here now than at any time since Le Feÿ's heyday in the mid-eighteenth century. But the supply of viable listed buildings is limited and progress has its downside. Highways or electric power networks run ever closer to fine châteaux; some properties nestle in villages where the mayor's pride is the number of *petits pavillons* he can get constructed for his electors, ruining the landscape of the great house. Still more châteaux have been spoiled by tasteless modernization and, let's face it, others are simply ugly in the first place.

How lucky we are at Le Feÿ! State forest protects our back and in front, roads, railroad tracks, and power lines hug the river valley, mercifully shielded from our sight by the steep hill and a copse of trees. We are an island of rural peace that is becoming ever rarer, less than 100 miles from Paris. Our front terrace still enjoys an unmatched view, and drinks outside are a summer ritual when the wind drops around sundown. "Didn't you know," said my mother, "a west wind, like an honest man, always goes to bed at night."

Our local sparkling white wine, *crémant,* is an inexpensive source of apéritifs. For Kir, the classic Burgundian addition is a teaspoon of black currant cassis (in our case homemade by Madame Milbert, page 68), named for Canon Kir, the wartime mayor of Dijon and a resistance hero and bon viveur. Blackberry, raspberry, and wild peach liqueur are equally tasty additions to *crémant* and we've tried a couple of other variants: one vanilla, very much in vogue, and one a kind of adult fizzy lemonade.

PREVIOUS PAGES: *Château du Feÿ, bottom right, rides high above the village of Villecien. At left, bunches of mistletoe are plentiful in the woods but can be a challenge to gather for Christmas decorations. Above, our fastigiated oaks are older than the château itself. Their dusting of snow invites my call to Christmas dinner.* PAGE 265: *Locally made chocolate-covered cherries are always welcome.* OPPOSITE: *Our local sparkling crémant white wine is the basis of many a celebration at Château du Feÿ. Here it is mixed with Madame Milbert's black currant cassis liqueur to make the classic Kir.*

Vanilla Syrup for Kir

For 1 cup/250 ml of vanilla syrup, heat 1 cup/200 g sugar with 1 cup/250 ml water over low heat until the sugar dissolves, stirring only once or twice. Bring the syrup to a boil and simmer for 5 minutes. Split 4 vanilla beans lengthwise to loosen the seeds and add them to the syrup. Continue simmering for 8 to 10 more minutes, until it is reduced to about a cup. Let the syrup cool, then strain it—it will be slightly sticky and cloudy with vanilla seeds. (The beans can be used again if you rinse and dry them, particularly for a recipe such as Frédéric's roasted pineapple on page 236.) For a cocktail, put 1 to 2 teaspoons of vanilla syrup and a teaspoon of rum or bourbon in a Champagne glass and fill with chilled sparkling white wine, stirring to mix. You'll be surprised at the intensity of the vanilla flavor. For a nonalcoholic cocktail, use cranberry juice instead of rum and lemonade instead of white wine. Vanilla syrup is also good for macerating fresh berries and for flavoring the syrup for poaching fruit.

One evening, a neighbor pressed this apéritif recipe on a tatty bit of paper into my hand. "The good life is with your back to the fire and belly to the table," he joked. "You must try this." The very Burgundian quantities suggested that six bottles of wine would serve 10 people, possibly "a few more at a pinch." Need I say that my servings have been scaled down.

Marquise Apéritif

Pare the zests from 3 medium lemons and reserve them. With a serrated knife, cut away and discard the bitter white pith. Thinly slice the lemon flesh and add the zests to ¾ cup/150 g of sugar. Stir in a bottle of dry white wine—we find that the local Aligoté is just right, or else try a Sauvignon Blanc. Cover tightly and leave to macerate for 24 hours in the refrigerator. Just before serving, stir in a chilled bottle (also 750 ml) of sparkling white *crémant*. Serve very cold for 10 to 12.

Summer means village fêtes and it's a feeble community indeed that does not have some kind of gathering. Our village of Villecien, with fewer than 300 inhabitants, musters a Bastille Day parade followed by a *verre de l'amitié* (glass of friendship) for which we contribute hors d'oeuvre such as my mother's favorite cheese sablés (opposite). There are drum majorettes (they seem to get younger every year) and a brass band led by Henri the carpenter who beats a vast drum as if he were hammering an outsize nail. Our mayor of fifteen years, Jean-Louis Potier, gives a short speech. A village mayor is important in France, elected by the residents and personally answerable to the state for public order and safety. "I am part manager, part sheriff, part confessor," says Monsieur Potier, who knows exactly what's going on in the community but discreetly keeps his mouth shut. To run for election, no qualifications are needed beyond paying taxes within the community. "It's open to any andouille!" grins Jean-Louis Potier. Luckily Monsieur Potier is not any old sausage, but a business executive. He manages a substantial budget (the village church, associated with Saint Vincent de Paul, has just been reroofed with state funds) and conducts Villecien's marriages and even burials. Farsighted and fair, he devotes much time to what is essentially an honorary position. "You never know what may come next," he says. "I've been called out in the night to certify the death of a baby or on Sunday morning to reconnect the water supply."

When we first arrived in Villecien in 1982, the village appeared to be dying. Over a period of a century it had taken several blows: first phylloxera, which spelled the end of the vines; then the seismic shock of World War I; and now the noise and nuisance of trucks thundering through our main street, past decaying houses, their shutters closed against the fumes. One truck driven by a *Britannique*—Monsieur Potier felt obliged to disclaim French responsibility—crashed into the churchyard and it was only when we went to inspect the damage that I realized that twenty villagers had laid down their lives in what is called the Great War, probably half of Villecien's youth. At last the trend seems to be reversed: a bypass has done much to reduce traffic and the village now has abundant water and main drains. Most important of all, young people are moving in, attracted by the gardens, the quiet, and the modest rents.

OPPOSITE AND ABOVE: *The band marching past the Villecien church is a fixture on Bastille Day. It is an amateur affair; the drum majorettes are scarcely old enough to parade, while in real life, drummer Henri, below, is a carpenter.*

My Mother's Cheese Sablés

With her coiffed white hair and choker of pearls, my mother had a great sense of style and a sharp sense of humor. To her, all politicians were rogues. She would tease my father, an arch political Conservative, by dangling the thought of voting for the Left, a fly to which he never failed to rise. Each evening she took her whiskey in a museum-quality crystal tumbler etched with roses commemorating Charles Stuart, Bonnie Prince Charlie. When the glass was drained, a hangman's gibbet emerged, etched on the bottom.

The cheese for these *sablés* should be very finely grated so they do not crumble. This recipe makes about three dozen *sablés* the size of a silver dollar.

> *2 cups/250 g flour*
> *1 teaspoon salt*
> *¼ teaspoon cayenne*
> *pinch of baking powder*
> *¾ cup plus 1 tablespoon/200 g butter*
> *1¼ cups/150 g grated Parmesan cheese*
> *1 egg, beaten to mix*
> *1 egg beaten with ½ teaspoon salt, for glaze*
> *paprika for sprinkling*

Put the flour, salt, cayenne, and baking powder in a food processor and work for 5 seconds until everything is well mixed. Cut the butter into pieces, add it to the flour, and work with the pulse button until it resembles coarse crumbs, ½ to 1 minute. Work in the cheese for about 10 seconds. Lastly add the egg and work until the mixture starts to form a ball, 30 to 40 seconds. Turn the dough onto a floured work surface and knead it with the heel of your hand, pushing it away and gathering it up with your fingers, until it peels off quite easily in one piece. This won't take long, 1 to 2 minutes.

Line 2 baking sheets with wax or parchment paper. Break off pieces of dough the size of a small walnut and roll them between your palms to form little balls. Set the balls on the baking sheets and flatten them to 2-inch/5-cm rounds with the back of a spoon. Brush them with the egg glaze and sprinkle with paprika. Chill them for 15 to 30 minutes until firm.

Heat the oven to 400°F/200°C. Bake the *sablés* until golden and lightly browned around the edges, 15 to 18 minutes. Transfer them to a rack to cool.

With a bit of persistence, you could visit a different fête every day according to the *Yonne Républicaine,* our local newspaper, which chronicles the sports events, the school graduations, the births and deaths (particularly on the roads) of our department. Concerts and art exhibitions vie with enormously popular *vide-greniers* (attic emptiers), where for a small fee you can park your junk on the sidewalk in the hope of a sale. The snail festival at Bassou tempts me, though I shy away from the climactic snail-eating contest—last year's winner ate 210 snails in fifteen minutes! At the nature park of Boutissaint, friends organize a Fête de la Nature et des Animaux Sauvages, a massive roundup of forest animals including deer and wild boar, simply for the spectacle.

At St. Fargeau in midsummer, 600 performers act out a sound and light show, one of the most vivid in France. This fifteenth-century castle served as prison for La Grande Mademoiselle, who was exiled for rubbing King Louis XIV the wrong way. The castle's majestic profile of pepperpot towers forms a backdrop for a fast-moving historical panorama involving hundreds of people, crack horsemen, creaking farm carts, and vehicles from World War II. A stout pig plods past, next a rare team of working oxen, then the trumpets sound, the lights blaze, all part of the Greatest Show on Earth to rival Madison Square Garden. After the blaze of fireworks that ends the performance, we go backstage to the dimly lit stables, packed now with odorous horses and a crowd congratulating the actors, who are all local volunteers. Our host, Joel Henrion, was for years a leading participant and he introduces us around. "You've come for a second show, have you!" teases one stalwart, stripping off his smock to reveal a muscled brown torso.

Joel recounts the story of how, only twenty years ago, St. Fargeau was abandoned, its roofs sagging and the wooden floors rotting away. But a visionary named Jacques Guyot saw something more. Determined to rescue a national treasure, he bought the property from the town for one franc on condition he undertake the restoration of one of the largest piles of masonry in France. Undaunted, Jacques has shown exactly what can be done, an adventure that has earned him national recognition and become a model for other owners of vast, forbidding properties (Le Feÿ, thank goodness, is on a human scale). Now St. Fargeau is alive: dozens of city children vacation there, sleeping in the attics; hundreds of visitors roam the refurbished rooms after each evening show to view an exhibition by local artists and inspect the latest renovations. Irrepressible and some would say crazy, Jacques Guyot now has an immense new project: to build a medieval castle from the foundations up, following ancient techniques with apprentice labor, thus introducing young people to the old ways.

Joel is our painter—"no, no, not interior designer," he insists. A charming, erratic blond, he has flamboyant taste and no sense of time. To ensure he turns up for a meeting, it's best to invite him to lunch. Joel runs classes in painting furniture and trompe l'oeil, and he and his wife Christine have founded an association of local young artisans—a lively group of painters (the river is always an attraction), cabinet-makers, and a potter or two—who meet to exchange views and arrange exhibitions, for example at the annual Journée de la Patrimoine when châteaux join in a national free opening day. Joel is a master of the very French skill of faux marbre, painting surfaces to resemble marble, stone, or wood. He's executed a smart chimney breast for us at Le Feÿ, and his restoration of a salon at St. Fargeau is impressive. Few old buildings that are left empty are safe for long. The family château of Clothilde de Drouas, who used to live at Le Feÿ, was raided one weekend and all the stone fireplaces were stolen. No doubt they ended up at a dealer in *matériaux anciens*; certainly the depot just along the road from us has a fine display of mantels among the stone basins, floor tiles, and great oak beams, all at vast prices.

Barbecued Quail with Asian Dips

Before the show at St. Fargeau, we met Joel's young family around a barbecue—even in France recipes such as Barbecued Quail with Asian Dips are recognized as ideal summer fare.

I am often surprised at how many of these little birds people will eat—we usually allow at least two per person, so the eight quail here should serve three to four.

> 8 quail
> 3 tablespoons olive oil
> 2 to 3 tablespoons lemon juice
> salt and pepper
>
> FOR THE GINGER-SCALLION DIP
> a 1-inch piece of fresh gingerroot, grated or finely
>   chopped
> 3 scallions, sliced
> 1/3 cup/75 ml peanut oil
> 2 tablespoons dark sesame oil
>
> FOR THE CHILE-SOY DIP
> 2 small fresh jalapeño chile peppers
> 2 tablespoons peanut oil
> 2 garlic cloves, chopped
> 1/3 cup/75 ml dark soy sauce
> 3 tablespoons rice wine vinegar
> juice of 1 lime
> 3 tablespoons chopped cilantro
>
> 6 to 8 wooden or metal skewers

OPPOSITE: *The ginger-scallion and chile-soy dips suggested for barbecued quail go well with barbecued chicken, too.*

If using wooden skewers, soak them in water so they do not scorch. To prepare the quail, put the birds on a board, breast down. Cut along each side of the backbone with poultry shears and remove the backbone (you can add them to the stockpot later). Turn the birds breast-side up and, with a sharp downward movement of the heel of your hand, flatten them, cracking the breastbones. Thread the flattened quail crosswise on 2 skewers, inserting one skewer through the wings and the second through the legs to hold the birds flat. Depending on the length of your skewers, you should be able to thread 2 or 3 quail on each pair. Set them on a shallow tray.

In a small bowl, whisk together the olive oil, lemon juice, salt, and pepper and brush the mixture over the quail. Cover and leave them to marinate at room temperature for up to an hour, turning them occasionally.

For the ginger-scallion dip, put the ginger and scallions in a small bowl with salt and pepper. Heat the peanut oil until very hot but not yet smoking, add the sesame oil, and pour the hot oil over the flavorings. Leave the dip to cool.

For the chile-soy dip, core the chiles, then finely chop them, including the seeds. (Be careful not to touch your face or eyes after handling the chiles.) Heat the oil in a small pan, add the chiles and garlic, and fry just until fragrant, 1 to 2 minutes. Remove the pan from the heat, stir in the soy sauce, vinegar, lime juice, and cilantro, and let the dip cool.

To finish, light the broiler or grill. Grill the quail about 3 inches/7.5 cm from the heat for 5 to 6 minutes, until brown and slightly charred. Turn them and brown the other side, 5 to 6 minutes longer. The quail should remain pink and juicy in the center but if they are plump they may need 4 to 5 minutes' more cooking on each side. Serve them very hot, with the dips in individual bowls.

The August harvest festival at Etigny, near Sens, marks the high point of our summer. The sun beats down with Mediterranean intensity and faces, brown now from vacation days outdoors, are moist with sweat. This is no religious festival, but a stirring re-creation of bygone harvesting with participants in white lace mobcaps, long dark skirts, and clogs, the men in straw hats and even in jeans. Dress is comfortable, casual, and as a result looks totally natural. As you stroll the lanes, here a farrier is shoeing a mule, there the *tonnelier* (barrel maker) bends his staves over the fire; you can try your hand at laundry, kneeling to beat the clothes with a wooden bat, or join the half-dozen lacemakers tossing their bobbins in the shade of an apple tree. Lace is not a local specialty but a recently formed group has grown to over 200 in ten years, so strong is the pull toward old crafts. Pausing under a shady tree, I suddenly smell roast pork—is it possible? There, over the fence, is a family placidly seated eating their Sunday lunch, oblivious of the crowd of thousands just outside their gate.

Like most French families, we eat a lot of pork, finding it just as tasty as veal and much less expensive. This idea for pork marinated in a sweet spiced brine, in effect half curing it, comes from Randall Price, as a reflection of his German ancestry.

Half-Cured Pork with Peaches

The pork is stuffed with cherries and dried peaches and garnished with baked peaches, serving six to eight. Don't worry about the number of ingredients in the brine; it is really very simple.

> *a 3-lb/1.4-kg boneless pork loin roast*
> *8 to 10 dried peaches or apricots (about 3 oz/90 g)*
> *½ lb/250 g fresh cherries, pitted*
> *2 to 3 tablespoons sugar*
> *1 tablespoon vegetable oil*
> *1 tablespoon butter*
> *5 small fresh peaches*
> *2 cups/500 ml veal or chicken stock*
> *salt and pepper*
>
> **FOR THE BRINE**
>
> *1¼ quarts/1.25 liters water*
> *¼ cup/60 g coarse salt*
> *¼ cup/50 g sugar*
> *3 bay leaves*
> *1 cinnamon stick*
> *1 teaspoon whole cloves*
> *2 garlic cloves, unpeeled*
> *1 teaspoon black peppercorns*
> *5 to 6 fresh thyme sprigs*
> *2 slices of fresh gingerroot*
> *1 small dried chile*
> *1 teaspoon crushed fennel seed*
> *3 to 4 star anise*

For the brine, heat the water with the salt and sugar until dissolved, stirring occasionally. Add the bay leaves, cinnamon, cloves, garlic, peppercorns, thyme, ginger, chile, fennel, and anise, bring to a boil, and simmer for 5 minutes. Let the brine mixture cool. When completely cool, butterfly the pork loin by cutting it lengthwise, leaving it joined at one side like an open book. Lay it flat in a shallow nonreactive dish and pour over the brine with its flavorings. Cover tightly with plastic wrap and refrigerate for 6 to 12 hours, turning the meat once or twice.

To roast the pork, heat the oven to 350°F/175°C. Drain the meat and pat it dry with paper towels, discarding the brine and seasonings. For the fruit stuffing, cut the dried fruit into chunks. Set half the cherries aside for gravy, and mix the rest with the dried fruit and a spoonful of sugar (if the cherries are sweet you will need very little). Arrange half of this stuffing along the center of the cut side of pork, reserving the rest to stuff the peaches. Reshape the meat to enclose the fruit and tie it with string to form a neat cylinder. Heat the oil and butter in a roasting pan over medium-high heat and brown the pork on all sides—it scorches easily because of the sugar cure. Cover the pan loosely with foil and roast the meat in the oven for 50 to 60 minutes.

To bake the peaches, halve them, discard the pits, and set them in a buttered baking dish. Pile the reserved fruit stuffing in the hollows left from the pits. Put the peaches in the oven with the pork and bake until they are just tender when pierced with a knife, 15 to 20 minutes. Set them aside to keep warm.

The pork is done when a skewer inserted in the center of the meat is hot to the touch when withdrawn after 30 seconds or a meat thermometer registers 165°F/72°C. The cooking time is shorter than usual since the meat is already partly cured. Transfer it to a board and cover it with foil to keep warm. Pour off and discard any fat from the roasting pan, set it on the stove to heat, and add the veal stock and remaining cherries. Simmer, stirring to dissolve the pan juices, until the cherries are tender and the gravy is reduced by half, 10 to 15 minutes. Work the gravy through a sieve into a saucepan; be sure to push down on the cherries in the sieve so the gravy is thickened with pulp. Reheat the gravy, taste, and adjust the seasoning with sugar, salt, and pepper. Discard the strings from the pork and cut it into ¾-inch/2-cm medallions, or thinner slices, whichever you prefer. Arrange the meat on a platter, spoon over some gravy, and add the stuffed peach garnish.

Cranberry Confit

In winter, instead of serving peaches and cherries with the half-cured pork, I substitute cranberries, which are now quite widely available in France. In the stuffing for the pork, add fresh cranberries instead of cherries. Then cook more of the berries with sugar as a confit (a preserve), using it to thicken the gravy and to serve as a colorful accompaniment.

Pick over 1 lb/500 g cranberries and spread them in a baking dish in a single layer so they all touch the bottom. Sprinkle them with ¾ cup/150 g sugar and cover with foil. Bake them in a 350°F/175C° oven with the pork, stirring them occasionally, until the berries just start to pop, 40 to 50 minutes. The confit is deliberately quite tart, but you can add more sugar if you like.

Etigny had its moment of fame in 1576, when Catherine de Medici signed a treaty there with her rebellious son, the Duc d'Anjou. Then, as now, the massive cathedral of Sens to the north must have been a presence as it is still clearly visible, riding high above the fields of grain, neither dwarfed by new buildings nor changed in 900 years. At the festival, a dozen ancient reapers and threshers are parked around a standing field of wheat, which grows ever smaller as each machine takes its turn. Passersby pick up discarded ears, bunching seven together to be tied with a strand of wool as a *porte-bonheur,* a symbol of good luck. Under a makeshift tent, the village baker is working at full stretch with a wood-fired bread oven, kneading, shaping, raising, and baking puffy round loaves—so much easier to handle than the finicky modern baguette that came into style in the mid-nineteenth century thanks to steam injection ovens. He's baking rustic leek and cheese *flamiches,* too, and fresh fruit tarts, which are snapped up the minute they are pulled from the oven on the long, spade-shaped wooden peel.

Flamiche is a robust version of quiche made with bread dough, and it needs a pungent filling of leeks, or perhaps of well-aged cheese.

274

Leeks in a Bread Crust
Flamiche aux Poireaux

As the name suggests, bread-based *flamiche* is Flemish, a reminder that in the fourteenth century, the dukes of Burgundy ruled as far as Flanders and the North Sea. Personally, I like to work with generous amounts of bread dough, so this recipe makes two *flamiches*, each enough for eight people. You'll find a cheese filling below as an alternative to the leek, so you can make two flavors and offer a choice. Simply divide the filling amounts in half to make one of each.

FOR THE BREAD DOUGH

1 ½ cups/300 ml milk
1 tablespoon/10 g active dry yeast
4 cups/500 g flour, more if needed
2 tablespoons sugar
1 ½ teaspoons salt
2 eggs, beaten to mix
1 cup/250 g butter

FOR THE LEEK FILLING

1 ½ lb/750 g leeks
2 tablespoons/30 g butter
2 to 3 tablespoons chopped thyme or sage
salt and pepper
2 egg yolks
⅓ cup/75 ml heavy cream

two 10-inch springform pans

To make the bread dough, scald the milk in a small saucepan and let it cool to tepid. Pour about a quarter cup into a small bowl, sprinkle the yeast on top, and leave it until dissolved, about 5 minutes. Sift the flour into a bowl with the sugar and salt and make a well in the center. Add the remaining milk, eggs, and yeast mixture. With your hand, gradually work the flour into the liquid ingredients to form a smooth dough—it should be quite soft, but if very sticky, add more flour. Alternatively, use a heavy-duty electric mixer with a dough hook to combine the ingredients.

To knead the dough by hand, lift it up and throw it down on a floured work surface until it is very elastic and resembles the texture of chamois leather, about 5 minutes. Work in more flour if necessary so that at the end of kneading the dough is somewhat sticky but holds together in one piece. Cream the butter and add it to the dough, squeezing with your fist until the butter is incor-

porated, about 5 minutes. You can also knead the dough and add the butter in the mixer—it will take about half the time. After kneading, transfer the dough to a buttered bowl, turn it over so the top is buttered, and cover the bowl with a damp cloth. Leave it in a warm place to rise until doubled in bulk, about an hour.

Meanwhile, make the filling. Trim the leeks, discarding most of the green tops, cut them lengthwise, and slice them into ¼-in/6-cm slices. Wash them thoroughly to remove any grit and drain them in a colander. Melt the butter in a medium pan, add the leeks with the thyme or sage, salt, and pepper, and press a piece of foil on top. Cover the pan with the lid and sweat the leeks over low heat until they are very tender, 20 to 30 minutes. Do not let them brown.

Generously butter the pans. When the dough is risen, knead it lightly to knock out the air and divide it in half. On a floured surface, roll or pat each piece of dough to a 15-in/40-cm round—it will be quite soft and floppy. Line the pans with dough, letting it drape over the rims. Spread the leeks on the dough. Whisk the egg yolks and cream with salt and pepper until mixed, and spoon this custard over the leeks. Fold the overhanging dough on top of the filling to half cover it, pleating it toward the center. Leave to rise in a warm place until almost doubled, 20 to 30 minutes. Heat the oven to 400°F/200°C and set a baking sheet low down to heat.

Bake the *flamiches* until the crust is browned and starts pulling from the sides of the pan; the filling should be set. Allow 40 to 50 minutes' cooking time and, if in doubt, bake longer as the dough is slow to cook. If the top browns too quickly, cover loosely with foil. Let the *flamiches* cool for 5 minutes before unmolding. Serve them freshly baked and warm with a green salad alongside.

Cheese in a Bread Crust
Flamiche au Fromage

As a quick filling for *flamiche,* we often use leftover cheese—the stronger the better. Dice, slice, or crumble the cheese, allowing about ¾ lb/375 g cheese for two *flamiches.* Scatter the cheese over the bread dough after lining the pans and before folding over the edges. Top with custard made by mixing 1 egg, 1 egg yolk, and ⅓ cup/75 ml heavy cream with salt and plenty of pepper (this makes enough custard for two flamiches). Fold dough on top, let rise, and bake as for Flamiche aux Poireaux.

Christmas for us, and for much of France, is a family affair and dinner is a combined effort. Simon supplies the caviar from his Russian sources and Emma fries the blini to go with them (page 202), while Mark is in charge of the wine. The bird and its trimmings are my responsibility. All my life the Christmas feast has centered around a fat goose, a Yorkshire tradition I've carried to Washington, D.C., Normandy, and now to Burgundy. The greatest treat is a bird fattened for foie gras as it supplies a maximum of crispy skin, so you can imagine my satisfaction when I found a producer in the Joigny market who is only too happy to off-load his meaty birds once the liver has been removed. He got the better of me one year, though. Geese are notoriously tricky to raise, some fattening with buxom white breasts and others remaining gaunt and bony. Foolishly I'd accepted the wrapped bird without inspection—never again!

ABOVE: *A basket of mistletoe, gathered from the overabundance in our fruit trees.* OPPOSITE: *A golden goose, with trimmings, awaits diners at our Christmas table.*

Roast Goose with Chestnuts and Wild Mushrooms

It was a Burgundian farmer, Madame Fournillon, who gave me this recipe for goose, which puts the chestnuts from our avenue of trees to good use with wild mushrooms from the market. Goose, like duck, is a bony bird and does not go far—you can generally count on one bird to serve six to eight, although our family of four have been known to strip the carcass at one sitting. At Christmas, the type of wild mushrooms available varies and I often mix them, aiming for a contrast of color with black trumpets, golden girolles, and white sheep's feet or oyster mushrooms.

a 10-lb/4.5-kg goose, with giblets
1 onion, sliced
1 carrot, sliced
2 tablespoons softened butter
salt and pepper
2 lb/1 kg fresh chestnuts
2 cups/500 ml milk, more if needed
2 cups/500 ml veal or chicken stock

FOR THE MUSHROOMS
1½ lb/750 g wild mushrooms
½ cup/125 g butter
2 shallots, very finely chopped
1 garlic clove, very finely chopped
2 tablespoons finely chopped parsley

trussing needle and string

Heat the oven to 450°F/230°C. Truss the goose using a trussing needle (see glossary) and set it on its back in a large roasting pan. Scatter the sliced onion, carrot, and the giblets around the bird (reserve the liver for another use). Spread the bird with the softened butter and sprinkle it with salt and pepper. Roast it, basting occasionally, until it is golden brown, about 40 minutes. Prick the bird all over with a fork to release fat under the skin. Lower the oven heat to 350°F/175°C and continue roasting, basting and pouring off the excess fat from the pan for 2 to 2½ hours. Reserve the fat.

Meanwhile, cook the chestnuts. Poke a hole in each chestnut with the point of a knife, put them in a pan of cold water, bring to a boil, and simmer for 2 minutes. Remove from the heat but leave the chestnuts in the water. Lift out a few chestnuts at a time on a draining spoon, let them cool slightly, and then strip off the skin and peel. Continue with the rest. Alternatively, you can strip off the skin and peel with a knife. Either way, this is a tiresome job, but once a year it's worth it.

Put the peeled chestnuts in a pan with enough milk to cover and add the lid. Bring them to a boil and simmer until almost tender, 15 to 20 minutes. You don't want them too soft, or they will fall apart when roasted. Put 2 to 3 tablespoons of the reserved fat in a baking dish, drain, and add the chestnuts with salt and pepper. Stir to coat them with fat and roast them in the oven with the goose (after the heat has been lowered to 350°F/175°C) until they are glazed and very tender, 20 to 30 minutes.

For the mushrooms, trim the stems of the mushrooms, discarding any earth; wash them only if they are very sandy, draining them well. Melt a tablespoon of the butter in a frying pan, add the mushrooms with salt and pepper, and cook, tightly covered, over very low heat until the juices run, 5 to 8 minutes. Remove the lid, raise the heat, and cook until the liquid evaporates, stirring occasionally. The cooking time varies from 5 to 10 minutes, depending on the type of mushroom and their size. Cream the butter with the shallots, garlic, parsley, salt, and pepper and set it aside.

If you like your goose to be pink, test it after it has been roasting for a total of about 3 hours by pricking the thigh with a fork—the juices should run pink but not red, and the thigh should be slightly flexible when you wiggle it. If you prefer goose well done, as we do, continue cooking until the juices from the leg run clear and the meat starts shrinking from the knuckle bone; the thigh will be almost loose.

When the goose is cooked, transfer it to a platter, cover it loosely with foil, and keep it warm. For the gravy, pour off the fat from the roasting pan, leaving behind the juices. Add the stock and simmer for 10 or 15 minutes, stirring to dissolve the pan juices. Strain the gravy into a small saucepan, taste it, and adjust the seasoning.

To finish, reheat the chestnuts and mushrooms if necessary. Discard the trussing strings from the goose and pile the chestnuts around it on the platter. Stir the shallot butter into the mushrooms and pile them in a warm serving dish. Moisten the goose with a little gravy and serve the rest separately.

The accompaniments to goose are just as important as the bird itself. Ours reflect our peripatetic life—often we have American wild rice (Minnesota is a popular stop of mine), or it may be kasha from Russia. The gravy is a French jus, dark, concentrated, and without thickening. Instead of stuffing, which I find tends to stew and steam inside a bird, we've always had plain onions, roasted until they are caramelized and almost black. Rather than adding them to the goose, I usually cook them separately so they are easier to control.

Burnt Onions

For 6 people, peel and slice 12 medium onions (I allow 2 per person as they collapse so thoroughly during cooking). Pour 6 to 8 tablespoons of fat from the roasting goose into a baking dish, add the onions, stir them to coat with fat, and sprinkle with salt and pepper. (Bacon fat is good for frying onions, too.) Roast the onions in the oven at 350°F/175°C with the goose, stirring from time to time, until they are very soft and colored to a deep golden brown. This will take an hour or more. If you like, continue until they are very dark brown and slightly bitter—that's the way I like them.

ABOVE: *Roast goose is surrounded with wild mushrooms, Brussels sprouts from our garden, and chestnuts from the avenue outside the gate, as well as bowls of rutabaga purée and simply braised red cabbage.*

Rutabaga Purée

My mother always had rutabaga (called a swede in England) purée with goose, so this is in her honor.

For 6 people, peel 2 lb/1 kg rutabagas, and cut them into large chunks. Put them in a pan of cold salted water, cover, and bring to a boil. Simmer until very tender, 30 to 40 minutes. Drain the rutabagas, return them to the pan, and heat gently for 2 or 3 minutes to dry them. Mash the chunks with a potato masher or fork— the purée will always be slightly fibrous. Work in 3 to 4 tablespoons butter (more if you are reckless) with a generous grate of nutmeg, taste, and adjust the seasoning.

Fresh Mincemeat Pies

Dessert on our Christmas table has varied from year to year. Sometimes it is pecan pie (we have a Southern friend who owns a pecan orchard). For years I made real mincemeat using ground cooked beef, suet, dried fruits, and spices, leaving it to mature at least six months before baking mince pies. A mouse found the crock one year, so I was forced to substitute this fresh mincemeat pie and since then we've never looked back. This recipe makes ten or twelve individual pies.

> *2 tart apples*
> *grated zest and juice of ½ lemon*
> *6 oz/175 g seedless grapes, halved*
> *½ cup/75 g dark raisins*
> *½ cup/75 g golden raisins*
> *⅓ cup/90 g light brown sugar*
> *¼ cup/22 g slivered almonds*
> *1 tablespoon chopped candied orange peel*
> *½ teaspoon ground cinnamon*
> *½ teaspoon ground allspice*
> *¼ teaspoon ground cloves*
> *2 tablespoons Cognac*
> *1 egg white for glaze*
> *granulated sugar for sprinkling*
>
> **FOR THE PÂTE BRISÉE**
> *4 cups/500 g flour*
> *3 egg yolks*
> *3 tablespoons sugar*
> *1 teaspoon salt*
> *⅓ cup/90 ml cold water, more if needed*
> *1 cup/250 g butter*
>
> *10 to 12 tartlet molds (4-in/10-cm diameter)*
> *4- and 5-in/10- and 12-cm fluted cookie cutters*

Prepare the pâte brisée dough using the ingredients above and the technique described in the glossary (page 298). Wrap and chill the dough for 30 minutes or more.

Meanwhile, make the mincemeat filling. Peel, core, and dice the apples, and mix them in a large bowl with the grated lemon zest and juice so the apples do not discolor. Stir in the grapes, dark and golden raisins, brown sugar, almonds, candied orange peel, cinnamon, allspice,

We always serve mincemeat pies with hard sauce, lifting the lid of the hot pie to insert a nugget of sauce so it melts into the filling. Scrumptious, as Dickens would have remarked.

and cloves until evenly mixed. Lastly stir in the Cognac.

Brush the tartlet molds with butter. Roll out half the dough and stamp out as many 5-in/12-cm rounds as possible. Use them to line the molds, pressing the dough well down into the base. Press the dough trimmings into the remaining dough, roll it out, and cut more 5-in/12-cm rounds with enough 4-in/10-cm lids to cover all the molds.

Spread the filling in the tartlet shells and top with lids. Do not seal the lids to the base, but leave them unattached so that they can be pried open at the table to sneak in a spoonful of Brandy Hard Sauce (below). With the point of a knife, slash each lid with a Christmas tree, or some other festive design of your choosing. Lightly whisk the egg white and brush the lids. Sprinkle the tops with granulatd sugar, letting it fall through a small sieve. Set the pies on a baking sheet and chill them until firm, 15 to 30 minutes. Heat the oven to 375°F/190°C.

Bake the pies low down in the oven until the tops are lightly browned and the filling starts to bubble, 25 to 30 minutes. A skewer inserted in the center of the pie should be hot to the touch when withdrawn after 30 seconds. Let the pies cool slightly, then unmold them. Serve them hot with hard sauce in a separate bowl.

Brandy Hard Sauce

As a child, my contribution to Christmas dinner was always the brandy butter (aka hard sauce) for mincemeat pies. We had no electric mixer and on a cold day quite vigorous beating was needed to bring the butter and sugar mixture to the necessary fluffy texture. If I shirked it, the brandy separated, and my father would wrinkle his nose at such sloth.

For 10 to 12 people, cream 1 cup/250 g butter. Beat in 1 cup/200 g sugar and continue beating until soft and light, 3 to 5 minutes. Beat in 5 to 6 tablespoons Cognac, or more to your taste, adding it a little at a time so it is evenly absorbed. Don't stint on the Cognac—with too little the sauce tastes bland and fatty. Chill it until firm, then shape into balls with an ice cream scoop or cut it in cubes, and pile in a serving bowl. Chill the sauce until serving.

In 1987, when we'd been at Château du Feÿ for five years, we

gave a party. Everything came out in multiples of seven. Both Mark and I were forty-nine, the date was the seventh day of the seventh month, we had been married for twenty-one years and, of course, we had to put seven guests at each table. A couple of weeks beforehand we counted over eighty acceptances, so we would need all hands to help. I knew that cooking was assured by Chefs Claude and Chambrette who would come down from La Varenne in Paris for the occasion. For days before, they were folding, shaping, and baking little puff pastry edibles with zesty little stuffings run up by Chambrette from cans of olives and anchovies that were years beyond their sell-by date. We had real potato chips, using garden potatoes that were freshly deep-fried. More recently, chefs have taken to frying a variety of roots to make what I call rainbow chips. Irresistible!

Rainbow Chips

We fire up the deep fat pan for only two treats: Indian poppadums brought from the gourmet grocery near my mother in Yorkshire and classic, freshly fried potato chips. This recipe is an upmarket, party version of chips that uses several different roots, preferably of different colors—the more variety, the better. Mix the chips in a bowl for a rainbow effect. They can be fried several hours ahead. This recipe makes enough chips to satisfy four people.

> ½ lb/250 g beets
> ½ lb/250 g potatoes
> ½ lb/250 g sweet potatoes
> ½ lb/250 g Jerusalem artichokes or celery root
> juice of ½ lemon
> oil for deep frying
> salt

Trim and peel all the vegetables. Depending on their shape and size, they may be left whole or may need to be cut into manageable chunks in order to slice them. Slice them as thinly as possible, preferably using a mandoline. Set the sliced beets aside; keep the sliced potatoes in separate bowls of cold water, and the sliced artichokes or celery in water acidulated with the lemon juice. Soaking not only prevents discoloration, it also reduces starch in the vegetables so the chips are lighter and stick together less in hot oil.

Heat the oil to 375°F/190°C. Drain one type of vegetable at a time and pat the slices dry on paper towels. Fry them in the hot oil until crisp and golden brown, 2 to 3 minutes, stirring gently with a draining spoon to separate the slices. Drain the chips on paper towels.

Fry the remaining vegetables in batches in the same way—the order does not matter. Take care with sweet potatoes, which tend to brown quickly. Sprinkle with salt just before serving.

Guests are invited for seven o'clock. Pink-cheeked Monsieur Branger, former mailman, is in charge of service—as a holdover from the de Drouas days, he knows the house well. Portuguese Maria washes up in one kitchen, Madame Milbert in the other. Monsieur Milbert brings out his hand-painted PARKING sign, used once a year, and opens the gate to the dry moat, while sweet, frail Claudine, the housekeeper, is set to welcome guests at the gate. Before the party begins, we have a formal photograph taken under the great oak tree, which is higher than the house and probably older too. My father, upright despite his arthritis and eighty-four years (another septimal number!), looks proudly into the lens; this family is his legacy for I am an only child with no relatives barring a single cousin who lives in Italy. My mother is more elegant than all of us in navy chiffon and a discreet twinkle of diamond, while Emma wears her first strapless dress, sure it will gape too revealingly, with Grandma's earrings and my pearls around her neck. Simon, in his first tuxedo, is a carbon copy of Dad, whose thirty-year-old outfit is showing the strain. And for my part I look excited, about to bounce out of the frame to the kitchen, the terrace, the dining room, anywhere so as not to stand still.

Soon we are downing Champagne in high sun on the terrace. By some blessing of fate the weather always seems benign when we entertain and only once in fifteen years have we had to retreat indoors. Mark opens the festivities with an elegant speech in French and English on the theme of the number seven and reads a well-wisher's message: "May you all be in seventh heaven." We settle down to a concert of chamber music in the salon, a Burgundian tradition signaled by the horn and lyre carved in the paneling above the fireplace. Across the way, the dining room is adorned with a glass and carafe— these rooms were designed for just such occasions. As we listen to the familiar strains of Mozart, a pleasant cross breeze brings the scent of lavender and rose. For dinner I had asked each chef to create a personal dessert and not surprisingly, they turned to wine (recipes overleaf).

OPPOSITE: *Our family lines up for a souvenir shot before the party. From left, Mark, my father, Simon, Emma, my mother, and me.* ABOVE: *A trumpet, lyre, and sheet of music, carved in the* boiserie *of the salon, call guests to the dance.*

Strawberry and Wine Mousse

I prefer this mousse made with a sweet white wine such as the rich Muscat from Beaumes de Venise or Frontignan. This recipe makes six individual mousses, plus a brilliant strawberry coulis to serve with them.

> 1½ quarts/500 g strawberries
> ½ bottle (375 ml) sweet white wine
> 1 tablespoon/7 g powdered gelatin
> ¼ cup/50 g sugar, more for the coulis
> 1 cup/250 ml heavy cream
>
> 6 ramekins (¾-cup/175-ml capacity each)

Set aside 6 small strawberries for decoration and hull the rest, washing them only if they are sandy. Slice half of them. Put about a quarter of the white wine in a small pan, sprinkle over the gelatin, and leave it until spongy, about 5 minutes. Put the remaining white wine in a small saucepan, add the sugar, and heat gently until the sugar is dissolved. Bring the wine and sugar just to a boil, pour it over the gelatin, and stir until the gelatin is melted. Leave to cool slightly.

Meanwhile, beat the cream until it holds a soft peak. Put the ramekins to chill in a bath of ice water. Set the wine mixture over ice and chill it, stirring gently, until very cold and starting to set. Take it off the ice and fold in the whipped cream. The gelatin mixture sets rapidly once it is cold, so work quickly—if it sets before you've added the cream, warm it briefly over a simmering bain-marie until melted, then chill it again.

To mold the mousse, ladle about half the wine and cream mixture into the chilled ramekins and let it set for 2 to 3 minutes. Top it with the sliced strawberries—the mousse should be firm enough so that the berries don't sink. Top with the remaining mousse mixture, filling the ramekins almost full. Cover and chill the mousses until firm, at least 2 hours. They can be kept up to 24 hours.

For the strawberry coulis, puree the remaining strawberries in a food processor or with a hand-held immersion blender. Work in sugar to taste.

To finish, immerse a ramekin in warm water for 5 to 10 seconds to loosen the mousse without melting it. Run a knife around the edge of the mousse and turn it onto a chilled individual dessert plate. Repeat with the rest. Spoon strawberry coulis around each mousse, set a whole strawberry on top, and serve lightly chilled.

Red Wine Tart

Chef Chambrette, of course, has to do something a bit different, a twist he's never tried before. Goodness knows where he came across the recipe for this curious Red Wine Tart, perfect in a Burgundian setting.

He was particularly pleased by the juxtaposition of local red wine with the ground cinnamon so favored by his American students. A Pinot Noir is good for this tart, nothing too expensive but with plenty of fruit. One tart can be divided into four to six wedges for serving.

> 2 eggs
> ½ cup/100 g sugar
> 2 teaspoons cornstarch
> 2 teaspoons ground cinnamon
> 1 cup/250 ml red wine
> ½ cup/125 ml heavy cream for decoration
>
> FOR THE PÂTE SUCRÉE
> 1½ cups/175 g flour
> ½ teaspoon salt
> ½ cup/100 g sugar
> 3 egg yolks
> 1 teaspoon vanilla extract
> 7 tablespoons/100 g butter
>
> a 9-in/22-cm pie pan with removable base
> pastry bag and small star tube

Heat the oven to 375°F/190°C and put a baking sheet to heat low down in the oven. Prepare and blind-bake the pâte sucrée tart shell using the ingredients listed above and the technique described in the glossary (page 000). Leave the oven on.

For the filling, whisk the eggs with the sugar, cornstarch, and cinnamon just until mixed—don't let any froth form, as it spoils the smooth surface of the tart. Stir in the wine. Pour the filling into the blind-baked pie shell and bake it on a shelf low down in the oven until it is set, 20 to 25 minutes. Let the tart cool for 5 minutes, then unmold it, and let it cool completely.

Shortly before you serve the tart, beat the cream until it holds a stiff peak. Fill it into the piping bag with the star tube and pipe very small rosettes of whipped cream around the edge of the tart, just inside the pastry edge.

Later the band strikes up again, for dancing this time, and my father looks nostalgic —he was a champion waltzer in his day. Simon tries hard not to tread on his grandmother's toes while I find myself whirling in the arms of a neighbor who has somewhere learned the steps of the Gay Gordons, a Scottish reel. After midnight it grows darker, though never too dark as the drive and walks are lit with little 5-franc candles like fireflies. Toward dawn Chef Chambrette is sighted naked in the pool, but his subsequent claim to have found a nine-year-old nymphet in similar guise was never confirmed. Emma, however, undoubtedly received her first improper proposal from a bibulous guest as she complained indignantly about it for a week afterward. The house was full with thirty or more, though many never went to bed, and as we listened from our aerie in one of the towers, Mark started looking ahead to the next likely celebration—a family wedding, Burgundian style. Simon or Emma—whose would it be?

ABOVE: *Nothing matches Chef Chambrette's Red Wine Tart when it comes to intensity of flavor and color.*

It was Emma! Her engagement to Todd, a quiet American whom we had known and come to appreciate, was a pleasure for us all. If anyone could tame talented, headstrong Emma, it was he. But when she announced the grand scale of her plans for a July 4 wedding, we were taken aback. Two hundred guests, bridesmaids to be dressed in trendy black, a rehearsal dinner, Dad in a top hat. What next! As for a bridal shower, to Europeans this means a wet wedding day. But Emma is nothing if not persistent and gradually we were won over.

The first vital question was whether a wedding ceremony was even possible at the château. We consulted Monsieur Potier, the village mayor. He would be delighted to come. "I'll simply tuck Marianne and the official portrait of President Chirac under my arm," he declared. Marianne proved to be a large plaster bust, crowned with laurel as befits an emblem of the French state. When decked out with a corsage on her very generous bosom, she became a member of the wedding party. But about one thing the mayor was adamant. By law the ceremony had to take place in the *mairie*. As so often in France, *"tout s'arrange* (everything can be arranged)." In this case the arrangement was a double wedding, the first part of the ceremony to be held in the morning at the *mairie,* with the full panoply on the steps of the château later in the day.

Back to the château. Yes, I agreed, we probably could find room for forty special guests to sleep somewhere on the property for several days before the wedding. Mark seized the excuse to install yet another bathroom, making the eighteenth on the property. (When the hot water heater gave up the struggle shortly after the first guests arrived, no one complained, that's *la vie de château.*) We settled down to explore what we would eat. Plenty of poultry, we agreed, ham, a leg or two of lamb, and of course, vegetables from the garden. It would be the season for strawberries, raspberries, and all of the currant family, including cassis (black currants) and gooseberries. Peas might be over but we'd have buckets of baby green beans, zucchini, fresh garlic, lettuces, and perhaps some new potatoes. We alerted Monsieur Milbert that the strain on his supplies would be considerable. Madame Milbert promised extras of *tilleul,* the dried lime blossoms from the avenue trees that make a soothing herb tea. I would need plenty of that, I could see.

An urn of flowers, arranged at the last possible minute in Emma's preferred colors of yellow and white, dresses the steps where the bride will stand.

How could we involve our friends the artisanal food producers who make this area, for me, the heart of Burgundy? Monsieur Parret the *fromager* came to mind. He would anchor the pre-dinner reception on the terrace with a spread of dozens of regional cheeses, labeled and divided to make sampling easy. Sadly Le Feÿ's ancient bread oven seemed too remote from the festivities to use. But why not fire it up for the dreaded Day After, when the newlyweds would be gone and listless guests would drift by at all hours to say good-bye. We would ask Monsieur Haumonté to make pizza for us all.

That left the dinner itself. Emma agreed that conventional wedding food was not for us. "Let's have a country buffet," she said, "with all those delicious pâtés and sausages, and lots of salads." And so we did, with some interesting twists provided by a local chef, Claude Godard. Guests found their place-cards, each table identified by a different herb, then lined up for chicken galantine with pistachios and foie gras, a pâté of confit leg of lamb, poached nuggets of salmon, assorted sausages, and a diversity of salads. Waiters served the main course of guinea hen in a rich cream sauce. At the time, neither I nor Emma realized how uncannily this menu echoed another wedding feast, given for Gustave Flaubert's Emma Bovary in the Norman countryside a century and a half ago. On that table were "four sirloins of beef, six dishes of chicken fricassee, casseroled veal, three legs of lamb and, in the center, a charming roast suckling pig, flanked by four andouille sausages flavored with sorrel."

For both Emmas, the feast culminated in a grandiose *pièce montée,* one of the great sugar fantasy sculptures that date back to the Middle Ages. The Bovary table boasted a three-tiered colonnaded temple embellished with petits fours of almond, angelica, raisins, and orange quarters, all crowned with Cupid perched on a peak of chocolate. On the Château du Feÿ cake, Chef Randall Price went equally to town. The base of the cake was a pound cake flavored with white chocolate and pistachio, imbibed with lemon syrup and Scotch whisky. The layers were filled with lemon and raspberry curd and our own fresh raspberries. Randall gathered blossoms of white lilac and painstakingly candied them with egg white and fine sugar to a crisp, ethereal white.

Assembly was a feat of engineering. Randall sheathed the cake layers in protective pistachio marzipan, then coated and decorated them with lemon and white chocolate buttercream. An hour or two before show time, the cake was built, tier upon tier, on sugar columns. What we didn't see was the ingenious scaffolding of plastic straws within the layers themselves. Can you wonder that such an oeuvre took weeks to prepare, with preliminary sketches and trials to get the cake and fillings just right?

OPPOSITE: *The cake is carried in stages to be assembled in the kitchen. Setting sunlight catches the table-settings. Right, party planner Rebecca Berry pulls some roses for arrangements.* ABOVE: *Chairs await cleaning before being moved to the supper tent.*

One-Tiered Wedding Cake

Only a professional with plenty of time would embark on the multitiered confection Randall created in Emma's honor. But the same ingredients in this simplified version make a splendid gala gâteau, rich but light with intriguing flavor. It serves ten generously. Decoration on top is very much up to you—fresh flowers such as orange blossoms, violets, or roses are a charming touch but they do not hold up long and get in the way when serving. A border of raspberries arranged in concentric circles, or even a complete covering, brings the cake closer to a dessert. The professional approach would be to add rosettes of piped buttercream (you may need more); candied violets and toasted whole nuts are another possibility.

FOR THE PISTACHIO CAKE
1 ¼ cups/150 g shelled pistachios
2 ½ cups/300 g flour
1 ½ tablespoons baking powder
½ teaspoon salt
6 oz/175 g white chocolate, chopped
½ cup/125 g butter
1 cup/200 g sugar
grated zest of 1 lemon
6 egg yolks
6 tablespoons/90 ml whiskey
1 cup/250 ml milk

FOR THE FILLING
1 cup Raspberry or Lemon Curd (opposite)
1 pint/175 g fresh raspberries

FOR THE LEMON-WHITE CHOCOLATE
BUTTERCREAM
½ lb/250 g white chocolate, chopped
½ cup/100 g sugar
½ cup/125 ml lemon juice
¼ cup/60 ml water
4 egg yolks
1 cup/250 g butter

FOR DECORATION
¾ cup/100 g shelled pistachios, chopped
decorative finishes of your choice

two 9-in/23-cm layer pans

Make the raspberry or lemon curd and let it cool. Heat the oven to 350°F/175°F. Finely grind the whole pistachios with about half of the flour in a food processor, then stir them into the remaining flour with the baking powder and salt. Melt the white chocolate, then leave it to cool. Brush the cake pans with melted butter and line each with a round of wax or parchment paper. Brush the paper with butter, then sprinkle the pans with flour, tapping the sides to coat them evenly and discarding the excess.

To make the cake, cream the butter in an electric mixer, beat in the sugar and lemon zest, and continue beating until the mixture is soft and light, 3 to 5 minutes. Beat in the egg yolks one by one, beating well after each addition. Beat in the melted chocolate (it must be cool or it will melt the butter), followed by 2 tablespoons of the whiskey; save the remaining whiskey for sprinkling after baking. Sprinkle about a third of the flour/nut mixture over the chocolate batter and fold them together. Fold in about half of the milk. Add the remaining flour/nut mixture in 2 batches with the milk.

Spread the batter in the cake pans. Bake the cakes until risen and brown, 25 to 30 minutes; they will be slightly shrunk from the sides of the pan and will spring back when pressed with a fingertip. Turn them onto a rack, remove the paper, then turn them bottom downward on the rack to become firm and cool.

Meanwhile, make the lemon-white chocolate buttercream. Melt the chocolate and leave it to cool. Heat the sugar, lemon juice, and water in a small saucepan until the sugar is dissolved. Reserve about half the syrup to sprinkle on the cake. Bring the remaining syrup to a boil and boil it to the soft ball stage (239°F/115°C on a candy thermometer).

Meanwhile, beat the egg yolks just until mixed. Still beating constantly, gradually pour in the very hot syrup and continue beating until the mixture is cool and forms a thick mousse, about 5 minutes. (This is most easily done in a standing mixer, which leaves your hand free to pour the hot syrup.) Cream the butter and beat it into the cooled mousse mixture—if it is warm, it will melt the butter. Beat in the cooled chocolate. Do not chill the buttercream.

To assemble the cake, sprinkle both cakes with the reserved syrup and the remaining whiskey. Spread the top of one cake with a generous amount of Raspberry or Lemon Curd—you may have some left over. Top the curd with the fresh raspberries. Set the second cake, top downward, on the raspberry filling—the upturned bottom of the cake provides an ideal flat surface for the buttercream frosting. Press the 2 cakes firmly together and set them on a round of cardboard or a flat plate so they are easy to handle. Chill them thoroughly, at least half an hour.

Spread the buttercream over the top of the assembled cake, coating the sides as well. Chop the reserved pistachios and press them around the sides of the cake. Add the decoration of your choice and chill the cake thoroughly before serving—it will keep for several days and the flavors will mellow. Fresh flowers should be added at the last minute.

Raspberry or Lemon Curd

I was brought up on lemon curd, but raspberry curd was a novelty when Randall introduced me to it. The color is purplish, rather strange unless you add a bit of food coloring, but the flavor is spectacular. If you have curd left over from the One-Tiered Wedding Cake (opposite), it is delicious spread on hot toast.

For raspberry curd, puree 1 pint/175 g raspberries in a food processor and put them in a pan with ½ cup/125 g butter and ½ cup/100 g sugar. Heat gently, stirring constantly, until the ingredients are melted and combined. Let them cool to tepid, then stir in 4 lightly beaten eggs. Set the pan back on the heat and continue to cook over very low heat, stirring all the time, until the curd thickens enough to coat the back of the spoon, 20 to 25 minutes. Don't let the curd cook too fast or get too hot as it will curdle. Work the curd through a sieve to remove the seeds (or the zest from the lemons). This makes 2 cups/500 ml of curd, more than enough for the One-Tiered Wedding Cake.

For lemon curd, in the recipe for Raspberry Curd, replace the raspberry purée with the grated zest and juice of 4 large lemons and cook the curd less—10 minutes is probably enough.

Preparation of a wedding cake starts weeks before its assembly on the morning of the party. Above, icing is piped to glue the second tier of the cake to the base. Below, Chef Randall Price tries on the crowning touch, a bower of sugar columns decorated with candied blossoms of white lilac, for size.

While we were planning the menus, Mark was conferring with Rebecca Berry, an American party planner who providentially was accustomed to setting up microphones, chairs, flowers, carpets of honor, and all the impedimenta of a one-time reception. She even knew a tent man, flashy Monsieur Fleuchet, who shinned up poles with the agility of an acrobat, clad in the shortest and most suggestive of shorts. Mark tracked down musicians, a local group recommended by Michel Gandolfo, a lycée teacher who over the years had kept Simon and Emma's French language up to scratch. (Simon had to be bribed with tennis lessons, an exchange that proved a lasting bond.)

The wedding, we'd decided, would take place on the front steps of Le Feÿ with the guests sitting in the courtyard facing the mayor and the bust of Marianne. As father of the bride, Mark went scouting conveyances to deliver him and Emma to the ceremony and he found a stylish coach and pair. The coachman is a story in himself. Antoine Frombach lives in a fortified farmhouse on the outskirts of Sens, with a secret collection of old carriages in his barns. His museum-class parade includes a "milord" once used by George Sand and an eighteenth-century traveling *berline* with a slot for love letters in the door, said to have belonged to a *petite amie* of Louis XV. Monsieur Frombach was once the village baker and when we went to settle about the carriage, he proudly showed us one of the earliest commercial electric mixers still fitted with its balloon whisk and giant copper bowl for beating egg whites. He remembers using it when he began his ten-year career as a baker, but "the hours were too long," he says with a rueful smile. We are climbing into the car when he rushes out with a treasure, a *banneton,* one of the linen-lined wicker bread baskets used to shape long French baguettes. This one is for loaves of two kilos, he says. "All you need do is wash the linen, no soap of course. Take it, it's for you."

It seemed that almost everyone we knew in the Yonne would be somehow involved in Emma's wedding, but the guests came from far and wide. Todd's family lives in Kansas, so a big American contingent was assured, supplemented by Simon and Emma's friends from college in the United States. Many of our contemporaries came over from England for the weekend, using the tunnel and autoroute that bring London within seven hours' drive of Le Feÿ. Dutch Hans, Russian Igor and Shaila (an Ismaili born in Tanzania) became very much part of the wedding group. Gustave Flaubert describes just such a motley group of guests at the Bovarys'. Like them, we invited relatives from both sides of the family; like them, "we renewed broken friendships and half-forgotten acquaintances." I can only wish our Emma a rosier future than her ill-fated namesake.

Emma and Todd exchange vows on the steps of Château du Feÿ in the pre-sence of the mayor, Jean-Louis Potier, and of Marianne, symbol of the French nation whose bust (partly obscured by guests) is on the steps at right.

For me, the actual wedding ceremony and reception passed in the haze that surrounds events of high tension. I remember small things: Simon holding my hand as we walk in procession to the steps. Zigzag our Dalmatian performing his hereditary act as a carriage dog trotting behind Emma and Mark in the post chaise, drawn by matched Comtois horses. In his wedding speech, Mark quotes Groucho Marx: "Marriage is a wonderful institution, but who wants to live in an institution?" He also repeats my own father's words to him when we were married thirty-two years before. "I always think that the most important quality in a husband, or wife, is a really kindly nature. If there is genuine kindness, so many other things flow from it and you can't go far wrong." At that moment I almost became the classic, weeping mother of the bride.

Later, much later, I start to register more normally. Goddamnit, we're running late. Why are half the tables without wine? How is it that the terrace candles aren't lit? Who will serve the coffee? Simon calms me down and takes me to the microphone where, to loud applause, I don a La Varenne apron and announce the arrival of the wedding cake. Chef Randall and a helper march gingerly up the ramp bearing the five-tiered cake on a huge plank, nicknamed, irresistibly, "the bier." Simon steps forward and with bravado sabres the neck of a bottle of Champagne with a scimitar from the desert of Morocco. (No secret, this. Simply strip the capsule and wire seal from the bottle and find the seam running up the glass to the neck, the weak point of the bottle. Holding the neck away from you, run the blunt, back edge of a heavy knife—or sword—up this seam to hit the lip of the bottle sharply. It will split like magic. The cork, with attached ring of glass, ejects like a rocket, so be sure no one is in the line of fire.)

Cake cutting is followed by fireworks, and fireworks by dancing. Despite the unaccustomed high heels I find my feet are in fine form. I start to dance and go on and on, passing from partner to partner in a kind of free-form cotillion. The precocious pianist, aged only eighteen and still in high school, gives a performance of virtuoso brilliance, fueled by bottles of Evian water. Around me, young and old whirl on a parquet floor made for dancing, to the invitation offered by the horn and lyre in the *boiseries* above our heads. Oblivious of time, we dance through the night until the sun is high. Happiness is the best Champagne.

295

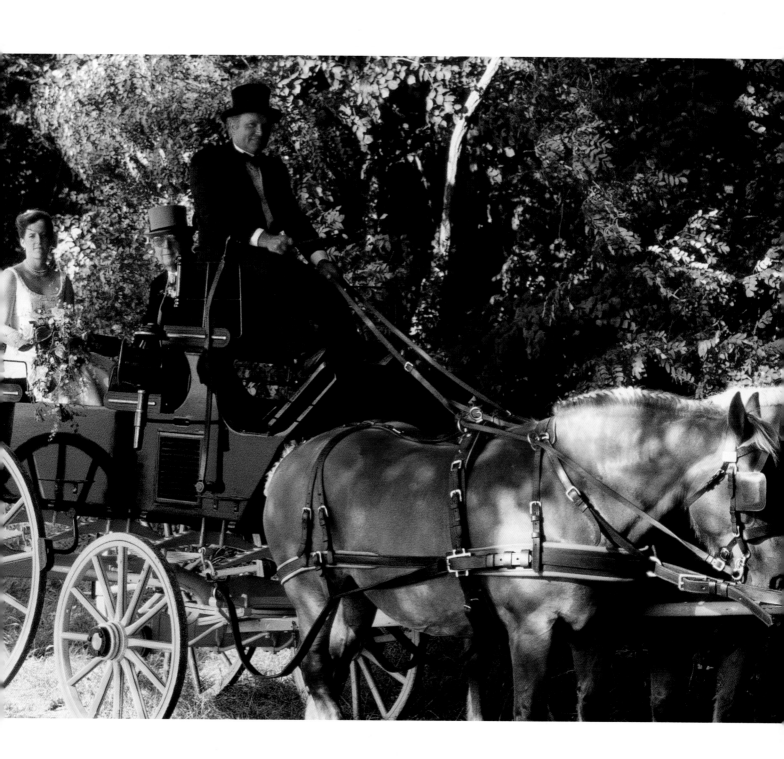

*Emma with her favorite yellow flowers and Mark in his top hat are carried
in style to the wedding ceremony by a matched pair of Comtois horses.*

GLOSSARY

Bouquet Garni

A bundle of aromatic herbs used for flavoring braises, ragoûts, stocks, and sauces. It should include a sprig of thyme, a bay leaf, and several sprigs of parsley, tied together with string. Green leek and celery tops may also be included.

Crème Fraîche

This thick French cream has a slightly tart flavor that is particularly good in sauces. If crème fraîche is unavailable, it is quite easily re-created using heavy cream and cultured buttermilk. The cream should be high in butterfat, and the buttermilk must be labeled "active." To make 1 quart/1 liter, stir together in a saucepan 3 cups/750 ml heavy cream, 1 cup/250 ml buttermilk, and the juice of 1 lemon. Heat gently, stirring, until just below body temperature (75°F/25°C). Pour the cream into a container and partly cover it. Keep it in a warm place, 70° to 80°F/21° to 27°C, until it thickens and develops a slightly tart flavor; this will take anywhere from 12 to 24 hours depending on the buttermilk culture and the temperature of the cream.

How to Cut Up Raw Poultry

Depending on the recipe and the size of the bird, you may want to cut it into 4 or 8 pieces. Either way, begin by grabbing hold of one of the legs and tugging it slightly so it pulls away from the body. Then, with a sharp knife, cut the skin between the leg and body, following the outline of the thigh until the leg joint is visible. Flip the bird so you can locate the "oyster" piece of meat lying against the backbone, and cut around it so that it remains attached to the thigh. Twist the leg sharply outward to break the thigh joint. Cut forward to detach the leg completely from the body, including the oyster. Turn the bird and repeat with the second leg. With a knife or poultry shears, cut away and remove the backbone. Cut along the breastbone to halve the carcass. Cut off the wingtips. (Save the backbone and wingtips for the stockpot.) The bird is now in 4 pieces.

To cut into 8 pieces, divide each breast crosswise in half, cutting diagonally through the meat, then through the breast and rib bones so a portion of breast meat remains attached to each wing. Trim the ends of the rib bones. Then, cut the legs in half through the joint, using the white line of fat on the underside as a guide. Trim the drumsticks and any protruding bones with poultry shears.

How to Cut Up a Rabbit

The aim is to cut the rabbit into equal-size pieces that will cook at the same speed. Trim and discard the flaps of belly skin, the tips of the forelegs, and any other protruding bones. Using a heavy knife or cleaver, divide the rabbit crosswise into three sections: back legs, back, and forelegs, including the rib cage. Cut between the back legs to separate them, and then trim off the tail end of the backbone. Separate the two forelegs in a similar fashion by chopping between the shoulders. Then cut the back, or saddle portion, crosswise into 2 or 3 pieces, depending on the size of the rabbit. You should have 6 or 7 pieces. For 8 or 9 pieces, divide the hind legs in two by cutting through the knee joint.

How to Truss Poultry with a Trussing Needle

Trussing encloses any stuffing and keeps a bird in shape so it cooks evenly. This method using a trussing needle and string takes a bit more time than a simple truss with string, but it is best when roasting a large bird such as goose, turkey, or good-sized chicken. First, remove the wishbone to make carving easier. Lift the neck skin and, with a small sharp knife, outline the wishbone and cut it free from the breastbone.

Set the bird breast up with the legs facing you, and with both hands, firmly push the legs back and down so the ends of the legs are sticking straight up in the air. Insert the trussing needle through one leg at the knee joint, then across and out through the other leg joint. Turn the bird over onto its breast and push the needle through both sections of one wing and then into the neck skin, under the backbone of the bird, and out the other side. Now catch the second wing in the same way as the first. Pull the ends of the string from the leg and wing firmly together and tie securely.

Rethread the trussing needle and turn the bird breast-side up. Tuck the fatty, spade-shaped tail into the cavity of the bird. Insert the needle into the end of one drumstick, make a stitch through the skin, which should be overlapping to cover the cavity, and then push the needle through the end of the other drumstick. Turn the bird over and push the needle through the tail. Tie the string ends together.

How to Truss Poultry with String Only

This method is good for small birds such as quail, pigeon, and small chickens. Even with this more casual approach to trussing, it's a good idea to first remove the wishbone to make carving easier. Lift the neck skin and, with a small sharp knife, outline the wishbone and cut it free from the breastbone.

Tuck the neck skin and wings under the bird. Set it on its back. Pass a long string under the tail and knot it over the leg joints and around the tail, tying a double knot. Take the strings back along the sides of the body, passing them between the legs and breast. Flip the bird over onto its breast and loop the strings under each wing pinion. Tie the strings tightly, again with a double knot, and turn the bird over onto its back. You'll see that both legs and wings are held firmly to the body and the bird sits flat on the board.

How to Sterilize and Pack Preserving Jars

To sterilize jars and lids for preserving, bring a large pan of water to a boil. Add the jars and lids and boil for about 10 minutes. Remove them from the water and leave to dry on clean paper towels—don't wipe them dry. Arrange the jars on a wooden board. If the preserves have cooled at all, take care to reheat them until very hot —otherwise the jars will not seal properly. Ladle the very hot preserves into the jars, using a widemouthed canning funnel for jellies and thin jams, and pouring others from a heatproof measuring cup. Take care to keep the rim clean, wiping it as necessary with a very clean towel. Anything on the rim may cause the seal to fail. Fill to within ⅜ inch/1 cm of the rim and, while still hot, cover with a lid, fastening tightly. Cover the jars with a clean cloth in case of leakage and turn them upside down so the preserves touch the lids; leave to cool. When completely cooled, turn the jars upright. You'll find that a vacuum has been created under the lid and enough air has been expelled to prevent spoilage. No further seal is needed.

Pasta Dough

This recipe makes enough to serve 6 to 8 when shaped into fettuccine, vermicelli, or other noodles. For ravioli or other filled pastas, simply cut the recipe amounts in half and do not bother dividing the original ball of dough into 2 pieces when rolling it.

Put 3 cups/375 g flour on a work surface and make a well in the center. Lightly beat 4 eggs and add them to the well along with 1 tablespoon olive oil and 1 teaspoon salt. With your fingertips, gradually mix in the flour from the sides, drawing in more flour to make coarse, slightly sticky crumbs. Add more flour if the crumbs seem moist, as pasta dough should be drier than pastry dough; if, on the other hand, the crumbs are very dry, moisten them with 1 to 2 tablespoons more water. Briefly work the dough until it comes together in a rather shaggy-looking ball; the rollers of the pasta machine will do most of the kneading for you.

Set the rollers of the pasta machine on their widest setting and divide the dough into 2 parts. Flatten each slightly so that it will just squeeze through the rollers. Feed the dough through the rollers, gathering up any crumbs that fall off and pressing them back onto the dough. The dough will appear ragged and patchy at first. Fold the strip to make a square that will fit sideways through the machine, and feed it through again, starting with one of the open ends. Repeat this kneading process of rolling and folding 3 to 5 times, until the dough becomes smooth and like chamois leather. Then cut the dough into 4 pieces so that it does not become unmanageable. Do not fold the pasta piece again, but continue rolling, decreasing the spacing of the rollers one notch each time until the pasta is rolled to the thickness of a postcard. The first time you try this, it may help to have an extra set of hands to catch the pasta sheets as they come out of the machine. Drape the sheets over the backs of chairs or use broom handles to create a makeshift pasta drier. Repeat with the remaining pieces of pasta dough. Cut and shape the sheets while they are still somewhat moist. They will become brittle and unmanageable if you let them dry for too long.

Pastry Doughs

Puff Pastry (Pâte Feuilletée)

To make enough pastry for 6 to 8 individual pastries, feuilletées, or an 8-in/20-cm tart or vol-au-vent, have ready 1 cup/250 g of chilled butter. Sift 2 cups/250 g flour onto a marble slab or work surface and make a well in the center. Add 2 to 3 tablespoons of the butter, cut into pieces, to the well with ½ cup/125 ml cold water. Work together with your fingertips until well mixed, then gradually draw in the flour with your hand and a pastry scraper to make crumbs. Work just until the dough is mixed, adding more water if it is dry. Shape the dough into a ball, wrap in plastic, and let it rest in the refrigerator for 15 minutes. This ball of dough is the *détrempe* and should be quite rough looking; avoid the mistake of overworking it into a smooth dough or it will become elastic.

Lightly flour the remaining butter, put it between 2 sheets of wax or parchment paper, and flatten it with a rolling pin. Fold it, replace it between the paper, and continue pounding and folding until it is pliable but not sticky—the butter should be the same consistency as the *détrempe*. Shape the butter into a 6-inch/15-cm square and flour it lightly. Roll out the dough to a 12-inch/30-cm square, slightly thicker in the center than at the sides. Set the butter diagonally in the center, and fold the dough around it like an envelope, pinching the edges to seal the package.

Make sure the work surface is well floured. Place the dough seam-side down and lightly pound it with a rolling pin to flatten it slightly. Roll it out into an 18 x 6-inch/45 x 15-cm rectangle. Fold the rectangle into three, like a business letter. Press the ends lightly with the rolling pin to seal the edges and turn the dough a quarter turn (90°) so the seam is to your left. This is called a turn. Roll out the rectangle again and fold it again in three. Keep a note of the number of turns by marking the corner of the dough with the appropriate number of fingerprints. Wrap the dough and chill it until firm, 20 to 30 minutes.

Repeat this rolling, folding, and turning process until you have rolled and folded the dough 6 times, with a refrigerated rest between every 2 turns. Chill the pastry for at least 30 minutes before using it.

French Pie Pastry (Pâte Brisée)

You'll find the ingredient measurements for this pie pastry in the individual recipes.

Sift the flour onto the work surface and make a well in the center. Put the eggs or egg yolks, salt, and water in the well along with any flavorings such as sugar. Pound the butter with a rolling pin to soften it, add it to the other ingredients in the well, and work them with the fingers of one hand until thoroughly mixed. Using a pastry scraper, gradually draw in flour from the sides and continue working with the fingers of both hands until coarse crumbs are formed. If the crumbs seem dry, sprinkle with another tablespoon of water; it should be soft but not sticky. Press the dough together into a ball, but don't overwork it; the dough will be uneven and unblended at this point.

Blend the dough quickly so the butter doesn't become too warm. Put the dough in front of you and use the heel of one hand to push away a bit at a time and flatten it against the work surface; this flattening motion evenly blends the butter with the other ingredients without overworking the dough. When the entire ball of dough has been blended in this fashion, gather it up with a scraper into a rough ball, and repeat this process of blending with the heel of your hand until the dough is pliable and pulls away from the work surface in one piece, 1 to 2 minutes. Shape it into a ball, wrap in plastic, and chill it until firm, at least 30 minutes.

French Sweet Pie Pastry (Pâte Sucrée)

The ingredient measurements for each pie or tart shell are in the individual recipes. Sift the flour onto the work surface and make a well in the center. Put the salt, sugar, egg yolks, and vanilla in the well. Pound the butter with a rolling pin to soften it, add it to the other ingredients in the well, and work them with the fingers of one hand until thoroughly mixed and the sugar is partially dissolved. Using a pastry scraper, gradually draw in flour then work the dough and chill it as for the French Pie Pastry, above.

Blind-Baking

Pastry shells are blind-baked (empty) before the filling is added. This procedure is used if the filling is not to be cooked in the shell, or when a filling is especially moist and might soak the pastry during baking. The dried beans or rice can be kept and used again for blind-baking.

Heat the oven to 375°F/190°C and put a baking sheet to heat low down in the oven. Roll out the dough to about 2 in/5 cm larger than the pie pan. Line the buttered pie pan with the dough and chill it until firm, at least 15 minutes. Line the pastry shell with parchment paper, pressing the paper well into the corners, and fill the shell with dried beans or rice. Bake it until the edges are set and starting to brown, 15 to 20 minutes. Remove the paper and beans and continue baking until the base is firm and dry, 4 to 5 minutes if the pie is to be baked with the filling, or until well browned, 8 to 10 minutes, to bake the shell completely.

Stocks

Brown Beef Stock

For about 2½ quarts/2½ liters of stock, roast 5 lb/2.3 kg veal bones in a very hot oven for 20 minutes (you may use half veal bones and half beef bones, if you like). Add 2 quartered carrots and 2 quartered onions and continue roasting until they are very brown, about 30 minutes more. Transfer the roasted bones and vegetables to a stockpot, leaving behind any rendered fat in the roasting pan. Add a bouquet garni (page 296), 1 tablespoon peppercorns, 1 tablespoon tomato puree or paste, and about 5 quarts/5 liters cold water, or enough to cover the bones and vegetables by a couple of inches.

Bring the stock slowly to a boil, and then simmer, uncovered, for 4 to 5 hours, skimming the surface occasionally. Strain the stock, taste and, if the flavor is not concentrated, boil it until it is well reduced. Chill and skim off any fat from the stock before using. It can be refrigerated for up to 3 days, and it freezes well.

White Veal Stock

Proceed as for Brown Beef Stock (above), using only veal bones, but skip the step of browning the bones and vegetables, and omit the tomato puree or paste. Instead, keep the stock light colored by blanching the bones. Put the bones in a stockpot filled with cold water. Bring slowly to a boil, skim, and then simmer the bones for 3 to 5 minutes. Drain, discard the water, rinse the bones, and proceed with the recipe.

Chicken Stock

Duck, other poultry bones, and even rabbit bones can be substituted for the chicken in this recipe. For about 2½ quarts/2½ liters of stock, combine 3 lb/1.4 kg chicken backs, necks, and bones with 1 quartered onion, 1 quartered carrot, 1 celery stalk cut into pieces, a bouquet garni (page 296), 1 teaspoon peppercorns, and about 4 quarts/4 liters cold water, or enough to cover the bones by about an inch. Bring slowly to a boil, and then simmer the stock, uncovered, for 2 to 3 hours, skimming often. Strain, taste, and if the stock is not concentrated, boil it until well reduced. Refrigerate it and, before using, skim off any solidified fat from the surface. Stock can be kept for up to 3 days in the refrigerator or it can be frozen.

Fish and Shellfish Stock

For about 1½ quarts/1½ liters of stock, break 2 lb/1 kg fish bones into pieces and wash them thoroughly. In a large pot, cook 1 sliced onion in 1 tablespoon butter until soft but not brown, 5 to 7 minutes. Add the fish bones, 1½ quarts/1½ liters water, a bouquet garni (page 296), 10 peppercorns, and 1½ cups/375 ml dry white wine. Bring to a boil and simmer quite briskly, uncovered, for 20 minutes, skimming often. Strain and cool.

For Shellfish Stock, halve the amount of fish bones and add the shells from ¾ lb/375 g medium shrimp along with the fish.

INDEX

NOTE: *Page numbers in italics refer to illustrations.*

CONVERSION CHART

Equivalent Imperial and Metric Measurements

American cooks use standard containers, the 8-ounce cup and a tablespoon that takes exactly 16 level fillings to fill that cup level. Measuring by cup makes it very difficult to give weight equivalents, as a cup of densely packed butter will weigh considerably more than a cup of flour. The easiest way therefore to deal with cup measurements in recipes is to take the amount by volume rather than by weight. Thus the equation reads:

1 cup = 250 ml = 8 fl. oz.   ½ cup = 125 ml = 4 fl. oz.

It is possible to buy a set of American cup measures in major stores around the world.

In the States, butter is often measured in sticks. One stick is the equivalent of 8 tablespoons. One tablespoon of butter is therefore the equivalent to ½ ounce/15 grams.

LIQUID MEASURES

Fluid Ounces	U.S.	Imperial	Milliliters
	1 teaspoon	1 teaspoon	5
¼	2 teaspoons	1 dessertspoon	10
½	1 tablespoon	1 tablespoon	15
1	2 tablespoons	2 tablespoons	30
2	¼ cup	4 tablespoons	60
4	½ cup		125
5		¼ pint or 1 gill	150
6	¾ cup		175
8	1 cup		250
9			275
10	1¼ cups	½ pint	300
12	1½ cups		375
15		¾ pint	450
16	2 cups		500
18	2¼ cups		550
20	2½ cups	1 pint	600
24	3 cups		750

SOLID MEASURES

U.S. and Imperial Measures		Metric Measures	
Ounces	Pounds	Grams	Kilos
1		30	
2		60	
3½		105	
4	¼	125	
5		150	
6		180	
8	½	250	
9		280	¼
12	¾	360	
16	1	500	
18		560	½
20	1¼	610	
24	1½	720	

OVEN TEMPERATURE EQUIVALENTS

Fahrenheit	Celsius	Gas Mark	Description
225	110	¼	Cool
250	130	½	
275	140	1	Very Slow
300	150	2	
325	160	3	Slow
350	175	4	Moderate
375	190	5	
400	200	6	Moderately Hot
425	220	7	Fairly Hot
450	230	8	Hot
475	240	9	Very Hot
500	250	10	Extremely Hot

all-purpose flour—plain flour   cornstarch—cornflour   heavy cream—double cream
coarse salt—kitchen salt   half and half—12% fat milk   light cream—single cream